THE BURDEN AND THE GLORY

Books by John F. Kennedy

THE BURDEN AND THE GLORY *(edited by Allan Nevins)*
TO TURN THE TIDE *(edited by John W. Gardner)*
THE STRATEGY OF PEACE *(edited by Allan Nevins)*
PROFILES IN COURAGE
WHY ENGLAND SLEPT

PRESIDENT JOHN F. KENNEDY

THE HOPES AND PURPOSES OF

PRESIDENT KENNEDY'S SECOND AND THIRD

YEARS IN OFFICE AS REVEALED IN

HIS PUBLIC STATEMENTS AND ADDRESSES

THE BURDEN

AND THE GLORY

Edited by Allan Nevins

Foreword by President Lyndon B. Johnson

Harper & Row, Publishers

New York, Evanston, and London

Contents

Foreword

Two months ago today he died—and a part of America died with him. He was so loving and so beloved, so wise and so courageous, so good and great a man, that we who must carry on his mission shall forever miss him more than we even know.

"No nation," President Kennedy told the Congress two years ago, "has ever been so ready to seize the burden and the glory of freedom"—and certainly no other man of our time has ever been so equipped to accept the burdens and glory of the Presidency.

To the tangled intricacies of public policy—whether fiscal, foreign or domestic—he brought a keen insight and a fresh outlook.

To the explosive problems of peace and war he brought matchless courage and ceaseless patience.

To this nation's moral and constitutional crisis of human rights he brought a cool head and a compassionate heart.

Above all, he was a builder of hope—new hope for peace and freedom and our fellow man, new hope for our nation and all the world. Those hopes, along with all the qualities mentioned above, are eloquently expressed in the pages that follow.

No book will have a more treasured place in my library—no book will be opened more often. For the speeches and statements of John Fitzgerald Kennedy are among the richest legacies he left us. They offer thoughtful guidance to the solution of almost every major problem. They provide wisdom from the past which can enlighten the future. And they remind us all of our unfinished tasks—the heights we have climbed and the summits that still lie ahead.

"The pressures of life," he said in this same passage of two years ago, "are not always distributed by choice." Nor, he might have added, are the hazards of death. But in death as in life, John Kennedy stirred the hearts of all mankind—and with his words and works to guide us and inspire us, his life will not have been in vain.

PRESIDENT LYNDON B. JOHNSON

The White House
January 22, 1964

Introduction

To tens of millions on November 22, 1963, the skies seemed suddenly darkened at midday. A sense of spaciousness was taken out of American life, a feeling that the nation's future was shot through with imagination and hope disappeared, and an exhilarating absorption in the adventures before us was lost. One gallant personality had thrown its radiance into a multitude of lives from the Atlantic to the Pacific. It seemed incredible that this radiance was so swiftly quenched; people walked that afternoon in a stunned incredulity, which haunted them for days. John F. Kennedy had given the country not only new ideas and a sharper challenge but graces of comprehension and humanity. The youngest man ever elected to the Presidency, he had imbued our public atmosphere with the vibrancy of youth. Within his influence lassitude and cynicism gave way to confident energy.

The memory of his distinctions of heart and action will live in the mind of our time, and in the histories written by generations to come. The first President born in the new century, he died at the height of his powers and, as his recent receptions in Germany, Italy, and Ireland had attested, of his international fame. He had shown a maturity of discretion and a power of decision that belied his years. No President ever displayed a quicker mastery of his administration, although it was an administration of strong men. He had climbed to the heights by rare political skill, but once there he proved a breadth of view and elevation of purpose not found in mere politicians. Although he was a thinker of cultured background, he was also a man of action, and at times very tough, practical action.

He was impatient in two senses of the word. He was impatient, as he repeatedly said, with a society which used hardly half its industrial capacity, which let children go hungry while food surpluses piled up, which allowed Russia to produce twice as many scientists and technologists, and which grossly neglected its natural resources. He was also impatient in the sense that he was in a hurry. Seeing so much that needed to be done, he urged upon his first Congress a program so large and varied that full execution was impossible. At the end of his White House years some of his best hopes were still unfulfilled, primarily because his urgent aims were so numerous, because his reach exceeded his grasp. But in how much, at the same time, he had succeeded!

When Theodore Roosevelt had been in the White House only a little longer than Kennedy's tenure, he quoted a passage from the fine old Elizabethan bishop Richard Hooker pertinent to Roosevelt's unfinished work and to President Kennedy's.

"He that goeth about to persuade a multitude that they are not so well governed as they ought to be," wrote Hooker, "shall never want attentive and favorable readers, because they know the manifold defects whereunto every kind of regimen is subject; but the secret lets and difficulties, which in public proceedings are innumerable and inevitable, they have not ordinarily the judgment to consider." The Presidents who are boldest in initiative and most fertile in undertakings would particularly endorse this statement. Mr. Kennedy might have quoted another pertinent statement of Hooker's: "Have patience with me for a small time, and by the help of Almighty God I shall pay the whole." But the small time was not vouchsafed him; he was snatched away while he was striving hardest.

President Kennedy perceived clearly that ours is a revolutionary age; he saw several important revolutions approaching completion, and strove to awaken the American people to them before it was too late. One was international in character. The United States had emerged from the Second World War a rich and powerful nation standing before a weak and shattered Europe, a chaotic Asia, and a still-unawakened Africa. It bestrode the world like a colossus. Partly because America assisted other nations in the Marshall Plan and later with unexampled generosity, partly because the mature industrial countries revived with astonishing celerity, and partly because much war ruin is simply a clearance of facilities that would soon be

obsolete anyway, the reconstruction of the Old World was rapid.
When Kennedy took office, Britain, France, West Germany, Italy
and Japan were more productive than ever before.

The consequence was a shift in the world balance which few
Americans grasped. Gone were the days of the colossus! America
had to compete with lusty, independent-minded nations, economically self-assertive. Our goods found penetration into overseas markets
more and more difficult. The dollar lost its old-time power. Both
politically and industrially, the United States was reduced from the
status of patron to that of equal. Taking Western Europe as a whole,
this country could no longer confidently claim even equality with
that complex and its rate of growth. President Kennedy knew that
leading Europeans marveled at our slow comprehension of the new
situation, and he tried desperately to drive home its meaning to
the country.

In domestic affairs, meanwhile, revolutionary changes had developed by 1960 with which neither public opinion nor the American frame of government seemed equipped to deal. Most Americans
still lived in the pre-Keynesian age. They had been slow to absorb
the fact that fiscal statesmanship can no longer be summed up in
budget balancing and debt reduction; that indeed a precipitate and
heedless effort to balance the budget can mean deflation and a
consequent recession.

Mr. Kennedy was passionately concerned about the lagging growth
of the national economy because he thought it too slow to maintain
our strength, which is the chief single pillar of the free world. He
was passionately concerned lest our economic drift, with far too
little reinvestment in industrial plant, cause us to fail the coming
generation. Places have somehow to be found for 26,000,000 young
people who will crowd into the labor market during the next decade.
He was passionately concerned about labor opportunities for minority
elements like the Negroes, the Puerto Ricans, and the Mexican-
Americans, usually the last to be hired and the first to be discharged.
He was passionately anxious that retraining programs be offered to
workers forced out of their jobs by inexorable technological change,
especially automation. And he was still more passionately concerned
about the possibility of a new recession, a stone in the road that

might perilously jolt our great careening vehicle of 190,000,000 people.

Among the social revolutions of the time, the revolt of the Negroes against the wrongs and exclusions they had suffered throughout the century since emancipation concerned him more and more deeply. The worst impediment he met, next to the intrenched obstructionism of Congressional committees, was the apathy of vast numbers of people; the difficulty of arousing public opinion. But this apathy had one healthy exception. The Negroes made their discontent peaceably but plainly visible. Mr. Kennedy knew the truth of Lloyd George's remark, "When the people rebel the people are always right." The United States could not hold its head high among the free nations until it did full justice to its colored citizens.

"The United States Government is sitting down at Geneva with the Soviet Union," President Kennedy told one news conference. "I can't understand why the city council of Albany, Georgia, cannot do the same for American citizens."

In an apathetic nation, a country far too much addicted to ambling down the middle of the road, President Kennedy's passion for reform and advancement—and *speedy* reform and advancement—was refreshing. He was continuously anxious to improve our educational equipment, and never tired of quoting Thomas Jefferson: "If a nation expects to be ignorant and free, in a state of civilization, it expects what never was and never will be." The opposition defeated his great measure for the assistance of primary and secondary schools; but in other areas he did more for education than any previous President. He was anxious to provide health insurance and hospital care for the aged. Again an opposition, in which some leaders of organized medicine resorted to downright misrepresentation, unhappily defeated him; but he felt sure of ultimate victory. He had a passionate realization that the United States could never remain healthy and free in a diseased and fettered world. Look at Brazil, he said, with a swollen population growing far too fast; two persons out of five under twenty; great areas illiterate; an unchecked inflation; the people living on an average income of $100 a year—can we stand by and refuse help? The Alliance for Progress, a greater effort than the Marshall Plan but undertaken with less money, was especially near his heart.

Above all, he became more and more intensely interested in the promotion of world peace. At the outset he laid emphasis on heavy expenditures for defense, including a build-up of tactical weapons and manpower to lessen our nearly total reliance on massive retaliation; during his campaign he gave too much countenance to talk of a "missile gap" which didn't exist as a "gap" so much as an arm which needed to be strengthened. But he had always spoken eloquently for peace, and in the end his greatest achievements were won in its behalf. His confrontation of Russia in the Cuban crisis in the autumn of 1962 did much to clear the air between the Soviet Union and the United States, and it is noteworthy that in this crisis he laid the quarrel before the United Nations, and always left a generous road of retreat open to Chairman Khrushchev. The treaty ending atmospheric tests of nuclear weapons was a great and hopeful step toward world understanding and concord. When he was so tragically taken from our midst, he was the most devoted and influential champion of peace on the world scene, and the mourning of all peoples acknowledged the fact.

ALLAN NEVINS

". . . it is the fate of this generation—of you in the Congress and of me as President—to live with a struggle we did not start, in a world we did not make. But the pressures of life are not always distributed by choice. And while no nation has ever faced such a challenge, no nation has ever been so ready to seize the burden and the glory of freedom."

—President John F. Kennedy,
State of the Union Message to Congress,
January 11, 1962

I

THE SHAPE
AND THE AIMS
OF GOVERNMENT

1 : The Second State of the Union Message

WASHINGTON, D.C.

JANUARY 11, 1962*

... This week we begin anew our joint and separate efforts to build the American future. But, sadly, we build without a man who linked a long past with the present and looked strongly to the future. "Mister Sam" Rayburn is gone. Neither this House nor the nation is the same without him.

Members of the Congress, the Constitution makes us not rivals for power but partners for progress. We are all trustees for the American people, custodians of the American heritage. It is my task to report the state of the Union; to improve it is the task of us all.

In the past year, I have traveled not only across our own land, but to

---

* The second session of the Eighty-seventh Congress, to which the President addressed this important state paper, was heavily Democratic in both Chambers, with 263 Democrats facing 174 Republicans in the House and 64 Democrats facing 36 Republicans in the Senate. But such figures give a totally illusory picture of administration strength. The alliance between conservative Republicans and immovable Southern Democrats that had plagued the government for four years reappeared in full force. Nor was administration leadership on the legislative scene as vigorous as it might have been had Speaker Sam Rayburn and Lyndon Johnson remained in their controlling positions.

Looking back to 1961, Kennedy had just told the nation: "It has been a tough first year, but then they're all going to be tough." He intended to press hard for the more liberal trade and tariff policies that he had just told the country were a necessity; for legislation protecting and broadening civil rights; for price and wage stability; and for progress with world disarmament. Fortunately, the economic condition of the country was fairly favorable. It was destined to escape a recession, which he always feared and which seemed possible when the stock market plunged downward in May. Business recovery continued, although its pace was slower than he had hoped.—A. N.

3

other lands—to the North and the South, and across the seas. And I have found, as I am sure you have in your travels, that people everywhere, in spite of occasional disappointments, look to us—not to our wealth or power, but to the splendor of our ideals. For our nation is commissioned by history to be either an observer of freedom's failure or the cause of its success. Our overriding obligation in the months ahead is to fulfill the world's hopes by fulfilling our own faith.

That task must begin at home. For if we cannot fulfill our own ideals here, we cannot expect others to accept them. And when the youngest child alive today has grown to the cares of manhood, our position in the world will be determined first of all by what provisions we make today—for his education, his health, and his opportunities for a good home and a good job and a good life.

At home, we began the year in the valley of recession; we completed it on the highroad of recovery and growth. With the help of new Congressionally approved or administratively increased stimulants to our economy, the number of major surplus labor areas has declined from 101 to 60; nonagricultural employment has increased by more than a million jobs; and the average factory work week has risen to well over forty hours. At year's end the economy which Mr. Khrushchev once called a "stumbling horse" was racing to new records in consumer spending, labor income and industrial production.

We are gratified, but we are not satisfied. Too many unemployed are still looking for the blessings of prosperity. As those who leave our schools and farms demand new jobs, automation takes old jobs away. To expand our growth and job opportunities, I urge on the Congress three measures:

First, the Manpower Development and Training Act, to stop the waste of able-bodied men and women who want to work, but whose only skill has been replaced by a machine, or moved with a mill, or shut down with a mine.

Second, the Youth Employment Opportunities Act, to help train and place not only the one million young Americans who are both out of school and out of work, but the 26 million young Americans entering the labor market in this decade.

Third, the 8 percent tax credit for investment in machinery and equipment, which, combined with planned revisions of depreciation allowances, will spur our modernization, our growth and our ability to compete abroad.

Moreover, pleasant as it may be to bask in the warmth of recovery, let us not forget that we have suffered three recessions in the last seven years. The time to repair the roof is when the sun is shining, by filling three basic gaps in our antirecession protection. We need:

First, Presidential stand-by authority, subject to Congressional veto, to adjust personal income tax rates downward within a specified range and time, to slow down an economic decline before it has dragged us all down.

Second, Presidential stand-by authority, upon a given rise in the rate of unemployment, to accelerate federal and federally aided capital improvement programs.

Third, a permanent strengthening of our unemployment compensation system, to maintain for our fellow citizens searching for a job who cannot find it, their purchasing power and their living standards without constant resort, as we have seen in recent years by Congress and the administrations, to temporary supplements.

If we enact this six-part program, we can show the whole world that a free economy need not be an unstable economy, that a free system need not leave men unemployed, and that a free society is not only the most productive but the most stable form of organization yet fashioned by man.

But recession is only one enemy of a free economy; inflation is another. Last year, 1961, despite rising production and demand, consumer prices held almost steady and wholesale prices declined. This is the best record of over-all price stability of any comparable period of recovery since the end of World War II.

Inflation too often follows in the shadow of growth, while price stability is made easy by stagnation or controls. But we mean to maintain both stability and growth in a climate of freedom.

Our first line of defense against inflation is the good sense and public spirit of business and labor, keeping their total increases in wages and profits in step with productivity. There is no single statistical test to guide each company and each union. But I strongly urge them, for their country's interest and for their own, to apply the test of the public interest to these transactions.

Within this same framework of growth and wage-price stability, this administration has helped keep our economy competitive by widening the access of small business to credit and government contracts, and by stepping up the drive against monopoly, price-fixing and racketeering. We will submit a Federal Pay Reform bill aimed at giving our classified, postal and other employees new pay scales more comparable to those of private industry. We are holding the fiscal 1962 budget deficit far below the level incurred after the last recession in 1958. And, finally, I am submitting for fiscal 1963 a balanced federal budget.

This is a joint responsibility, requiring Congressional cooperation on appropriations, and on three sources of income in particular.

First, an increase in postal rates, to end the postal deficit.

Second, passage of the tax reforms previously urged, to remove unwarranted tax preferences, and to apply to dividends and to interest the same withholding requirements we have long applied to wages.

Third, extension of the present excise and corporation tax rates, except for those changes, which will be recommended in a message, affecting transportation.

But a stronger nation and economy require more than a balanced budget. They require progress in those programs that spur our growth and fortify our strength.

A strong America depends on its cities, America's glory and sometimes America's shame. To substitute sunlight for congestion and progress for decay, we have stepped up existing urban renewal and housing programs, and launched new ones; redoubled the attack on water pollution; speeded aid to airports, hospitals, highways and our declining mass transit systems; and secured new weapons to combat organized crime, racketeering and youth delinquency, assisted by the coordinated and hard-hitting efforts of our investigative services: the FBI, the Internal Revenue, the Bureau of Narcotics and many others. We shall need further anticrime, mass transit and transportation legislation, and new tools to fight air pollution. And with all this effort under way, both equity and common sense require that our nation's urban areas, containing three-fourths of our population, sit as equals at the Cabinet table. I urge a new Department of Urban Affairs and Housing.

A strong America also depends on its farms and natural resources. American farmers took heart in 1961, from a billion-dollar rise in farm income and from a hopeful start on reducing the farm surpluses. But we are still operating under a patchwork accumulation of old laws, which cost us $1 billion a year in CCC carrying charges alone, yet fail to halt rural poverty or boost farm earnings.

Our task is to master and turn to fully fruitful ends the magnificent productivity of our farms and farmers. The revolution on our own countryside stands in the sharpest contrast to the repeated farm failures of the Communist nations and is a source of pride to us all. Since 1950 our agricultural output per man-hour has actually doubled! Without new, realistic measures, it will someday swamp our farmers and our taxpayers in a national scandal or a farm depression.

I will therefore submit to the Congress a new comprehensive farm program, tailored to fit the use of our land and the supplies of each crop to the long-range needs of the sixties, and designed to prevent chaos in the sixties with a program of common sense.

We also need for the sixties, if we are to bequeath our full national estate to our heirs, a new, long-range conservation and recreation program—expansion of our superb national parks and forests, preservation of our authentic wilderness areas, new starts on water and power projects as our population steadily increases, and expanded REA generation and transmission loans.

But America stands for progress in human rights as well as economic affairs, and a strong America requires the assurance of full and equal rights to all its citizens, of any race or of any color. This administration has shown as never before how much could be done through the full use of Executive powers, through the enforcement of laws already passed by the Congress, through persuasion, negotiation and litigation, to secure the constitutional rights of all: the right to vote, the right to travel without hindrance across state lines, and the right to free public education.

I issued last March a comprehensive order to guarantee the right to equal employment opportunity in all federal agencies and contractors. The Vice President's Committee thus created has done much, including the voluntary "Plans for Progress" which, in all sections of the country, are achieving a quiet but striking success in opening up to all races new professional, supervisory and other job opportunities.

But there is much more to be done—by the Executive, by the courts and by the Congress. Among the bills now pending before you, on which the Executive departments will comment in detail, are appropriate methods of strengthening these basic rights which have our full support. The right to vote, for example, should no longer be denied through such arbitrary devices on a local level, sometimes abused, such as literacy tests and poll taxes. As we approach the one hundredth anniversary, next January, of the Emancipation Proclamation, let the acts of every branch of the government, and every citizen, portray that "righteousness does exalt a nation."

Finally, a strong America cannot neglect the aspirations of its citizens—the welfare of the needy, the health care of the elderly, the education of the young. For we are not developing the nation's wealth for its own sake. Wealth is the means, and people are the ends. All our material riches will avail us little if we do not use them to expand the opportunities of our people.

Last year we improved the diet of needy people, provided more hot lunches and fresh milk to schoolchildren, built more college dormitories, and, for the elderly, expanded private housing, nursing homes, health services and Social Security. But we have just begun.

To help those least fortunate of all, I am recommending a new public welfare program, and training for useful work instead of prolonged dependency.

To relieve the critical shortage of doctors and dentists—and this is a matter which should concern us all—and expand research, I urge action to aid medical and dental colleges and scholarships and to establish new National Institutes of Health.

To take advantage of modern vaccination achievements, I am proposing a mass immunization program, aimed at the virtual elimination of such ancient enemies of our children as polio, diphtheria, whooping cough and tetanus.

To protect our consumers from the careless and the unscrupulous, I shall recommend improvements in the Food and Drug laws—strengthening inspection and standards, halting unsafe and worthless products, preventing misleading labels and cracking down on the illicit sale of habit-forming drugs.

But in matters of health no piece of unfinished business is more important or more urgent than the enactment under the Social Security System of health insurance for the aged.

For our older citizens have longer and more frequent illnesses, higher hospital and medical bills and too little income to pay them. Private health insurance helps some, but its cost is high and its coverage limited. Public welfare cannot help those too proud to seek relief but hard pressed to pay their own bills. Nor can their children or grandchildren always sacrifice their own health budgets to meet this constant drain.

Social Security has long helped to meet the hardships of retirement, death and disability. I now urge that its coverage be extended without further delay to provide health insurance for the elderly.

Equally important to our strength is the quality of our education. Eight million adult Americans are classified as functionally illiterate. This is a disturbing figure, reflected in Selective Service rejection rates, reflected in welfare rolls and crime rates. And I shall recommend plans for a massive attack to end this adult illiteracy.

I shall also recommend bills to improve educational quality, to stimulate the arts and, at the college level, to provide federal loans for the construction of academic facilities and federally financed scholarships.

If this nation is to grow in wisdom and strength, then every able high school graduate should have the opportunity to develop his talents. Yet nearly half lack either the funds or the facilities to attend college. Enrollments are going to double in our colleges in the short space of ten years. The annual cost per student is skyrocketing to astronomical levels—now averaging $1,650 a year, although almost half of our families earn less than $5,000. They cannot afford such costs, but this nation cannot afford to maintain its military power and neglect its brainpower.

But excellence in education must begin at the elementary level. I

sent to the Congress last year a proposal for federal aid to public
school construction and teachers' salaries. I believe that bill, which
passed the Senate and received House Committee approval, offered
the minimum amount required by our needs and, in terms of across-
the-board aid, the maximum scope permitted by our Constitution. I
therefore see no reason to weaken or withdraw that bill, and I urge
its passage at this session. "Civilization," said H. G. Wells, "is a race
between education and catastrophe." It is up to you in this Congress
to determine the winner of that race.

These are not unrelated measures addressed to specific gaps or
grievances in our national life. They are the pattern of our intentions and the foundation of our hopes. "I believe in democracy,"
said Woodrow Wilson, "because it releases the energy of every human
being." The dynamic of democracy is the power and the purpose
of the individual, and the policy of this administration is to give
to the individual the opportunity to realize his own highest possibilities.

Our program is to open to all the opportunity for steady and
productive employment, to remove from all the handicap of arbitrary
or irrational exclusion, to offer to all the facilities for education and
health and welfare, to make society the servant of the individual and
the individual the source of progress, and thus to realize for all the
full promise of American life.

All of these efforts at home give meaning to our efforts abroad.
Since the close of the Second World War, a global civil war has
divided and tormented mankind. But it is not our military might
or our higher standard of living that has most distinguished us from
our adversaries. It is our belief that the state is the servant of the
citizen and not his master.

This basic clash of ideas and wills is but one of the forces reshaping our globe, swept as it is by the tides of hope and fear, by crises
in the headlines today that become mere footnotes tomorrow. Both
the successes and the setbacks of the past year remain on our agenda
of unfinished business. For every apparent blessing contains the seeds
of danger; every area of trouble gives out a ray of hope; and the one
unchangeable certainty is that nothing is certain or unchangeable.

Yet our basic goal remains the same: a peaceful world community of free and independent states, free to choose their own future and their own system, so long as it does not threaten the freedom of others.

Some may choose forms and ways that we would not choose for ourselves, but it is not for us that they are choosing. We can welcome diversity; the Communists cannot. For we offer a world of choice; they offer the world of coercion. And the way of the past shows clearly that freedom, not coercion, is the wave of the future. At times our goal has been obscured by crisis or endangered by conflict, but it draws sustenance from five basic sources of strength: the moral and physical strength of the United States; the united strength of the Atlantic Community; the regional strength of our hemispheric relations; the creative strength of our efforts in the new and developing nations; and the peace-keeping strength of the United Nations.

Our moral and physical strength begins at home, as already discussed. But it includes our military strength as well. So long as fanaticism and fear brood over the affairs of men, we must arm to deter others from aggression.

In the past twelve months our military posture has steadily improved. We increased the previous defense budget by 15 percent, not in the expectation of war but for the preservation of peace. We more than doubled our acquisition rate of Polaris submarines. We doubled the production capacity for Minuteman missiles and increased by 50 percent the number of manned bombers standing ready on fifteen-minute alert. This year the combined force levels planned under our new defense budget, including nearly three hundred additional Polaris and Minuteman missiles, have been precisely calculated to insure the continuing strength of our nuclear deterrent.

But our strength may be tested at many levels. We intend to have at all times the capacity to resist nonnuclear or limited attacks, as a complement to our nuclear capacity, not as a substitute.We have rejected any all-or-nothing posture which would leave no choice but inglorious retreat or unlimited retaliation.

Thus we have doubled the number of ready combat divisions in the Army's strategic reserve, increased our troops in Europe, built up the Marines, added new sealift and airlift capacity, modernized our weapons and ammunition, expanded our antiguerrilla forces, and increased the active fleet by more than seventy vessels and our tactical air forces by nearly a dozen wings.

Because we needed to reach this higher long-term level of readiness more quickly, 155,000 members of the Reserve and National Guard were activated under the Act of this Congress. Some disruptions and distress were inevitable. But the overwhelming majority bore their burdens, and their nation's burdens, with admirable and traditional devotion.

In the coming year, our reserve programs will be revised. Two Army divisions will, I hope, replace those Guard divisions on duty, and substantial other increases will boost our Air Force fighter units, the procurement of equipment and our continental defense and warning efforts. The nation's first serious civil defense shelter program is under way, identifying, marking and stocking fifty million spaces; and I urge your approval of federal incentives for the construction of public fallout shelters in schools and hospitals and similar centers.

But arms alone are not enough to keep the peace; it must be kept by men. Our instrument and our hope is the United Nations, and I see little merit in the impatience of those who would abandon this imperfect world instrument because they dislike our imperfect world. For the troubles of a world organization merely reflect the troubles of the world itself. And if the organization is weakened, these troubles can only increase. We may not always agree with every detailed action taken by every officer of the United Nations, or with every voting majority. But as an institution, it should have in the future, as it has had in the past since its inception, no stronger or more faithful member than the United States of America.

In 1961 the peace-keeping strength of the United Nations was reinforced. And those who preferred or predicted its demise, envisioning a troika in the seat of Hammarskjöld or Red China inside the Assembly, have seen instead a new vigor, under a new Secretary General and a fully independent Secretariat. In making plans for a new forum and principles on disarmament, for peace-keeping in outer space, for a decade of development effort, the UN fulfilled its Charter's lofty aim.

Eighteen months ago the tangled, turbulent Congo presented the UN with its gravest challenge. The prospect was one of chaos, or certain big-power confrontation, with all of its hazards and all of its risks, to us and to others. Today the hopes have improved for peaceful conciliation within a united Congo. This is the objective of our policy in this important area.

No policeman is universally popular, particularly when he uses his stick to restore law and order on his beat. Those members who are willing to contribute their votes and their views, but very little else, have created a serious deficit by refusing to pay their share of special UN assessments. Yet they do pay their annual assessments to retain their votes, and a new UN bond issue, financing special operations for the next eighteen months, is to be repaid with interest from these regular assessments. This is clearly in our interest. It will not only keep the UN solvent, but require all voting members to pay their fair share of its activities. Our share of special operations has long been much higher than our share of the annual assessment, and the bond issue will in effect reduce our disproportionate obligation, and for these reasons I am urging Congress to approve our participation.

With the approval of this Congress, we have undertaken in the past year a great new effort in outer space. Our aim is not simply to be first on the moon, any more than Charles Lindbergh's real aim was to be the first to Paris. His aim was to develop the techniques of our own country and other countries in the field of air and the atmosphere, and our objective in making this effort, which we hope will place one of our citizens on the moon, is to develop in a new frontier of science, commerce and cooperation the position of the United States and the free world.

This nation belongs among the first to explore it, and among the first, if not the first, we shall be. We are offering our know-how and our cooperation to the UN. Our satellites will soon be providing other nations with improved weather observations. And I shall soon send to the Congress a measure to govern the financing and operation of an International Communications Satellite system, in a manner consistent with the public interest and our foreign policy.

But peace in space will help us naught once peace on earth is gone. World order will be secured only when the whole world has laid down these weapons which seem to offer us present security but threaten the future survival of the human race. That armistice day seems very far away. The vast resources of this planet are being devoted more and more to the means of destroying, instead of enriching, human life.

But the world was not meant to be a prison in which man awaits his execution. Nor has mankind survived the tests and trials of thousands of years to surrender everything, including its existence, now. This nation has the will and the faith to make a supreme effort to break the log jam on disarmament and nuclear tests; and we will persist until we prevail, until the rule of law has replaced the ever-dangerous use of force.

I turn now to a prospect of great promise: our hemispheric relations. The Alliance for Progress is being rapidly transformed from proposal to program. Last month in Latin America I saw for myself the quickening of hope, the revival of confidence and the new trust in our country, among workers and farmers as well as diplomats. We have pledged our help in speeding their economic, educational and social progress. The Latin-American republics have in turn pledged a new and strenuous effort of self-help and self-reform.

To support this historic undertaking, I am proposing, under the authority contained in the bills of the last session of the Congress, a special long-term Alliance for Progress fund of $3 billion. Combined with our Food for Peace, Export-Import Bank and other resources, this will provide more than $1 billion a year in new support for the Alliance. In addition, we have increased twelvefold our Spanish- and Portuguese-language broadcasting in Latin America, and improved hemispheric trade and defense. And while the blight of Communism has been increasingly exposed and isolated in the Americas, liberty has scored a gain. The people of the Dominican Republic, with our firm encouragement and help, and those of our sister republics of this hemisphere, are safely passing the treacherous course from dictatorship through disorder toward democracy.

Our efforts to help other new or developing nations, and to strengthen their stand for freedom, have also made progress. A newly unified Agency for International Development is reorienting our foreign assistance to emphasize long-term development loans instead of grants, more economic aid instead of military, individual plans to meet the individual needs of the nations, and new standards on what they must do to marshal their own resources.

A newly conceived Peace Corps is winning friends and helping people in fourteen countries, supplying trained and dedicated young men and women, to give these new nations a hand in building a society, and a glimpse of the best that is in our country. If there is a problem here, it is that we cannot supply the spontaneous and mounting demand.

A newly expanded Food for Peace Program is feeding the hungry of many lands with the abundance of our productive farms, providing lunches for children in school, wages for economic development, relief for the victims of flood and famine, and a better diet for millions whose daily bread is their chief concern.

These programs help people; and, by helping people, they help freedom. The views of their governments may sometimes be very different from ours, but events in Africa, the Middle East and Eastern Europe teach us never to write off any nation as lost to the Communists. That is the lesson of our time. We support the independence of those newer or weaker states whose history, geography, economy or lack of power impels them to remain outside "entangling alliances" —as we did for more than a century. For the independence of nations is a bar to the Communists' "grand design"; it is the basis of our own.

In the past year, for example, we have urged a neutral and independent Laos, regained there a common policy with our major allies, and insisted that a cease-fire precede negotiations. While a workable formula for supervising its independence is still to be achieved, both the spread of war, which might have involved this country also, and a Communist occupation have thus far been prevented.

A satisfactory settlement in Laos would also help to achieve and safeguard the peace in Vietnam, where the foe is increasing his tactics of terror, where our own efforts have been stepped up, and where the local government has initiated new programs and reforms to broaden the base of resistance. The systematic aggression now bleeding that country is not a "war of liberation," for Vietnam is already free. It is a war of attempted subjugation, and it will be resisted.

Finally, the united strength of the Atlantic Community has flourished in the last year under severe tests. NATO has increased both the number and the readiness of its air, ground and naval units, both its nuclear and nonnuclear capabilities. Even greater efforts by all its members are still required. Nevertheless our unity of purpose and will has been, I believe, immeasurably strengthened.

The threat to the brave city of Berlin remains. In these last six months the Allies have made it unmistakably clear that our presence in Berlin, our free access thereto and the freedom of two million West Berliners would not be surrendered either to force or through appeasement; that to maintain those rights and obligations, we are prepared to talk, when appropriate, and to fight, if necessary. Every member of NATO stands with us in a common commitment to preserve this symbol of free man's will to remain free.

I cannot now predict the course of future negotiations over Berlin. I can only say that we are sparing no honorable effort to find a peaceful and mutually acceptable resolution of this problem. I believe such a resolution can be found, and with it an improvement in our relations with the Soviet Union, if only the leaders in the Kremlin will recognize the basic rights and interests involved, and the interest of all mankind in peace.

But the Atlantic Community is no longer concerned with purely military aims. As its common undertakings grow at an ever-increasing pace, we are, and increasingly will be, partners in aid, trade, defense, diplomacy and monetary affairs.

The emergence of the new Europe is being matched by the emergence of new ties across the Atlantic. It is a matter of undramatic daily cooperation in hundreds of workaday tasks: of currencies kept in effective relation, of development loans meshed together, of standardized weapons and concerted diplomatic positions. The Atlantic Community grows, not like a volcanic mountain, by one mighty explosion, but like a coral reef, from the accumulating activity of all.

Thus we in the free world are moving steadily toward unity and cooperation, in the teeth of that old Bolshevik prophecy, and at the very time when extraordinary rumbles of discord can be heard across the Iron Curtain. It is not free societies which bear within them the seeds of inevitable disunity.

On one special problem, of great concern to our friends, and to us, I am proud to give the Congress an encouraging report. Our efforts to safeguard the dollar are progressing. In the eleven months preceding last February 1, we suffered a net loss of nearly $2 billion in gold. In the eleven months that followed, the loss was just over half a billion dollars. And our deficit in our basic transactions with the rest of the world—trade, defense, foreign aid and capital, excluding volatile short-term flows—has been reduced from $2 billion for 1960 to about one-third that amount for 1961. Speculative fever against the dollar is ending, and confidence in the dollar has been restored.

We did not, and could not, achieve these gains through import restrictions, troop withdrawals, exchange controls, dollar devaluation or choking off domestic recovery. We acted not in panic, but in perspective. But the problem is not yet solved. Persistently large deficits would endanger our economic growth and our military and defense commitments abroad. Our goal must be a reasonable equilibrium in our balance of payments. With the cooperation of the Congress, business, labor and our major allies, that goal can be reached.

We shall continue to attract foreign tourists and investments to our shores, to seek increased military purchases here by our Allies, to maximize foreign aid procurement from American firms, to urge increased aid from other fortunate nations to the less fortunate, to seek tax laws which do not favor investment in other industrialized nations or tax havens, and to urge coordination of Allied fiscal and monetary policies so as to discourage large and disturbing capital movements.

Above all, if we are to pay for our commitments abroad, we must expand our exports. Our businessmen must be export-conscious and export-competitive. Our tax policies must spur modernization of our plants. Our wage and price gains must be consistent with productivity to hold the line on prices. Our export credit and promotion campaigns for American industries must continue to expand.

But the greatest challenge of all is posed by the growth of the European Common Market. Assuming the accession of the United Kingdom, there will arise across the Atlantic a trading partner behind a single external tariff similar to ours with an economy which nearly equals our own. Will we in this country adapt our thinking to these new prospects and patterns, or will we wait until events have passed us by?

This is the year to decide. The Reciprocal Trade Act is expiring. We need a new law, a wholly new approach, a bold new instrument of American trade policy. Our decision could well affect the unity of the West, the course of the Cold War and the economic growth of our nation for a generation to come.

If we move decisively, our factories and farms can increase their sales to their richest, fastest-growing market. Our exports will increase. Our balance-of-payments position will improve. And we will have forged across the Atlantic a trading partnership with vast resources for freedom.

If, on the other hand, we hang back in deference to local economic pressures, we will find ourselves cut off from our major allies. Industries—and I believe this is most vital—industries will move their plants and jobs and capital inside the walls of the Common Market, and jobs therefore will be lost here in the United States if they cannot otherwise compete for its consumers. Our farm surpluses will pile up. Our balance of trade, as you all know, to Europe, to the Common Market, in farm products, is nearly three or four to one in our favor, amounting to one of the best earners of dollars in our balance-of-payments structure. Without entrance to this market, without the ability to enter it, our farm surpluses will pile up in the Middle West, tobacco in the South, and other commodities which have gone through Western Europe for fifteen years. Our balance-of-payments position will worsen. Our consumers will lack a wider choice of goods at lower prices. And millions of American workers, whose jobs depend on the sale or the transportation or the distribution of exports or imports, or whose jobs will be endangered by the movement of our capital to Europe, or whose jobs can be maintained only in an expanding economy—these millions of workers in your home states and mine will see their real interests sacrificed.

Members of the Congress, the United States did not rise to greatness by waiting for others to lead. This nation is the world's foremost manufacturer, farmer, banker, consumer and exporter. The Common Market is moving ahead at an economic growth rate twice ours. The Communist economic offensive is under way. The opportunity is ours; the initiative is up to us; and I believe that 1962 is the time.

To seize that initiative, I shall shortly send to the Congress a new five-year Trade Expansion Act, far-reaching in scope but designed with great care to make certain that its benefits to our people far outweigh any risks. The bill will permit the gradual elimination of tariffs here in the United States and in the Common Market on those items in which we together supply 80 percent of the world's trade—mostly items in which our own ability to compete is demonstrated by the fact that we sell abroad, in these items, substantially more than we import. This step will make it possible for our major industries to compete with their counterparts in Western Europe for access to European consumers.

On the other hand, the bill will permit a gradual reduction of duties up to 50 percent, permit bargaining by major categories, and provide for appropriate and tested forms of assistance to firms and employees adjusting to import competition. We are not neglecting the safeguards provided by peril points, an escape clause or the National Security Amendment. Nor are we abandoning our non-European friends or our traditional "most-favored nation" principle. On the contrary, the bill will provide new encouragement for their sale of tropical agricultural products, so important to our friends in Latin America, who have long depended upon the European Common Market, who now find themselves faced with new challenges which we must join with them in overcoming.

Concessions, in this bargaining, must of course be reciprocal, not unilateral. The Common Market will not fulfill its own high promise unless its outside tariff walls are low. The dangers of restriction or timidity in our own policy have counterparts for our friends in Europe. For together we face a common challenge: to enlarge the prosperity of free men everywhere, to build in partnership a new trading community in which all free nations may gain from the productive energy of free competitive effort.

These various elements in our foreign policy lead, as I have said, to a single goal—the goal of a peaceful world of free and independent states. This is our guide for the present and our vision for the future: a free community of nations, independent but interdependent, uniting north and south, east and west, in one great family of man, outgrowing and transcending the hates and fears that rend our age.

We will not reach that goal today, or tomorrow. We may not reach it in our own lifetime. But the quest is the greatest adventure of our century. We sometimes chafe at the burden of our obligations, the complexity of our decisions, the agony of our choices. But there is no comfort or security for us in evasion, no solution in abdication, no relief in irresponsibility.

A year ago, in assuming the tasks of the Presidency, I said that few generations in all history had been granted the role of being the great defender of freedom in its hour of maximum danger. This is our good fortune; and I welcome it now as I did a year ago. For it is the fate of this generation—of you in the Congress and of me as President—to live with a struggle we did not start, in a world we did not make. But the pressures of life are not always distributed by choice. And while no nation has ever faced such a challenge, no nation has ever been so ready to seize the burden and the glory of freedom.

And in this high endeavor, may God watch over the United States of America.

2 : The Third State of the Union Message

WASHINGTON, D.C.
JANUARY 14, 1963*

I congratulate you all, not merely on your electoral victory, but on your selected role in history. For you and I are privileged to serve the great Republic in what could be the most decisive decade in its long history. The choices we make, for good or ill, will affect the welfare of generations yet unborn.

---

* A new Congress, the Eighty-eighth, was beginning with the new year. The Eighty-seventh Congress, which had adjourned October 13, 1962, had made an unsatisfactory record in domestic legislation. To

Little more than one hundred weeks ago, I assumed the office of the President of the United States. In seeking the help of the Congress and our countrymen, I pledged no easy answers. I pledged, and asked, only toil and dedication. These the Congress and the people have given in good measure. And today, having witnessed in recent months a heightened respect for our national purpose and power, having seen the courageous calm of a united people in a perilous hour, and having observed a steady improvement in the opportunities and well-being of our citizens, I can report to you that the state of this old but youthful Union is good.

---

be sure, it had passed more than four-fifths of the bills the administration had sponsored. The new Trade Act, which authorized the President to negotiate on tariff reductions with enlarged power, and contained other liberal features, was especially important. The President had carried a housing bill, a debt limit extension, a foreign aid bill providing $4.9 billions, a strengthening of minimum wage legislation, a drug control bill, and measures providing for the support of national defense and the Peace Corps. Some of these measures, however, passed in unsatisfactory form, and some of them were essentially continuations of existing legislation. The drug control bill represented less a genuine passion for reform than a wave of emotion generated by the horrible effects of the drug thalidomide on some babies. Much of the country was bitterly disappointed by the failure of President Kennedy's broad measure to strengthen education, and by the defeat of his bill for medical care of the aged. People hoped for a better showing by the Eighty-eighth Congress—though when it made little progress the first year, the President reminded critics that it should be measured by its record in its full life of two years.

The administration still had its large numerical majority in both houses of Congress. In the mid-term elections of 1962 the Democrats had more than held their strength; they gained four seats in the Senate, and although they apparently lost four in the House, the effect of reapportionment under the census of 1960 was to give the President more real supporters. But the coalition of conservative Republicans and conservative Southern Democrats still kept the margin between administration adherents and opponents slender on important domestic measures, ten or a dozen votes sometimes determining the outcome.—A. N.

In the world beyond our borders, steady progress has been made in building a world of order. The people of West Berlin remain free and secure. A settlement, although still precarious, has been reached in Laos. The spearpoint of aggression has been blunted in South Vietnam. The end of the agony may be in sight in the Congo. The doctrine of troika is dead. And, while danger continues, a deadly threat has been removed from Cuba.

At home, the recession is behind us. Well over a million more men and women are working today than were working two years ago. The average factory work week is once again more than forty hours; our industries are turning out more goods than ever before; and more than half of the manufacturing capacity that lay silent and wasted one hundred weeks ago is humming with activity.

In short, both at home and abroad there may now be a temptation to relax. For the road has been long, the burden heavy, and the pace consistently urgent.

But we cannot be satisfied to rest here. This is the side of the hill, not the top. The mere absence of war is not peace. The mere absence of recession is not growth. We have made a beginning, but we have only begun.

Now the time has come to make the most of our gains, to translate the renewal of our national strength into the achievement of our national purpose.

America has enjoyed twenty-two months of uninterrupted economic recovery. But recovery is not enough. If we are to prevail in the long run, we must expand the long-run strength of our economy. We must move along the path to a higher rate of growth and full employment. For this would mean tens of billions of dollars more each year in production, profits, wages and public revenues. It would mean an end to the persistent slack which has kept our unemployment at an above 5 percent rate for sixty-one out of the past sixty-two months, and an end to the growing pressures for such restrictive measures as the thirty-five-hour week, which alone could increase hourly labor costs by as much as 14 percent, start a new wage-price spiral of inflation and undercut our efforts to compete with other nations.

To achieve these greater gains, one step, above all, is essential:

the enactment this year of a substantial reduction and revision in federal income taxes.

For it is increasingly clear—to those in government, business and labor who are responsible for our economy's success—that our obsolete tax system exerts too heavy a drag on private purchasing power, profits and employment. Designed to check inflation in earlier years, it now checks growth instead. It discourages extra effort and risk. It distorts the use of resources. It invites recurrent recessions, depresses our federal revenues and causes chronic budget deficits.

Now, when the inflationary pressures of the war and the postwar years no longer threaten, and the dollar commands new respect—now, when no military crisis strains our resources—now is the time to act. We cannot afford to be timid or slow. For this is the most urgent task confronting the Congress in 1963.

In an early message, I shall propose a permanent reduction in tax rates which will lower liabilities by $13.5 billion. Of this, $11 billion results from reducing individual tax rates, which now range between 20 and 91 percent, to a more sensible range of 14 to 65 percent, with a split in the present first bracket. Two and a half billion dollars result from reducing corporate tax rates, from 52 percent—which gives the government today a majority interest in profits—to the permanent pre-Korean level of 47 percent. This is in addition to the more than $2 billion cut in corporate tax liabilities resulting from last year's investment credit and depreciation reform.

To achieve this reduction within the limits of a manageable budget deficit, I urge: First, that these cuts be phased over three calendar years, beginning in 1963 with a cut of some $6 billion at annual rates; second, that these reductions be coupled with selected structural changes, beginning in 1964, which will broaden the tax base, end unfair and unnecessary preferences, remove or lighten certain hardships, and in the net offset some $3.5 billion of the revenue loss; and, third, that budgetary receipts at the outset be increased by $1.5 billion a year, without any change in tax liabilities, by gradually shifting the tax payments of large corporations to a more current time schedule. This combined program, by increasing the amount of our national income, will in time result in still higher federal revenues.

It is a fiscally responsible program, the surest and the soundest way of achieving in time a balanced budget in a balanced full-employment economy.

This net reduction in tax liabilities of $10 billion will increase the purchasing power of American families and business enterprises in every tax bracket, with the greatest increase going to our low-income consumers. It will, in addition, encourage the initiative and risk-taking on which our free-enterprise system depends—induce more investment, production and capacity use, help provide the two million new jobs we need every year, and reinforce the American principle of additional reward for additional effort.

I do not say that a measure for tax reduction and reform is the only way to achieve these goals. No doubt a massive increase in federal spending could also create jobs and growth, but in today's setting private consumers, employers and investors should be given a full opportunity first. No doubt a temporary tax cut could provide a spur to our economy, but a long-run problem compels a long-run resolution. No doubt a reduction in either individual or corporation taxes alone would be of great help, but corporations need customers and job seekers need jobs. No doubt tax reduction without reform would sound simpler and more attractive to many, but our growth is also hampered by a host of tax inequities and special preferences which have distorted the flow of investment. And, finally, there are no doubt some who would prefer to put off a tax cut in the hope that ultimately an end to the Cold War would make possible an equivalent reduction in government expenditures, but that end is not in view and to wait for it would be costly and self-defeating.

In submitting a tax program which will, of course, temporarily increase the deficit but can, I believe, ultimately end it, and in recognition of the need to control expenditures, I will shortly submit a fiscal 1964 administrative budget which, while allowing for needed rises in defense, space and fixed-interest charges, holds total expenditures for all other purposes below this year's level.

This requires the reduction or postponement of many desirable programs, the absorption of a large part of last year's federal pay raise through personnel and other economies, the termination of certain installations and projects, and the substitution in several programs of private for public credit. But I am convinced that the enactment this year of tax reduction and tax reform overshadows all other domestic problems in this Congress. For we cannot for long lead the cause of peace and freedom if we ever cease to set the pace here at home.

Tax reduction alone, however, is not enough to strengthen our society, to provide opportunities for the four million Americans who are born every year, to improve the lives of 32 million Americans who live on the outskirts of poverty. The quality of American life must keep pace with the quantity of American goods. This country cannot afford to be rich and desperately poor.

Therefore, by keeping the budgetary cost of existing programs within the limitations I have set, it is both possible and imperative to adopt other new measures that we cannot afford to postpone.

These measures are based on a series of fundamental premises, grouped under four related headings.

First, we need to strengthen our nation by investing in our youth. The future of any country which is dependent upon the will and wisdom of its citizens is damaged, and irreparably damaged, whenever any of its children are not educated to the full extent of their talents, from grade school through graduate school. Today an estimated four out of every ten students in the fifth grade will never finish high school, and that is a waste that we cannot afford.

In addition, there is no reason why one million young Americans, out of school and out of work, should all remain unwanted and often untrained on our city streets when their energies can be put to good use.

Finally, the overseas success of our Peace Corps volunteers, most of them young men and women carrying skills and ideals to needy people, suggests the merits of a similar corps serving our own community needs: in mental hospitals, on Indian Reservations, in centers for the aged or for young delinquents, in schools for the illiterate or the handicapped. As the idealism of our youth has served world peace, so can it serve the domestic tranquillity.

Second, we need to strengthen our nation by safeguarding its health. Our working men and women, instead of being forced to ask for help from public charity once they are old and ill, should start contributing now to their own retirement health program through the Social Security System.

Moreover, all our miracles of medical research will count for little if we cannot reverse the growing nationwide shortage of doctors, dentists and nurses, and the widespread shortages of nursing homes and modern, urban hospital facilities. Merely to keep the present ratio of doctors and dentists from declining any further, this country must, over the next ten years, increase the capacity of our medical schools by 50 percent and our dental schools by 100 percent.

Finally, and of deep concern, I believe that the abandonment of the mentally ill and the mentally retarded to the grim mercy of custodial institutions too often inflicts on them and their families a needless cruelty which this nation should not endure. The incidence of mental retardation in the United States of America is three times as high as that of Sweden, for example, and that figure can and must be reduced.

Third, we need to strengthen our nation by protecting the basic rights of its citizens. The right to competent counsel must be assured to every man accused of crime in federal court, regardless of his means.

And the most precious and powerful right in the world, the right to vote in a free American election, must not be denied to any citizens on grounds of their race or their color. I wish that all qualified Americans permitted to vote were willing to vote, but surely, in this centennial year of the Emancipation, all those who are willing to vote should always be permitted.

Fourth, we need to strengthen our nation by making the best and most economical use of its resources and facilities.

Our economic health depends on having healthy transportation arteries, and I believe the way to a more modern, economical choice of national transportation service is through increased competition and decreased regulation. Local mass transit, faring even worse, is as essential a community service as highways. Nearly three-fourths of our citizens live in urban areas, which occupy only 2 percent of our land, and if local transit is to survive and relieve the congestion of these cities, it needs federal stimulation and assistance.

Next, the government is in the shortage and stockpile business to the melancholy tune of $16 billion. We must continue to support farm income, but we should not pile more farm surpluses on top of the $7.5 billion worth we already own. We must maintain a stockpile of strategic materials, but the $8.5 billion worth we have acquired, for reasons both good and bad, is much more than we need, and we should be empowered to dispose of some of the excess in ways which will not cause market disruption.

Finally, our already overcrowded National Parks and recreation areas will have twice as many visitors ten years from now as they do today. If we do not plan today for the future growth of these and other great natural assets—not only parks and forests, but wildlife and wilderness preserves and water projects of all kinds—our children and their children will be poorer in every sense of the word.

Proposals will be made to the Congress in the coming days to meet these challenges.

These are not domestic concerns alone. For upon our achievement of greater vitality and strength here at home hang our fate and future in the world, our ability to sustain and supply the security of free men and nations, our ability to command their respect for our leadership, our ability to expand our trade without threat to our balance of payments, and our ability to adjust to the changing demands of Cold War competition and challenge.

We shall be judged more by what we do at home than by what we preach abroad. Nothing we could do to help the developing countries would help them half so much as a booming American economy, which consumes their raw materials; and nothing our opponents could do to encourage their own ambitions would encourage them half so much as a chronic lagging United States economy. These domestic tasks do not divert our energy or our security. They provide the very foundation for freedom's survival and success.

Turning to the world outside, it was only a few years ago—in Southeast Asia, Africa, Eastern Europe, Latin America, even in outer space—that Communism sought to convey the image of a unified, confident and expanding empire, closing in on a sluggish America and a free world in disarray. But few people would hold that picture today.

In these past months we have reaffirmed the scientific and military superiority of freedom. We have doubled our efforts in space, to assure us of being first in the future. We have undertaken the most far-reaching defense improvements in the peacetime history of this country, and we have maintained the frontiers of freedom from Vietnam to West Berlin. But complacency or self-congratulation can imperil our security as much as the weapons of our adversaries. A moment of pause is not a promise of peace. Dangerous problems remain from Cuba to the South China Sea. The world's prognosis prescribes, in short, not a year's vacation for us, but a year of obligation and opportunity.

Four special avenues of opportunity stand out: the Atlantic Alliance, the developing nations, the new Sino-Soviet difficulties and the search for world-wide peace.

First, how fares the Grand Alliance? Free Europe is entering into a new phase in its long and brilliant history. The era of colonial expansion has passed; the era of national rivalries is fading; and a new era of interdependence and unity is taking shape. Defying the old prophecies of Marx, consenting to what no conqueror could ever compel, the free nations of Europe are moving toward a unity of purpose and power and policy in every sphere of activity.

For seventeen years this movement has had our consistent support, both political and economic. Far from resenting the new Europe, we regard her as a welcome partner, not a rival. For the road to world peace and freedom is still very long, and these are burdens which only full partners can share—in supporting the common defense, in expanding world trade, in aligning our balance of payments, in aiding the emergent nations, in concerting political and economic policies, and in welcoming to our common effort other industrialized nations, notably Japan, whose remarkable political and economic development in the 1950's permits it now to play on the world scene a major, constructive role.

No doubt differences of opinion will continue to get more attention than agreements on action, as Europe moves from independence to more formal interdependence. But these are honest differences among honorable associates, more real and frequent, in fact, among our Western European allies than between them and the United States. For the unity of freedom has never relied on uniformity of opinion, fortunately. But the basic agreement of this alliance on fundamental issues continues.

The first task of the alliance remains the common defense. Last month, Prime Minister Macmillan and I laid plans for a new stage in our long, cooperative effort, one which aims to assist in the wider task of framing a common nuclear defense for the whole alliance. The Nassau Agreement recognizes that the security of the West is indivisible, and so must be our defense. But it also recognizes that this is an alliance of proud and sovereign nations, and works best when we do not forget it. It recognizes further that the nuclear defense of the West is not a matter for the present nuclear powers alone; that France will be such a power in the future; and that ways must be found, without increasing the hazards of nuclear diffusion, to increase the role of our other partners in planning, manning and directing a truly multilateral nuclear force within an increasingly intimate NATO Alliance. Finally, the Nassau Agreement recognizes that nuclear defense is not enough, that the agreed NATO levels of conventional strength must be met, and that the alliance cannot afford to be in a position of having to answer every threat with nuclear weapons or nothing.

We remain too near the Nassau decisions, and too far from their final realization, to know their place in history. But I believe that for the first time the door is open for the nuclear defense of the alliance to become a source of confidence, instead of a cause of contention.

The next most pressing concern of the alliance is our common economic goals of trade and growth. This nation continues to be concerned about its balance-of-payments deficit, which, despite its decline, remains a stubborn and troublesome problem. We believe, moreover, that closer economic ties among all free nations are essential to prosperity and peace. And neither we nor the members of the Common Market are so affluent that we can long afford to shelter high-cost farms or factories from the winds of foreign competition, or to restrict the channels of trade with other nations of the free world. If the Common Market should now move toward protectionism and restrictionism, it would undermine its own basic principles. This government means to use the authority conferred on it last year by the Congress to encourage trade expansion on both sides of the Atlantic and around the world.

Second, what of the developing and nonaligned nations? They were, I believe, shocked by the Soviets' sudden and secret attempt to transform Cuba into a nuclear striking base, and by Communist China's arrogant invasion of India. They have been reassured by our prompt assistance to India, by our support through the United Nations of the Congo's unification, by our patient search for disarmament, and by the improvement in our treatment of citizens and visitors whose skin does not happen to be white. And as the older colonialism recedes, and the neo-colonialism of the Communist powers stands out more starkly than ever, they realize more clearly that the issue in the world struggle is not Communism versus capitalism, but coercion versus a free choice.

They realize that the longing for independence is the same the world over, whether it is the independence of West Berlin or Vietnam. They realize that such independence runs athwart all Communist ambitions, but is in keeping with our own, and that our approach to their needs is resilient and resourceful, while the Communists rely on ancient doctrines and old dogmas.

Nevertheless, it is hard for any nation to focus on an external or subversive threat to its independence when its energies are drained in daily combat with the forces of poverty and despair. It makes little sense for us to assail, in speeches and resolutions, the horrors of Communism, to spend $50 billion a year to prevent its military advance, and then to begrudge spending, largely on American products, less than one-tenth of that amount to help other nations strengthen their independence and cure the social chaos in which Communism has always thrived.

I am proud, and I think most Americans are proud, of a mutual defense and assistance program, evolved with bipartisan support in three administrations, which has, with all of its recognized problems, contributed to the fact that not a single one of the nearly fifty United Nations members to gain independence since the Second World War has succumbed to Communist control.

I am proud of a program and of a country that has helped to arm and feed and clothe millions of people who live on the front lines of freedom. I am especially proud that this country has put forward for the sixties a vast cooperative effort to achieve economi꞉ growth and social progress throughout the Americas—the Alliance for Progress.

I do not underestimate the difficulties that we face in this mutual effort among our close neighbors, but the free states of this hemisphere, working in close collaboration, have begun to make this Alliance a reality. Today it is feeding one out of every four school-age children in Latin America an extra food ration from our farm surpluses. It has distributed 1.5 million schoolbooks and is building 17,000 classrooms. It has helped resettle tens of thousands of farm families on land they can call their own. It is stimulating our good neighbors to more self-help and reform—fiscal, social, institutional and land reforms. It is bringing housing and hope and health to millions who were forgotten. The men and women of this hemisphere know that the Alliance cannot succeed if it is only another name for United States handouts, that it can succeed only as the Latin-American nations themselves devote their best efforts to fulfilling its goals.

This story is the same in Africa, in the Middle East and in Asia. Wherever nations are willing to help themselves, we stand ready to help them build new bulwarks of freedom. We are not purchasing votes for the Cold War; we have gone to the aid of imperiled nations, neutrals and allies alike. What we do ask, and all that we ask, is that our help be used to the best advantage, and that their own efforts not be diverted by needless quarrels with other independent nations.

Despite all its past achievements, the continued progress of the Mutual Assistance Program requires a persistent discontent with present progress. We have been reorganizing this program to make it a more effective and efficient instrument, and that process will continue this year.

But free world development will still be an uphill struggle. Governmental aid can only supplement the role of private investment, trade expansion, commodity stabilization and, above all, internal self-improvement. The processes of growth are gradual, bearing fruit in a decade, not a day. Our successes will be neither quick nor dramatic. But if these programs were ever to be ended, our failures in a dozen countries would be sudden and would be certain.

Neither money nor technical assistance, however, can be our only weapon against poverty. In the end, the crucial effort is one of purpose, requiring the fuel of finance and also a torch of idealism. And nothing carries the spirit of this American idealism and expresses our hopes better and more effectively to the far corners of the earth than the American Peace Corps.

A year ago less than nine hundred Peace Corps volunteers were on the job. A year from now they will number more than nine thousand —men and women, aged eighteen to seventy-nine, willing to give two years of their lives to helping people in other lands. There are, in fact, nearly one million Americans serving their country and the cause of freedom in overseas posts, a record no other people can match.

Surely those of us who stay at home should be glad to help indirectly, by supporting our aid programs; by opening our doors to foreign visitors and diplomats and students; and by proving, day by day, by deed as well as by word, that we are a just and generous people.

Third, what comfort can we take from the increasing strains and tensions within the Communist bloc? Here hope must be tempered with caution. For the Soviet-Chinese disagreement is over means, not ends. A dispute over how to bury the West is no ground for Western rejoicing.

Nevertheless, while a strain is not a fracture, it is clear that the forces of diversity are at work inside the Communist camp, despite all the iron disciplines of regimentation and all the iron dogmatisms of ideology. Marx is proven wrong once again, for it is the closed Communist societies, not the free and open societies, which carry within themselves the seeds of internal disintegration.

This disarray of the Communist empire has been heightened by two other formidable forces. One is the historic force of nationalism and the yearning of all men to be free. The other is the gross inefficiency of their economies. For a closed society is not open to ideas of progress, and a police state finds it cannot command the grain to grow.

New nations asked to choose between two competing systems need only compare conditions in East and West Germany, Eastern and Western Europe, North and South Vietnam. They need only compare the disillusionment of Communist Cuba with the promise of a hemisphere Alliance for Progress. And all the world knows that no successful system builds a wall to keep its people in and freedom out, and that the wall dividing Berlin is a symbol of that Communist failure.

Finally, what can we do to move from the present pause toward enduring peace? I would counsel caution. I foresee no spectacular reversal in Communist methods or goals. But if all these trends and developments can persuade the Soviet Union to walk the path of peace, then let her know that all free nations will join with her. But until that choice is made, and until the world can develop a reliable system of international security, the free peoples have no choice but to keep their arms near.

This country, therefore, continues to require the best defense in the world, a defense which is suited to the sixties. This means, unfortunately, a rising defense budget, for there is no substitute for adequate defense, and no "bargain basement" way of achieving it. It means the expenditure of more than $15 billion this year on nuclear weapons systems alone, a sum which is about equal to the combined defense budgets of our European allies.

But it also means improved air and missile defenses, improved civil defense, a strengthened antiguerrilla capacity and, of prime importance, more powerful and flexible nonnuclear forces. For threats of massive retaliation may not deter piecemeal aggression, and a line of destroyers in a quarantine or a division of well-equipped men on a border may be more useful to our real security than the multiplication of awesome weapons beyond all rational need.

But our commitment to national safety is not a commitment to expand our military establishment indefinitely. We do not dismiss disarmament as an idle dream. For we believe in the end that it is the only way of insuring the security of all without impairing the interests of any. Nor do we mistake honorable negotiation for appeasement. While we shall never weary in the defense of freedom, neither shall we abandon the pursuit of peace.

In this quest, the United Nations requires our full and continued support. Its value in serving the cause of peace has been shown anew in its role in the West New Guinea settlement, in its use as a forum for the Cuban crisis and in its task of unification in the Congo. Today the United Nations is primarily the protector of the small and the weak and a safety valve for the strong. Tomorrow it can form the framework for a world of law, a world in which no nation dictates the destiny of another, and in which the vast resources now devoted to destructive means will serve constructive ends.

In short, let our adversaries choose. If they choose peaceful competition, they shall have it. If they come to realize that their ambitions cannot succeed; if they see their "wars of liberation" and subversion will ultimately fail; if they recognize that there is more security in accepting inspection than in permitting new nations to master the black arts of nuclear weapons and war; and if they are willing to turn their energies, as we are, to the great unfinished tasks of our own peoples—then, surely, the areas of agreement can be very wide indeed: a clear understanding about Berlin, stability in Southeast Asia, an end to nuclear testing, new checks on surprise or accidental attack and, ultimately, general and complete disarmament.

For we seek not the world-wide victory of one nation or system, but a world-wide victory of men. The modern globe is too small, its weapons are too destructive, they multiply too fast, and its disorders are too contagious to permit any other kind of victory.

To achieve this end, the United States will continue to spend a greater portion of its national production than any other people in the free world. For fifteen years no other free nation has demanded so much of itself. Through hots wars and cold, through recession and prosperity, through the ages of the atom and outer space, the American people have neither faltered nor has their faith flagged. If at times our actions seem to make life difficult for others, it is only because history has made life difficult for us all.

But difficult days need not be dark. I think these are proud and memorable days in the cause of peace and freedom. We are proud, for example, of Major Rudolf Anderson, who gave his life over the island of Cuba. We salute Specialist James Allen Johnson, who died on the border of South Korea. We pay honor to Sergeant Gerald Pendell, who was killed in Vietnam. They are among the many who in this century, far from home, have died for our country. Our task now, and the task of all Americans, is to live up to their commitment.

My friends, I close on a note of hope. We are not lulled by the momentary calm of the sea or the somewhat clearer skies above. We know the turbulence that lies below, and the storms that are beyond the horizon this year. But now the winds of change appear to be blowing more strongly than ever, in the world of Communism as well as our own. For 175 years we have sailed with those winds at our back, and with the tides of human freedom in our favor. We steer our ship with hope, as Thomas Jefferson said, "leaving fear astern."

Today we still welcome those winds of change, and we have every reason to believe that our tide is running strong. With thanks to Almighty God for seeing us through a perilous passage, we ask His help anew in guiding the good ship "Union."

3 : The Work Done and the Work Still to Do

AFL-CIO CONVENTION
NEW YORK, NEW YORK
NOVEMBER 15, 1963*

The other day I read in a newspaper that Senator Goldwater asked for labor's support before two thousand cheering Illinois businessmen. I've come here to ask labor's support for a program for the United States.

I'm glad to come to this convention, and I think the AFL-CIO at this convention, and looking back over the years, over this century,

---

* Despite a dilatory and disappointing record of legislative action during the first year of the Eighty-eighth Congress, the President not only looked forward to the second year, but also took pleasure in the support the AFL-CIO had given parts of his program. It had moved to raise the minimum wage to $1.25 an hour, and had increased the coverage of this wage for the first time in twenty years. Congress had passed what the President called "the best Housing Act since 1949." It had carried against grim opposition a bill (twice vetoed by President Eisenhower) furnishing assistance to districts suffering from chronic

can take pride in the actions it has taken, pride in the stands it has made, pride in the things it has done, not only for the American labor movement, but for the United States as a whole. It is no accident. . . .

With your help and support, with your concern, we have worked to try to improve the lot of the people of the United States.

In the last three years abroad we have doubled the number of nuclear weapons in our strategic alert forces; in the last three years we've increased by 45 percent the number of combat-ready Army divisions.

We've increased by 600 percent the number of our counterinsurgency forces, increased by 175 percent our procurement of airlift aircraft and doubled our Polaris and Minuteman programs. The United States is stronger today than ever before in our history. And with that strength we work for peace.

And here in the United States we've encouraged the peaceful desegregation of schools in 238 districts, theaters in 144 cities, restaurants in 129 cities and lunch counters in 100 cities, while at the same time taking Executive action to open doors to our citizens in transportation terminals and polling places and public and private employment.

And finally, we've been working to strengthen the economy of the United States through the Area Redevelopment Act of '61, through the Public Works Acceleration Act of '62, through the Manpower Development and Training Act of '62.

We've increased industry's ability and desire to hire men through

---

unemployment. It had passed legislation providing for long-range measures against water pollution. It had increased the benefits under Social Security, and lowered the Social Security retirement age for men from sixty-five to sixty-two. It had also secured the appropriation in 1962 of $435 million for a three-year program of occupational training. But, as the President here explains, much remained to be done, especially in the enactment of legislation to stimulate the economy and thus provide more employment. He was confident that organized labor would remain his staunch ally.—A. N.

the most extensive and promising Trade Expansion Act in our history, through the most comprehensive Housing and Urban Renewal Act of all time, through liberalized depreciation guidelines and through over a billion-dollar loan to small businessmen.

We have boosted the purchasing power and relieved the distress of some of those least able to take care of themselves—by increasing the minimum wage to $1.25, which is still much too low, and expanding its coverage by three and a half millions, which is still too little; by increasing Social Security benefits to men and women who can retire at the age of sixty-two; by granting for the first time in the history of the United States public assistance to several hundred thousand children of unemployed fathers; and by extending the benefits of nearly three million jobless workers.

By doing these things and others we have attempted to work for the benefit of our people. And I can assure you that if we could obtain —and I see no good reason why we should not—the prompt passage of the pending $11 billion tax reduction bill, we will be sailing by next April on the winds of the longest and strongest peacetime expansion in the history of the United States.

Our national output three years ago was $500 billion. In January, three years later, it will be $600 billion, a record rise of $100 billion in thirty-six months. For the first time in history we have seventy million men and women at work. For the first time in history factory earnings have exceeded $100 a week. And even the stock market has broken all records—though we only get credit when it goes down.

The average factory worker takes home ten dollars a week more than he did three years ago, and two and a half million people more are at work. In fact, if the economy during the last two and a half years had grown at the same lagging pace that it did in the last two and a half years of the fifties, unemployment today would be 8 percent. In short, we have made progress, but all of us know that more progress must be made. That's what we're here about.

I'm here today to talk about the right to work—the right to have a job in this country in a time of prosperity in the United States. That's the real right-to-work issue of 1963.

In spite of this progress, this country must move fast even to stand still. Productivity goes up so fast, the number of people coming into the labor market is so increased, ten million more jobs are needed in the next two and a half years.

Even with this astonishing economic progress, which in the last eighteen months has meant that the United States has grown faster economically than France and Germany, than any country in Europe but two—even with this extraordinary economic progress in the last eighteen months, we still have an unemployment rate of 5.5 percent with four million people out of work. Productivity goes up so fast, so many millions come into the labor market, that unless we have the most extraordinary economic progress in the history of our country we cannot possibly make a dent in the 5.5 percent figure.

So while we take some satisfaction in what we've done and tried to do, this group more than any knows how much we still have left to do, and I hope the day will never come—nor do I predict it—when the AFL-CIO will be satisfied with anything less than the best.

Four million people are out of work. All the people who opposed the efforts we're making to try to improve the economic climate of the United States, who talked to us so long about socialism and deficits and all the rest, should look at that figure: four million people out of work. And judging from last summer's statistics, three times that many have experienced some unemployment.

That hanging over the labor market makes it more difficult for those of you who speak for labor at the bargaining table to speak with force. When there are so many people out of work, it affects the whole economic climate. That's why I think that this issue of economic security, of jobs, is the basic issue facing the United States in 1963, and I wish we could get everybody talking about it.

A quarter of the people we're talking about are out of work fifteen weeks or longer, and their families feel it. This is a year of prosperity, of record prosperity, and 1954 was a year of recession, and yet our unemployment rate is as high today as it was in 1954.

Last year's loss of man-hours in terms of those willing but unable to find full-time work was a staggering one billion work days lost, equivalent to shutting down the entire country for three weeks with no pay. That is an intolerable waste for this rich country of ours.

And that's why I say that economic security is the No. 1 issue today. It is not so recognized by everyone. There are those who oppose the tax cut, the youth employment bill, who oppose more money for depressed areas and job retraining and other public needs.

And they are powerful and articulate. They are campaigning on a platform of so-called individual initiative. They talk loudly of deficits and socialism. But they do not have a single constructive job-creating program of their own, and they oppose the efforts that we are making. I do not believe that selling TVA is a program to put people to work.

There are those who support our efforts for jobs but say it isn't the No. 1 issue. Some may say that civil rights is the No. 1 issue. This nation needs the passage of our bill if we are to fulfill our constitutional obligations. But no one gains from a fair employment practice bill if there is no employment to be had. No one gains by being admitted to a lunch counter if he has no money to spend. No one gains from attending a better school if he doesn't have a job after graduation. No one thinks much of the right to own a good home, or to sleep in a good hotel, or go to the theater, if he has no work and no money. Civil rights legislation is important. But to make that legislation effective, we need jobs in the United States.

And some may say that the No. 1 domestic issue is education, and this nation must improve its education. What concerns me almost more than anything is the statistic that there will be eight million young boys and girls coming into the labor market in the sixties who have not been graduated from high school.

Where are they going to find jobs? Which of your unions is going to be able to put them to work? Eight million of them. But the best schools, the best teachers and the best books—all these are of no avail if there are no jobs. The out-of-work college graduate is just as much out of work as the school dropout. The family beset by unemployment cannot send a child to college. It may even encourage him to drop out of high school to find a job which he will not keep.

Education is a key to the growth of this country. We must educate our children as our most valuable resource. We must make it possible for those who have talent to go to college, but only if those who are educated can find a job.

If jobs are the most important domestic issue that this country faces, then clearly no single step can now be more important in sustaining the economy of the United States than the passage of our tax bill. For this will help consumer markets, and build investment demand, and build business incentive, and therefore provide jobs for a total addition to the economy of the United States in the next months of nearly $30 billion.

We dare not wait for this tax cut until it's too late, as perhaps some would have. On the average this nation's period of peacetime expansion before the downturn comes leading to a recession has lasted twenty-eight months since 1920 and thirty-two months since the end of the Second World War.

Today we are already in our thirty-third month of economic expansion, and we urgently need that tax cut as insurance against a recession next year. We need that cut where it will do the most good. And the benefits mostly will go to those two or three million people who out of that bill will find new jobs.

But tax cuts are not enough, and jobs are not enough, and higher earnings and greater growth and record prosperity are not enough—unless that prosperity is used to sustain a better society. We can take real pride in a $600 billion economy and seventy million jobs only when they are underwriting to the fullest extent possible to improve our schools, to rebuild our cities, to counsel our youth, to assure our health and to care for our aged and infirm.

Next Monday the House Ways and Means Committee will open its hearings on a bill too long delayed to provide hospital insurance for our older citizens. These hearings are desirable, but the facts are known.

Our older and retired workers are sick more often and for longer periods than the rest of the population. Their income is only half that of our younger citizens. They cannot afford either the rising cost of hospital care or the rising cost of hospital insurance. Their children cannot afford to pay hospital bills for three generations—for their children, for themselves and for their parents. I have no doubt that most children are willing to try to do it, but they cannot, and I think that the United States should heed its responsibilities as a proud and resourceful country.

I cannot tell whether we're going to get this legislation before Christmas, but I can say that I believe that this Congress will not go home next summer to the people of the United States without passing this bill. I think we should stay there till we do.

~§ II

THE CONTINUING

STRUGGLE FOR PEACE

4 : Constant Readiness for Fair Negotiations

UNIVERSITY OF WASHINGTON
SEATTLE, WASHINGTON
NOVEMBER 16, 1961*

... As long as we know what comprises our vital interests and our long-range goals, we have nothing to fear from negotiations at the appropriate time, and nothing to gain by refusing to play a part in them. At a time when a single clash could escalate overnight into a holocaust of mushroom clouds, a great power does not prove its firmness by leaving the task of exploring the other's intentions to sentries or those without full responsibility. Nor can ultimate weapons rightfully be employed, or the ultimate sacrifice rightfully demanded of our citizens, until every reasonable solution has been explored. "How many wars," Winston Churchill has written, "have been averted by patience and persisting good will! . . . . How many wars have been precipitated by firebrands!"

If vital interests under duress can be preserved by peaceful means, negotiations will find that out. If our adversary will accept nothing less than a concession of our rights, negotiations will find that out. And if negotiations are to take place, this nation cannot abdicate to

---

* President Kennedy used the centenary commemoration at the University of Washington in Seattle to pay tribute to Justin S. Morrill of Vermont for his authorship of the epochal Land Grant Act passed July 2, 1862, the basis for the creation of an imposing system of state universities and colleges. He then turned to the spirit in which the United States approached international problems. When he delivered this speech, his meeting with Khrushchev in Vienna on June 3-4, a proof of his willingness to explore possible paths toward peace, was fresh in public memory. He had said after that meeting, "No spectacular progress was either achieved or pretended." But he thought it had reduced the chances of a "dangerous misjudgment."—A. N.

43

its adversaries the task of choosing the forum and the framework and the time.

For there are carefully defined limits within which any serious negotiations must take place. With respect to any future talks on Germany and Berlin, for example, we cannot, on the one hand, confine our proposals to a list of concessions we are willing to make, nor can we, on the other hand, advance any proposals which compromise the security of free Germans and West Berliners, or endanger their ties with the West.

No one should be under the illusion that negotiations for the sake of negotiations always advance the cause of peace. If for lack of preparation they break up in bitterness, the prospects of peace have been endangered. If they are made a forum for propaganda or a cover for aggression, the processes of peace have been abused.

But it is a test of our national maturity to accept the fact that negotiations are not a contest spelling victory or defeat. They may succeed; they may fail. They are likely to be successful only if both sides reach an agreement which both regard as preferable to the status quo, an agreement in which each side can consider its own situation can be improved. And this is most difficult to obtain. . . .

5 : Nuclear Testing and Disarmament

TELEVISION ADDRESS TO THE PEOPLE
THE WHITE HOUSE
WASHINGTON, D.C.
MARCH 2, 1962*

Seventeen years ago man unleashed the power of the atom. He thereby took into his mortal hands the power of self-extinction. Throughout the years that have followed, under three successive

---

* The United States had warned the Soviet Government in June, 1961, that it must resume tests of nuclear weapons if Russia con-

Presidents, the United States has sought to banish this weapon from the arsenals of individual nations. For of all the awesome responsibilities entrusted to this office, none is more somber to contemplate than the special statutory authority to employ nuclear arms in the defense of our people and freedom.

But until mankind has banished both war and its instruments of destruction, the United States must maintain an effective quantity and quality of nuclear weapons, so deployed and protected as to be capable of surviving any surprise attack and devastating the attacker. Only through such strength can we be certain of deterring a nuclear strike, or an overwhelming ground attack, upon our forces and allies. Only through such strength can we in the free world, should that

---

tinued to delay the progress of talks on nuclear disarmament then under way in Geneva. Throughout the summer many leaders inside and outside Congress pressed strongly for resumption, on the ground that Russia might be making secret tests and gaining a lead. Despite numerous assurances that the Soviet Union would not explode new devices, Chairman Khrushchev at the end of August ordered new testing. This seemed the more alarming because it followed hard upon the East German steps to close the border between East and West Berlin by a barbed wire wall; and because it also followed an increase of the defense outlay in the Russian budget for 1961–62 to one-sixth of the total. The White House at once declared that Khrushchev's announcement freed the United States to resume testing. Early in September President Kennedy directed a resumption of laboratory and underground tests. Then at the beginning of November, with the approval of Prime Minister Macmillan and the support of ex-Presidents Truman and Eisenhower, he ordered preparations for atmospheric testing. The country reluctantly agreed that these decisions were a necessity.

But the President and the people were nevertheless anxious that the talks upon disarmament which Arthur Dean had been conducting at Geneva should be continued, and Mr. Macmillan was equally anxious to prosecute them. Mr. Kennedy's anxiety to hold the door open, and his readiness to study the views of the Russian Government carefully, were plainly manifest; and he was shortly to expound them at length in his speech at the American University in Washington.—A. N.

deterrent fail, face the tragedy of another war with any hope of survival. And that deterrent strength, if it is to be effective and credible when compared with that of any other nation, must embody the most modern, the most reliable and the most versatile nuclear weapons our research and development can produce.

The testing of new weapons and their effects is necessarily a part of that research and development process. Without tests, to experiment and verify, progress is limited. A nation which is refraining from tests obviously cannot match the gains of a nation conducting tests. And when all nuclear powers refrain from testing, the nuclear arms race is held in check.

That is why this nation has long urged an effective world-wide end to nuclear tests. And that is why in 1958 we voluntarily subscribed, as did the Soviet Union, to a nuclear test moratorium, during which neither side would conduct new nuclear tests and both East and West would seek concrete plans for their control.

But on September 1 of last year, while the United States and the United Kingdom were negotiating in good faith at Geneva, the Soviet Union callously broke its moratorium with a two-month series of more than forty nuclear tests. Preparations for these tests had been secretly under way for many months. Accompanied by new threats and new tactics of terror, these tests, conducted mostly in the atmosphere, represented a major Soviet effort to put nuclear weapons back into the arms race.

Once it was apparent that new appeals and proposals were to no avail, I authorized on September 5 a resumption of U.S. nuclear tests underground, and I announced on November 2, before the close of the Soviet series, that preparations were being ordered for a resumption of atmospheric tests, and that we would make whatever tests our security required in the light of Soviet gains.

This week the National Security Council has completed its review of this subject. The scope of the Soviet tests has been carefully reviewed by the most competent scientists in the country. The scope and justification of proposed American tests have been carefully reviewed, determining which experiments can be safely deferred, which can be deleted, which can be combined or conducted underground, and which are essential to our military and scientific progress. Careful attention has been given to the limiting of radioactive fallout, to the future course of arms control diplomacy and to our obligations to other nations.

Every alternative was examined. Every avenue of obtaining Soviet agreement was explored. We were determined not to rush into imitating their tests. And we were equally determined to do only what our own security required us to do. Although the complex preparations have continued at full speed while these facts were being uncovered, no single decision of this administration has been more thoroughly or more thoughtfully weighed.

Having carefully considered these findings, having received the unanimous recommendations of the pertinent department and agency heads, and having observed the Soviet Union's refusal to accept any agreement which would inhibit its freedom to test extensively after preparing secretly, I have today authorized the Atomic Energy Commission and the Department of Defense to conduct a series of nuclear tests, beginning when our preparations are completed, in the latter part of April, and to be concluded as quickly as possible (within two or three months), such series, involving only those tests which cannot be held underground, to take place in the atmosphere over the Pacific Ocean.

These tests are to be conducted under conditions which restrict the radioactive fallout to an absolute minimum, far less than the contamination created by last fall's Soviet series. By paying careful attention to location, wind and weather conditions, and by holding these tests over the open sea, we intend to rule out any problem of fallout in the immediate area of testing. Moreover, we will hold the increase in radiation in the Northern Hemisphere, where nearly all such fallout will occur, to a very low level.

Natural radioactivity, as everyone knows, has always been part of the air around us, with certain long-range biological effects. By conservative estimate, the total effects from this test series will be roughly equal to only one percent of those due to this natural background. It has been estimated, in fact, that the exposure due to radioactivity from these tests will be less than one-fiftieth of the difference which can be experienced, due to variations in natural radioactivity, simply by living in different locations in this country. This will obviously be well within the guides for general population health and safety, as set by the Federal Radiation Council; and considerably less than one-tenth of one percent of the exposure guides set for adults who work with industrial radioactivity.

Nevertheless, I find it deeply regrettable that any radioactive material must be added to the atmosphere, that even one additional individual's health may be risked in the foreseeable future. And however remote and infinitesimal those hazards are judged to be, I still exceedingly regret the necessity of balancing these hazards against the hazards to hundreds of millions of lives which would be created by any relative decline in our nuclear strength.

In the absence of a major shift in Soviet policies, no American President, responsible for the freedom and safety of so many people, could in good faith make any other decision. But because our nuclear posture affects the security of all Americans and all free men, because this issue has aroused such widespread concern, I want to share with you and all the world, to the fullest extent our security permits, all of the facts and thoughts which have gone into my decision.

Many of these facts are hard to explain in simple terms; many are hard to face in a peaceful world; but these are facts which must be faced and must be understood.

Had the Soviet tests of last fall reflected merely a new effort in intimidation and bluff, our security would not have been affected. But, in fact, they also reflected a highly sophisticated technology, the trial of novel designs and techniques, and some substantial gains in weaponry. Many of their tests were aimed at improving their defenses against missiles; others were proof tests, trying out existing weapons systems; but over one-half emphasized the development of new weapons, particularly those of greater explosive power.

A primary purpose of these tests was the development of warheads which weigh very little compared to the destructive efficiency of their thermonuclear yield. One Soviet test weapon exploded with the force of 58 megatons—the equivalent of 58 million tons of TNT. This was a reduced-yield version of their much-publicized hundred-megaton bomb. Today, Soviet missiles do not appear able to carry so heavy a warhead. But there is no avoiding the fact that other Soviet tests, in the one-to-five megaton range and up, were aimed at unleashing increased destructive power in warheads actually capable of delivery by existing missiles.

Much has also been said about Soviet claims for an antimissile missile. Some of the Soviet tests which measured the effects of high-altitude nuclear explosion—in one case over a hundred miles high—were related to this problem. While apparently seeking information on the effects of nuclear blasts on radar and communication which is important in developing an antimissile defense system, these tests did not, in our judgment, reflect a developed system.

In short, last fall's tests, in and by themselves, did not give the Soviet Union superiority in nuclear power. They did, however, provide the Soviet laboratories with a mass of data and experience on which, over the next two or three years, they can base significant analyses, experiments and extrapolations, preparing for the next test series which would confirm and advance their findings.

And I must report to you in all candor that further Soviet series, in the absence of further Western progress, could well provide the Soviet Union with a nuclear attack and defense capability so power-ful as to encourage aggressive designs. Were we to stand still while the Soviets surpassed us, or even appeared to surpass us, the free world's ability to deter, to survive and to respond to an all-out attack would be seriously weakened.

The fact of the matter is that we cannot make similar strides with-out testing in the atmosphere as well as underground. For, in many areas of nuclear weapons research, we have reached the point where our progress is stifled without experiments in every environment. The information from our last series of atmospheric tests in 1958 has all been analyzed and reanalyzed. It can tell us no more without new data. And it is in these very areas of research—missile penetration and missile defense, for example—that further major Soviet tests, in the absence of further Western tests, might endanger our deterrent.

In addition to proof tests of existing systems, two different types of tests have therefore been decided upon. The first and most important are called "effects tests"—determining what effect an enemy's nuclear explosions would have upon our ability to survive and respond. We are spending great sums of money on radar to alert our defenses and to develop possible antimissile systems; on the communications which enable our command and control centers to direct a response; on hardening our missile sites, shielding our missiles and their warheads from defensive action, and providing them with electronic guidance systems to find their targets. But we cannot be certain how much of this preparation will turn out to be useless: blacked out, paralyzed or destroyed by the complex effects of a nuclear explosion.

We know enough from earlier tests to be concerned about such phenomena. We know that the Soviets conducted such tests last fall. But until we measure the effects of actual explosions in the atmosphere under realistic conditions, we will not know precisely how to prepare our future defenses, how best to equip our missiles for penetration of an antimissile system, and whether it is possible to achieve such a system for ourselves.

Secondly, we must test in the atmosphere to permit the development of those more advanced concepts and more effective, efficient weapons which, in the light of Soviet tests, are deemed essential to our security. Nuclear weapon technology is still a constantly changing field. If our weapons are to be more secure, more flexible in their use and more selective in their impact; if we are to be alert to new breakthroughs, to experiment with new designs; if we are to maintain our scientific momentum and leadership; then our weapons progress must not be limited to theory or to the confines of laboratories and caves.

This series is designed to lead to many important, if not always dramatic, results. Improving the nuclear yield per pound of weight in our weapons will make them easier to move, protect and fire, more likely to survive a surprise attack, and more adequate for effective retaliation. It will also, even more importantly, enable us to add to our missiles certain penetration aids and decoys, and to make those missiles effective at higher-altitude detonations, in order to render ineffective any antimissile or interceptor system an enemy might someday develop.

Whenever possible, these development tests will be held underground. But the larger explosions can only be tested in the atmosphere. And while our technology in smaller weapons is unmatched, we know now that the Soviets have made major gains in developing larger weapons of low weight and high explosive content—of one to five megatons and upward. Fourteen of their tests last fall were in this category, for a total of thirty such tests over the years. The United States, on the other hand, had conducted, prior to the moratorium, a total of only twenty tests within this megaton range. . . .

If the Soviets should change their position, we will have an opportunity to learn it immediately. On the fourteenth of March, in Geneva, Switzerland, a new eighteen-power conference on disarmament will begin. A statement of agreed principles has been worked out with the Soviets and endorsed by the UN. In the long run, it is the constructive possibilities of that conference, and not the testing of new destructive weapons, on which rest the hopes of all mankind. However dim those hopes may sometimes seem, they can never be abandoned. And however far off most steps toward disarmament appear, there are some that can be taken at once.

The United States will offer at the Geneva conference, not in the advance expectation they will be rejected and not merely for purposes of propaganda, a series of concrete plans for a major "breakthrough to peace." We hope and believe that they will appeal to all nations opposed to war. They will include specific proposals for fair and enforceable agreements: to halt the production of fissionable materials and nuclear weapons and their transfer to other nations; to convert them from weapon stockpiles to peaceable uses; to destroy the warheads and the delivery systems that threaten man's existence; to check the dangers of surprise and accidental attack; to reserve outer space for peaceful use; and progressively to reduce all armed forces in such a way as ultimately to remove forever all threats and thoughts of war.

And of greatest importance to our discussion tonight, we shall, in association with the United Kingdom, present once again our proposals for a separate comprehensive treaty, with appropriate arrangements for detection and verification, to halt permanently the testing of all nuclear weapons, in every environment: in the air, in outer space, underground or underwater. New modifications will also be offered in the light of new experience.

The essential arguments and facts relating to such a treaty are well known to the Soviet Union. There is no need for further repetition, propaganda or delay. The fact that both sides have decided to resume testing only emphasizes the need for new agreement, not new argument. And before charging that this decision shatters all hopes for agreement, the Soviets should recall that we were willing to work out with them, for joint submission to the UN, an agreed statement of disarmament principles at the very time their autumn tests were being conducted. And Mr. Khrushchev knows, as he said in 1960, that any nation which broke the moratorium could expect other nations to be "forced to take the same road."

Our negotiators will be ready to talk about this treaty even before the conference begins on March 14, and they will be ready to sign well before the date on which our tests are ready to begin. That date is still nearly two months away. If the Soviet Union should now be willing to accept such a treaty, sign it before the latter part of April and apply it immediately—if all testing can thus be actually halted—then the nuclear arms race would be slowed down at last, the security of the United States and its ability to meet its commitments would be safeguarded, and there would be no need for our tests to begin. . . .

It is our hope and prayer that these grim, unwelcome tests will never have to be made, that these deadly weapons will never have to be fired, and that our preparations for war will bring us the preservation of peace. Our foremost aim is the control of force, not the pursuit of force, in a world made safe for mankind. But whatever the future brings, I am sworn to uphold and defend the freedom of the American people, and I intend to do whatever must be done to fulfill that solemn obligation.

6 : What Kind of Peace Do We Want?

THE AMERICAN UNIVERSITY
WASHINGTON, D.C.
JUNE 10, 1963*

"There are few earthly things more beautiful than a University," wrote John Masefield, in his tribute to the English universities, and his words are equally true here. He did not refer to spires and towers, to campus greens and ivied walls. He admired the splendid beauty of the university, he said, because it was "a place where those who hate ignorance may strive to know, where those who perceive truth may strive to make others see."

I have therefore chosen this time and this place to discuss a topic on which ignorance too often abounds and the truth is too rarely perceived, yet it is the most important topic on earth: world peace.

What kind of peace do I mean? What kind of peace do we seek? Not a *Pax Americana* enforced on the world by American weapons of war. Not the peace of the grave or the security of the slave. I am talking about genuine peace, the kind of peace that makes life on earth worth living, the kind that enables men and nations to grow and to hope and to build a better life for their children—not

---

* The generous attitude toward Russia expressed by President Kennedy in this speech, and his challenge to the principal powers to "find solutions that now seem beyond us," soon met a response. On July 14, W. Averell Harriman for the United States and Lord Hailsham for Great Britain arrived in Moscow for negotiations. Next day Khrushchev banteringly remarked to them: "Shall we begin by signing the agreement right away?" In a formal speech that week he went on to say that "hope now exists" that a treaty halting nuclear tests could be concluded. It seemed evident that Russia was taking a new attitude—the attitude that shortly led to the treaty prohibiting nuclear tests. Mr. Kennedy's painstaking effort to keep the door open had helped create this attitude.—A. N.

merely peace for Americans, but peace for all men and women; not merely peace in our time, but peace for all time.

I speak of peace because of the new face of war. Total war makes no sense in an age when great powers can maintain large and relatively invulnerable nuclear forces and refuse to surrender without resort to those forces. It makes no sense in an age when a single nuclear weapon contains almost ten times the explosive force delivered by all of the Allied air forces in the Second World War. It makes no sense in an age when the deadly poisons produced by a nuclear exchange would be carried by the wind and water and soil and seed to the far corners of the globe and to generations yet unborn.

Today the expenditure of billions of dollars every year on weapons acquired for the purpose of making sure we never need to use them is essential to keeping the peace. But surely the acquisition of such idle stockpiles, which can only destroy and never create, is not the only, much less the most efficient, means of assuring peace.

I speak of peace, therefore, as the necessary rational end of rational men. I realize that the pursuit of peace is not as dramatic as the pursuit of war, and frequently the words of the pursuer fall on deaf ears. But we have no more urgent task.

Some say that it is useless to speak of world peace or world law or world disarmament, and that it will be useless until the leaders of the Soviet Union adopt a more enlightened attitude. I hope they do. I believe we can help them do it. But I also believe that we must re-examine our own attitude, as individuals and as a nation, for our attitude is as essential as theirs. And every graduate of this school, every thoughtful citizen who despairs of war and wishes to bring peace, should begin by looking inward, by examining his own attitude toward the possibilities of peace, toward the Soviet Union, toward the course of the Cold War, and toward freedom and peace here at home.

First, let us examine our attitude toward peace itself. Too many of us think it is impossible. Too many think it unreal. But that is a dangerous, defeatist belief. It leads to the conclusion that war is inevitable, that mankind is doomed, that we are gripped by forces we cannot control.

We need not accept that view. Our problems are man-made; therefore they can be solved by man. And man can be as big as he wants. No problem of human destiny is beyond human beings. Man's reason and spirit have often solved the seemingly unsolvable, and we believe they can do it again.

I am not referring to the absolute, infinite concept of universal peace and goodwill of which some fantasts and fanatics dream. I do not deny the value of hopes and dreams, but we merely invite discouragement and incredulity by making them our only and immediate goal.

Let us focus instead on a more practical, more attainable peace, based not on a sudden revolution in human nature but on a gradual evolution in human institutions, on a series of concrete actions and effective agreements which are in the interest of all concerned. There is no single, simple key to this peace, no grand or magic formula to be adopted by one or two powers. Genuine peace must be the product of many nations, the sum of many acts. It must be dynamic, not static, changing to meet the challenge of each new generation. For peace is a process, a way of solving problems.

With such a peace there will still be quarrels and conflicting interests, as there are within families and nations. World peace, like community peace, does not require that each man love his neighbor; it requires only that they live together in mutual tolerance, submitting their disputes to a just and peaceful settlement. And history teaches us that enmities between nations, as between individuals, do not last forever. However fixed our likes and dislikes may seem, the tide of time and events will often bring surprising changes in the relations between nations and neighbors.

So let us persevere. Peace need not be impracticable, and war need not be inevitable. By defining our goal more clearly, by making it seem more manageable and less remote, we can help all peoples to see it, to draw hope from it, and to move irresistibly toward it.

Second, let us re-examine our attitude toward the Soviet Union. It is discouraging to think that their leaders may actually believe what their propagandists write. It is discouraging to read a recent authoritative Soviet text on military strategy and find, on page after page, wholly baseless and incredible claims—such as the allegation that

"American imperialist circles are preparing to unleash different types of wars . . . that there is a very real threat of a preventive war being unleashed by American imperialists against the Soviet Union . . . [and that] the political aims of the American imperialists are to enslave economically and politically the European and other capitalist countries . . . [and] to achieve world domination . . . by means of aggressive wars."

Truly as it was written long ago: "The wicked flee when no man pursueth." Yet it is sad to read these Soviet statements, to realize the extent of the gulf between us. But it is also a warning—a warning to the American people not to fall into the same trap as the Soviets, not to see only a distorted and desperate view of the other side, not to see conflict as inevitable, accommodation as impossible, and communication as nothing more than an exchange of threats.

No government or social system is so evil that its people must be considered as lacking in virtue. As Americans we find Communism profoundly repugnant as a negation of personal freedom and dignity. But we can still hail the Russian people for their many achievements —in science and space, in economic and industrial growth, in culture and in acts of courage.

Among the many traits the peoples of our two countries have in common, none is stronger than our mutual abhorrence of war. Almost unique among the major world powers, we have never been at war with each other. And no nation in the history of battle ever suffered more than the Soviet Union suffered in the course of the Second World War. At least twenty million lost their lives. Countless millions of homes and farms were burned or sacked. A third of the nation's territory, including nearly two-thirds of its industrial base, was turned into a wasteland—a loss equivalent to the devastation of this country east of Chicago.

Today, should total war ever break out again, no matter how, our two countries would become the primary targets. It is an ironical but accurate fact that the two strongest powers are the two in the most danger of devastation. All we have built, all we have worked for, would be destroyed in the first twenty-four hours. And even in the Cold War, which brings burdens and dangers to so many countries, including this nation's closest allies, our two countries bear the heaviest burdens. For we are both devoting massive sums of money to weapons that could be better devoted to combating ignorance, poverty and disease. We are both caught up in a vicious and dangerous cycle in which suspicion on one side breeds suspicion on the other and new weapons beget counterweapons.

In short, both the United States and its allies, and the Soviet Union and its allies, have a mutually deep interest in a just and genuine peace and in halting the arms race. Agreements to this end are in the interests of the Soviet Union as well as ours, and even the most hostile nations can be relied upon to accept and keep those treaty obligations, and only those treaty obligations, which are in their own interest.

So let us not be blind to our differences, but let us also direct attention to our common interests and to the means by which those differences can be resolved. And if we cannot end now our differences, at least we can help make the world safe for diversity. For in the final analysis our most basic common link is that we all inhabit this planet. We all breathe the same air. We all cherish our children's future. And we are all mortal.

Third, let us re-examine our attitude toward the Cold War, remembering that we are not engaged in a debate, seeking to pile up debating points. We are not here distributing blame or pointing the finger of judgment. We must deal with the world as it is and not as it might have been had the history of the last eighteen years been different.

We must, therefore, persevere in the search for peace in the hope that constructive changes within the Communist bloc might bring within reach solutions which now seem beyond us. We must conduct our affairs in such a way that it becomes in the Communists' interest to agree on a genuine peace. Above all, while defending our own vital interests, nuclear powers must avert those confrontations which bring an adversary to a choice of either a humiliating retreat or a nuclear war. To adopt that kind of course in the nuclear age would be evidence only of the bankruptcy of our policy or of a collective death wish for the world.

To secure these ends, America's weapons are nonprovocative, carefully controlled, designed to deter and capable of selective use. Our military forces are committed to peace and disciplined in self-restraint. Our diplomats are instructed to avoid unnecessary irritants and purely rhetorical hostility.

For we can seek a relaxation of tensions without relaxing our guard. And, for our part, we do not need to use threats to prove that we are resolute. We do not need to jam foreign broadcasts out of fear our faith will be eroded. We are unwilling to impose our system on any unwilling people, but we are willing and able to engage in peaceful competition with any people on earth.

Meanwhile we seek to strengthen the United Nations, to help solve its financial problems, to make it a more effective instrument of peace, to develop it into a genuine world security system—a system capable of resolving disputes on the basis of law, of insuring the security of the large and the small, and of creating conditions under which arms can finally be abolished.

7 : The Test Ban Treaty Announced

TELEVISION ADDRESS TO THE PEOPLE
THE WHITE HOUSE
WASHINGTON, D.C.
JULY 26, 1963*

I speak to you tonight in a spirit of hope. Eighteen years ago the advent of nuclear weapons changed the course of the world as well as the war. Since that time, all mankind has been struggling to escape from the darkening prospect of mass destruction on earth. In an age

---

* In Moscow on July 25 Averell Harriman, Lord Hailsham, and Chairman Khrushchev initialed an agreement to end all atmospheric and submarine tests of nuclear weapons, no restrictions being placed on underground tests. Inspection or policing of sites seemed unnecessary, for monitoring devices were now sufficiently acute to detect tests of the

when both sides have come to possess enough nuclear power to destroy the human race several times over, the world of Communism and the world of free choice have been caught up in a vicious circle of conflicting ideology and interest. Each increase of tension has produced an increase of arms; each increase of arms has produced an increase of tension.

In these years the United States and the Soviet Union have frequently communicated suspicion and warnings to each other, but very rarely hope. Our representatives have met at the summit and at the brink; they have met in Washington and in Moscow, in Geneva and at the United Nations. But too often these meetings have produced only darkness, discord or disillusion.

Yesterday a shaft of light cut into the darkness. Negotiations were concluded in Moscow on a treaty to ban all nuclear tests in the atmosphere, in outer space and underwater. For the first time, an agreement has been reached on bringing the forces of nuclear destruction under international control—a goal first sought in 1946 when Bernard Baruch presented a comprehensive control plan to the United Nations.

That plan and many subsequent disarmament plans, large and small, have all been blocked by those opposed to international inspection. A ban on nuclear tests, however, requires on-the-spot inspection only for underground tests. This nation now possesses a variety of techniques to detect the nuclear tests of other nations which are conducted in the air or underwater. For such tests produce unmistakable signs which our modern instruments can pick up.

The treaty initialed yesterday, therefore, is a limited treaty which

---

types forbidden. Underground tests of small weapons could not be discovered, but they did not augment the radioactive content of the atmosphere. It was generally believed in the United States and Great Britain that the readiness of the Soviet Union to sign this epochal agreement sprang in part from the increasing friction between the Russian and Chinese governments. The Russians, who had exploded a 58-megaton bomb, supposedly held a lead in such huge superweapons, but in other respects American technology was undoubtedly superior. France and China refused to sign the agreement.—A. N.

permits continued underground testing and prohibits only those tests that we ourselves can police. It requires no control posts, no on-site inspection, no international body.

We should also understand that it has other limits as well. Any nation which signs the treaty will have an opportunity to withdraw if it finds that extraordinary events related to the subject matter of the treaty have jeopardized its supreme interests; and no nation's right of self-defense will in any way be impaired. Nor does this treaty mean an end to the threat of nuclear war. It will not reduce nuclear stockpiles; it will not halt the production of nuclear weapons; it will not restrict their use in time of war.

Nevertheless, this limited treaty will radically reduce the nuclear testing which would otherwise be conducted on both sides; it will prohibit the United States, the United Kingdom, the Soviet Union and all others who sign it from engaging in the atmospheric tests which have so alarmed mankind; and it offers to all the world a welcome sign of hope.

For this is not a unilateral moratorium, but a specific and solemn legal obligation. While it will not prevent this nation from testing underground, or from being ready to conduct atmospheric tests if the acts of others so require, it gives us a concrete opportunity to extend its coverage to other nations and later to other forms of nuclear tests.

This treaty is in part the product of Western patience and vigilance. We have made clear, most recently in Berlin and Cuba, our deep resolve to protect our security and our freedom against any form of aggression. We have also made clear our steadfast determination to limit the arms race. In three administrations our soldiers and diplomats have worked together to this end, always supported by Great Britain. Prime Minister Macmillan joined with President Eisenhower in proposing a limited test ban in 1959, and again with me in 1961 and 1962.

But the achievement of this goal is not a victory for one side; it is a victory for mankind. It reflects no concessions either to or by the Soviet Union. It reflects simply our common recognition of the dangers in further testing.

This treaty is not the millennium. It will not resolve all conflicts, or cause the Communists to forgo their ambitions, or eliminate the dangers of war. It will not reduce our need for arms or allies or programs of assistance to others. But it is an important first step—a step toward peace, a step toward reason, a step away from war.

Here is what this step can mean to you and to your children and your neighbors.

First, this treaty can be a step toward reduced world tension and broader areas of agreement. The Moscow talks have reached no agreement on any other subject, nor is this treaty conditioned on any other matter. Under Secretary Harriman made it clear that any nonaggression arrangements across the division in Europe would require full consultation with our allies and full attention to their interests. He also made clear our strong preference for a more comprehensive treaty banning all tests everywhere and our ultimate hope for general and complete disarmament. The Soviet Government, however, is still unwilling to accept the inspection such goals require.

No one can predict with certainty, therefore, what further agreements, if any, can be built on the foundations of this one. They could include controls on preparations for surprise attack or on numbers and type of armaments. There could be further limitations on the spread of nuclear weapons. The important point is that efforts to seek new agreements will go forward.

But the difficulty of predicting the next step is no reason to be reluctant about this step. Nuclear test ban negotiations have long been a symbol of East-West disagreement. If this treaty can also be a symbol, if it can symbolize the end of one era and the beginning of another, if both sides can by this treaty gain confidence and experience in peaceful collaboration, then this short and simple treaty may well become an historic mark in man's age-old pursuit of peace.

Western policies have long been designed to persuade the Soviet Union to renounce aggression, direct or indirect, so that their people and all people may live and let live in peace. The unlimited testing of new weapons of war cannot lead toward that end, but this treaty, if it can be followed by further progress, can clearly move in that direction.

I do not say that a world without aggression or threats of war would be an easy world. It will bring new problems, new challenges from the Communists, new dangers of relaxing our vigilance or of mistaking their intent.

But those dangers pale in comparison to those of the spiraling arms race and a collision course toward war. Since the beginning of history, war has been mankind's constant companion. It has been the rule, not the exception. Even a nation as young and as peace-loving as our own has fought through eight wars. And three times in the last two years and a half I have been required to report to you as President that this nation and the Soviet Union stood on the verge of direct military confrontation in Laos, in Berlin and in Cuba.

A war today or tomorrow, if it led to nuclear war, would not be like any war in history. A full-scale nuclear exchange, lasting less than sixty minutes, with the weapons now in existence, could wipe out more than 300 million Americans, Europeans and Russians, as well as untold numbers elsewhere. And the survivors, as Chairman Khrushchev warned the Communist Chinese, "The survivors would envy the dead." For they would inherit a world so devastated by ex-plosions and poison and fire that today we cannot even conceive of its horrors. So let us try to turn the world from war. Let us make the most of this opportunity, and every opportunity, to reduce tension, to slow down the perilous nuclear arms race and to check the world's slide toward final annihilation.

Second, this treaty can be a step toward freeing the world from the fears and dangers of radioactive fallout. Our own atmospheric tests last year were conducted under conditions which restricted such fallout to an absolute minimum. But over the years the num-ber and the yield of weapons tested have rapidly increased and so have the radioactive hazards from such testing. Continued un-restricted testing by the nuclear powers, joined in time by other nations which may be less adept in limiting pollution, will increas-ingly contaminate the air that all of us must breathe.

Even then, the number of children and grandchildren with can-cer in their bones, with leukemia in their blood or with poison in their lungs might seem statistically small to some, in comparison with natural health hazards. But this is not a natural health hazard, and it is not a statistical issue. The loss of even one human life or the malformation of even one baby, who may be born long after we are gone, should be of concern to us all. Our children and grand-children are not merely statistics toward which we can be indifferent.

Nor does this affect the nuclear powers alone. These tests befoul the air of all men and all nations, the committed and the uncommitted alike, without their knowledge and without their consent. That is why the continuation of atmospheric testing causes so many countries to regard all nuclear powers as equally evil; and we can hope that its prevention will enable those countries to see the world more clearly, while enabling all the world to breathe more easily.

Third, this treaty can be a step toward preventing the spread of nuclear weapons to nations not now possessing them. During the next several years, in addition to the four current nuclear powers, a small but significant number of nations will have the intellectual, physical and financial resources to produce both nuclear weapons and the means of delivering them. In time, it is estimated, many other nations will have either this capacity or other ways of obtaining nuclear warheads, even as missiles can be commercially purchased today.

I ask you to stop and think for a moment what it would mean to have nuclear weapons in so many hands, in the hands of countries large and small, stable and unstable, responsible and irresponsible, scattered throughout the world. There would be no rest for anyone then, no stability, no real security and no chance of effective disarmament. There would only be the increased chance of accidental war and an increased necessity for the great powers to involve themselves in what otherwise would be local conflicts.

If only one thermonuclear bomb were to be dropped on any American, Russian or any other city, whether it was launched by accident or design, by a madman or by an enemy, by a large nation or by a small, from any corner of the world, that one bomb could release more destructive power on the inhabitants of that one helpless city than all the bombs dropped in the Second World War.

Neither the United States nor the Soviet Union nor the United Kingdom nor France can look forward to that day with equanimity. We have a great obligation—all four nuclear powers have a great obligation—to use whatever time remains to prevent the spread of nuclear weapons, to persuade other countries not to test, transfer, acquire, possess or produce such weapons.

This treaty can be the opening wedge in that campaign. It provides that none of the parties will assist other nations to test in the forbidden environments. It opens the door for further agreements on the control of nuclear weapons, and it is open for all nations to sign; for it is in the interest of all nations, and already we have heard from a number of countries who wish to join with us promptly.

Fourth and finally, this treaty can limit the nuclear arms race in ways which, on balance, will strengthen our nation's security far more than the continuation of unrestricted testing. For in today's world a nation's security does not always increase as its arms increase when its adversary is doing the same, and unlimited competition in the testing and development of new types of destructive nuclear weapons will not make the world safer for either side. Under this limited treaty, on the other hand, the testing of other nations could never be sufficient to offset the ability of our strategic forces to deter or survive a nuclear attack and to penetrate and destroy an aggressor's homeland.

We have, and under this treaty we will continue to have, the nuclear strength that we need. It is true that the Soviets have tested nuclear weapons of a yield higher than that which we thought to be necessary, but the hundred-megaton bomb of which they spoke two years ago does not and will not change the balance of strategic power. The United States has chosen, deliberately, to concentrate on more mobile and more efficient weapons, with lower but entirely sufficient yield, and our security is, therefore, not impaired by the treaty I am discussing.

It is also true, as Mr. Khrushchev would agree, that nations cannot afford in these matters to rely simply on the good faith of their adversaries. We have not, therefore, overlooked the risk of secret violations. There is at present a possibility that deep in outer space, hundreds and thousands of millions of miles away from the earth, illegal tests might go undetected. But we already have the capability to construct a system of observation that would make such tests almost impossible to conceal, and we can decide at any time whether such a system is needed in the light of the limited risk to us and the limited reward to others of violations attempted at that range. For any tests which might be conducted so far out in space which cannot be conducted more easily and efficiently and legally underground would necessarily be of such a magnitude that they would be extremely difficult to conceal. We can also employ new devices to check on the testing of smaller weapons in the lower atmosphere. Any violation, moreover, involves, along with the risk of detection, the end of the treaty and the world-wide consequences for the violator.

Secret violations are possible and secret preparations for a sudden withdrawal are possible, and thus our own vigilance and strength must be maintained, as we remain ready to withdraw and to resume all forms of testing if we must. But it would be a mistake to assume that this treaty will be quickly broken. The gains of illegal testing are obviously slight compared to their cost and the hazard of discovery, and the nations which have initialed and will sign this treaty prefer it, in my judgment, to unrestricted testing as a matter of their own self-interest, for these nations, too, and all nations, have a stake in limiting the arms race, in holding the spread of nuclear weapons and in breathing air that is not radioactive. While it may be theoretically possible to demonstrate the risks inherent in any treaty—and such risks in this treaty are small—the far greater risks to our security are the risks of unrestricted testing, the risk of a nuclear arms race, the risk of new nuclear powers, nuclear pollution and nuclear war.

This limited test ban, in our most careful judgment, is safer by far for the United States than an unlimited nuclear arms race. For all these reasons, I am hopeful that this nation will promptly approve the limited test ban treaty. There will, of course, be debate in the country and in the Senate. The Constitution wisely requires the advice and consent of the Senate to all treaties, and that consultation has already begun. All this is as it should be. A document which may mark an historic and constructive opportunity for the world deserves an historic and constructive debate.

It is my hope that all of you will take part in that debate, for this treaty is for all of us. It is particularly for our children and our grandchildren, and they have no lobby here in Washington. This debate will involve military, scientific and political experts, but it must not be left to them alone. The right and the responsibility are yours.

If we are to open new doorways to peace, if we are to seize this rare opportunity for progress, if we are to be as bold and farsighted in our control of weapons as we have been in their invention, then let us now show all the world on this side of the wall and the other that a strong America also stands for peace.

There is no cause for complacency. We have learned in times past that the spirit of one moment or place can be gone in the next. We have been disappointed more than once, and we have no illusions now that there are short cuts on the road to peace. At many points around the globe the Communists are continuing their efforts to exploit weakness and poverty. Their concentration of nuclear and conventional arms must still be deterred.

The familiar contest between choice and coercion, the familiar places of danger and conflict, are still there, in Cuba, in Southeast Asia, in Berlin and all around the globe, still requiring all the strength and the vigilance that we can muster. Nothing could more greatly damage our cause than if we and our allies were to believe that peace has already been achieved and that our strength and unity were no longer required.

But now, for the first time in many years, the path of peace may be open. No one can be certain what the future will bring. No one can say whether the time has come for an easing of the struggle. But history and our own conscience will judge us more harshly if we do not now make every effort to test our hopes by action, and this is the place to begin. According to the ancient Chinese proverb, "A journey of a thousand miles must begin with a single step."

My fellow Americans, let us take that first step. Let us, if we can, get back from the shadows of war and seek out the way of peace. And if that journey is one thousand miles, or even more, let history record that we, in this land, at this time, took the first step.

8 : The Tasks of the United Nations

THE UNITED NATIONS
NEW YORK, NEW YORK
SEPTEMBER 20, 1963*

... We meet again in the quest for peace.

Twenty-four months ago, when I last had the honor of addressing this body, the shadow of fear lay darkly across the world. The freedom of West Berlin was in immediate peril. Agreement on a neutral Laos seemed remote. The mandate of the United Nations in the Congo was under fire. The financial outlook for this organization was in doubt. Dag Hammarskjöld was dead. The doctrine of troika was being pressed in his place, and atmospheric nuclear tests had been resumed by the Soviet Union.

Those were anxious days for mankind, and some men wondered aloud whether this organization could survive. But the Sixteenth and Seventeenth General Assemblies achieved not only survival but progress. Rising to its responsibility, the United Nations helped reduce the tensions and helped to hold back the darkness.

Today the clouds have lifted a little so that new rays of hope can break through. The pressures on West Berlin appear to be temporarily eased. Political unity in the Congo has been largely restored. A neutral coalition in Laos, while still in difficulty, is at least in being.

---

* The President's regard for the United Nations never wavered. When Ex-President Hoover declared that it needed supplementary organizations of the free nations capable of taking action whenever the Communist countries blocked UN effort, Mr. Kennedy pointed out in one of his news conferences that such organizations had been brought into being, notably in NATO, SEATO and OAS. He added that Mr. Hoover's ideas deserved careful consideration. But in this address he made plain his faith in the continued usefulness of the greatest of all international organizations since history began.—A. N.

The integrity of the United Nations Secretariat has been reaffirmed. A United Nations Decade of Development is under way. And, for the first time in seventeen years of effort, a specific step has been taken to limit the nuclear arms race.

I refer, of course, to the treaty to ban nuclear tests in the atmosphere, outer space and underwater, concluded by the Soviet Union, the United Kingdom and the United States, and already signed by nearly one hundred countries. It has been hailed by people the world over who are thankful to be free from the fears of nuclear fallout, and I am confident that on next Tuesday at ten-thirty o'clock in the morning it will receive the overwhelming endorsement of the Senate of the United States.

The world has not escaped from the darkness. The long shadows of conflict and crisis envelop us still. But we meet today in an atmosphere of rising hope and at a moment of comparative calm. My presence here today is not a sign of crisis, but of confidence. I am not here to report on a new threat to the peace or new signs of war. I have come to salute the United Nations and to show the support of the American people for your daily deliberations.

For the value of this body's work is not dependent on the existence of emergencies, nor can the winning of peace consist only of dramatic victories. Peace is a daily, a weekly, a monthly process, gradually changing opinions, slowly eroding old barriers, quietly building new structures. And however undramatic the pursuit of peace, that pursuit must go on.

Today we may have reached a pause in the Cold War, but that is not a lasting peace. A test ban treaty is a milestone, but it is not the millennium. We have not been released from our obligations; we have been given an opportunity. And if we fail to make the most of this moment and this momentum, if we convert our new-found hopes and understandings into new walls and weapons of hostility, if this pause in the Cold War merely leads to its renewal and not to its end, then the indictment of posterity will rightly point its finger at us all. But if we can stretch this pause into a period of cooperation, if both sides can now gain new confidence and experience in concrete collaborations for peace, if we can now be as bold and farsighted in the control of deadly weapons as we have been in their creation, then surely this first small step can be the start of a long and fruitful journey.

The task of building the peace lies with the leaders of every nation, large and small. For the great powers have no monopoly on conflict or ambition. The Cold War is not the only expression of tension in this world, and the nuclear race is not the only arms race. Even little wars are dangerous in a nuclear world. The long labor of peace is an undertaking for every nation, and in this effort none of us can remain unaligned. To this goal none can be uncommitted.

The reduction of global tension must not be an excuse for the narrow pursuit of self-interest. If the Soviet Union and the United States, with all their global interests and clashing commitments of ideology, and with nuclear weapons still aimed at each other today, can find areas of common interest and agreement, then surely other nations can do the same—nations caught in regional conflicts, in racial issues or in the death throes of old colonialism. Chronic disputes which divert precious resources from the needs of the people or drain the energies of both sides serve the interests of no one, and the badge of responsibility in the modern world is a willingness to seek peaceful solutions.

It is never too early to try; and it is never too late to talk; and it is high time that many disputes on the agenda of this Assembly were taken off the debating schedule and placed on the negotiating table.

The fact remains that the United States, as a major nuclear power, does have a special responsibility in the world. It is, in fact, a threefold responsibility: a responsibility to our own citizens, a responsibility to the people of the whole world who are affected by our decisions, and to the next generation of humanity. We believe the Soviet Union also has these special responsibilities, and that those responsibilities require our two nations to concentrate less on our differences and more on the means of resolving them peacefully. For too long both of us have increased our military budgets, our nuclear stockpiles and our capacity to destroy all life—human, animal, vegetable—without any corresponding increase in our security.

Our conflicts, to be sure, are real. Our concepts of the world are different. No service is performed by failing to make clear our disagreements. A central difference is the belief of the American people in self-determination for all people.

We believe that the people of Germany and Berlin must be free to reunite their capital and their country.

We believe that the people of Cuba must be free to secure the fruits of the revolution that has been betrayed from within and exploited from without.

In short, we believe that in all the world—in Eastern Europe as well as Western, in Southern Africa as well as Northern, in old nations as well as new—people must be free to choose their own future, without discrimination or dictation, without coercion or subversion.

These are the basic differences between the Soviet Union and the United States, and they cannot be concealed. So long as they exist, they set limits to agreement, and they forbid the relaxation of our vigilance. Our defense around the world will be maintained for the protection of freedom, and our determination to safeguard that freedom will measure up to any threat or challenge.

But I would say to the leaders of the Soviet Union, and to their people, that if either of our countries is to be fully secure, we need a much better weapon than the H-bomb, a weapon better than ballistic missiles or nuclear submarines, and that better weapon is peaceful cooperation.

We have, in recent years, agreed on a limited test ban treaty, on an emergency communications link between our capitals, on a statement of principles for disarmament, on an increase in cultural exchange, on cooperation in outer space, on the peaceful exploration of the Antarctic, and on tempering last year's crisis over Cuba.

I believe, therefore, that the Soviet Union and the United States, together with their allies, can achieve further agreements—agreements which spring from our mutual interest in avoiding mutual destruction.

There can be no doubt about the agenda of further steps. We must continue to seek agreements on measures which prevent war by accident or miscalculation. We must continue to seek agreement on safeguards against surprise attack, including observation posts at key points. We must continue to seek agreement on further measures to curb the nuclear arms race, by controlling the transfer of nuclear weapons, converting fissionable materials to peaceful purposes and banning underground testing, with adequate inspection and enforcement. We must continue to seek agreement on a freer flow of information and people from East to West and West to East.

We must continue to seek agreement, encouraged by yesterday's affirmative response to this proposal by the Soviet Foreign Minister, on an arrangement to keep weapons of mass destruction out of outer space. Let us get our negotiators back to the negotiating table to work out a practicable arrangement to this end.

In these and other ways, let us move up the steep and difficult path toward comprehensive disarmament, securing mutual confidence through mutual verification and building the institutions of peace as we dismantle the engines of war. We must not let failure to agree on all points delay agreements where agreement is possible. And we must not put forward proposals for propaganda purposes.

Finally, in a field where the United States and the Soviet Union have a special capacity—in the field of space—there is room for new cooperation, for further joint efforts in the regulation and exploration of space. I include among these possibilities a joint expedition to the moon. Space offers no problems of sovereignty. By resolution of this Assembly, the members of the United Nations have forsworn any claim to territorial rights in outer space or on celestial bodies, and declared that international law and the United Nations Charter will apply. Why, therefore, should man's first flight to the moon be a matter of national competition? Why should the United States and the Soviet Union, in preparing for such expeditions, become involved in immense duplications of research, construction and expenditure? Surely we should explore whether the scientists and astronauts of our two countries—indeed, of all the world—cannot work together in the conquest of space, sending someday in this decade to the moon not the representatives of a single nation but the representatives of all our countries.

All these and other new steps toward peaceful cooperation may be possible. Most of them will require on our part full consultation with our allies, for their interests are as much involved as our own, and we will not make an agreement at their expense. Most of them will require long and careful negotiation. And most of them will require a new approach to the Cold War—a desire not to "bury" one's adversary, but to compete in a host of peaceful arenas: in ideas, in production and ultimately in service to all mankind.

The contest will continue—the contest between those who see a monolithic world and those who believe in diversity—but it should be a contest in leadership and responsibility instead of destruction, a contest in achievement instead of intimidation. Speaking for the United States of America, I welcome such a contest. For we believe that truth is stronger than error, and that freedom is more enduring than coercion. And in the contest for a better life, all the world can be a winner.

The effort to improve the conditions of man, however, is not a task for a few. It is the task of all nations, acting alone, acting in groups, acting in the United Nations; for plague and pestilence, and plunder and pollution, the hazards of nature and the hunger of children are the foes of every nation. The earth, the sea and the air are the concern of every nation. And science, technology and education can be the ally of every nation.

Never before has man had such capacity to control his own environment—to end thirst and hunger, to conquer poverty and disease, to banish illiteracy and massive human misery. We have the power to make this the best generation of mankind in the history of the world or to make it the last.

The United States since the close of the war has sent over $100 billion worth of assistance to nations seeking economic viability. And two years ago this week we formed a Peace Corps to help interested nations meet the needs for trained manpower. Other industrialized nations whose economies were rebuilt not so long ago with some help from us are now in turn recognizing their responsibility to the less developed nations.

The provision of development assistance by individual nations must go on. But the United Nations also must play a larger role in helping bring to all men the fruits of modern science and industry. A United Nations conference on this subject held earlier this year at Geneva opened new vistas for the developing countries. Next year a United Nations Conference on Trade will consider the needs of these nations for new markets. And more than four-fifths of the entire United

Nations system can be found today mobilizing the weapons of science and technology for the United Nations' Decade of Development.

But more can be done.

A world center for health communications under the World Health Organization could warn of epidemics and the adverse effects of certain drugs, as well as transmit the results of new experiments and new discoveries.

Regional research centers could advance our common medical knowledge and train new scientists and doctors for new nations.

A global system of satellites could provide communication and weather information for all corners of the earth.

A world-wide program of conservation could protect the forest and wild game preserves now in danger of extinction for all time, improve the marine harvest of food from our oceans, and prevent the contamination of air and water by industrial as well as nuclear pollution.

And, finally, a world-wide program of farm productivity and food distribution, similar to our country's "Food for Peace" program, could now give every child the food he needs.

But man does not live by bread alone, and members of this organization are committed by the Charter to promote and respect human rights. Those rights are not respected when a Buddhist priest is driven from his pagoda, when a synagogue is shut down, when a Protestant church cannot open a mission, when a cardinal is forced into hiding or when a crowded church service is bombed. The United States of America is opposed to discrimination and persecution on grounds of race and religion anywhere in the world, including our own nation. We are working to right the wrongs of our own country.

Through legislation and administrative action, through moral and legal commitment, this government has launched a determined effort to rid our nation of discrimination which has existed too long—in education, in housing, in transportation, in employment, in the Civil Service, in recreation and in places of public accommodation. And therefore, in this or any other forum, we do not hesitate to condemn racial or religious injustice, whether committed or permitted by friend or foe.

I know that some of you have experienced discrimination in this country. But I ask you to believe me when I tell you that this is not the wish of most Americans, that we share your regret and resentment, and that we intend to end such practices for all time to come, not only for our visitors but for our own citizens as well.

I hope that not only our nation but all other multiracial societies will meet these standards of fairness and justice. We are opposed to apartheid and all forms of human oppression. We do not advocate the rights of black Africans in order to drive out white Africans. Our concern is the right of all men to equal protection under the law; and since human rights are indivisible, this body cannot stand aside when those rights are abused and neglected by any member state.

New efforts are needed if this Assembly's Declaration of Human Rights, now fifteen years old, is to have full meaning. And new means should be found for promoting the free expression and trade of ideas, through travel and communication, and through increased exchanges of people and books and broadcasts. For as the world renounces the competition of weapons, competition in ideas must flourish, and that competition must be as full and as fair as possible.

The United States delegation will be prepared to suggest to the United Nations initiatives in the pursuit of all the goals. For this is an organization for peace, and peace cannot come without work and progress.

The peace-keeping record of the United Nations has been a proud one, though its tasks are always formidable. We are fortunate to have the skills of our distinguished Secretary General and the brave efforts of those who have been serving the cause of peace in the Congo, in the Middle East, in Korea and Kashmir, in West New Guinea and Malaysia. But what the United Nations has done in the past is less important than the tasks for the future. We cannot take its peace-keeping machinery for granted. That machinery must be soundly financed, which it cannot be if some members are allowed to prevent it from meeting its obligations by failing to meet their own. The United Nations must be supported by all those who exercise their franchise here. And its operations must be backed to the end.

Too often a project is undertaken in the excitement of a crisis, and then it begins to lose its appeal as the problems drag on and the bills pile up. But we must have the steadfastness to see every enterprise through.

It is, for example, most important not to jeopardize the extraordinary United Nations gains in the Congo. The nation which sought this organization's help only three years ago has now asked the United Nations' presence to remain a little longer. I believe this Assembly should do what is necessary to preserve the gains already made and to protect the new nation in its struggle for progress. Let us complete what we have started, for "No man who puts his hand to the plow and looks back," as the Scriptures tell us, "No man who puts his hand to the plow and looks back is fit for the Kingdom of God."

I also hope that the recent initiative of several members in preparing stand-by peace forces for United Nations call will encourage similar commitments by others. This nation remains ready to provide logistic and other material support.

Policing, moreover, is not enough without provision for pacific settlement. We should increase the resort to special missions of fact-finding and conciliation, make greater use of the International Court of Justice and accelerate the work of the International Law Commission.

The United Nations cannot survive as a static organization. Its obligations are increasing as well as its size. Its charter must be changed as well as its customs. The authors of that charter did not intend that it be frozen in perpetuity. The science of weapons and war has made us all, far more than eighteen years ago in San Francisco, one world and one human race, with one common destiny. In such a world absolute sovereignty no longer assures us of absolute security. The conventions of peace must pull abreast and then ahead of the inventions of war. The United Nations, building on its successes and learning from its failures, must be developed into a genuine world security system.

But peace does not rest in charters and covenants alone. It lies in the hearts and minds of all people. And in this world no act, no pact, no treaty, no organization can hope to preserve it without the support and the wholehearted commitment of all people.

So let us not rest all our hopes on parchment and on paper. Let us strive to build peace, a desire for peace, a willingness to work for peace, in the hearts and minds of all of our people. I believe that we can. I believe the problems of human destiny are not beyond the reach of human beings.

Two years ago I told this body that the United States had proposed, and was willing to sign, a limited test ban treaty. Today that treaty has been signed. It will not put an end to war. It will not remove basic conflicts. It will not secure freedom for all. But it can be a lever, and Archimedes, in explaining the principles of the lever, was said to have declared to his friends: "Give me a place where I can stand, and I shall move the world."

My fellow inhabitants of this planet, let us take our stand here in this Assembly of nations. And let us see if we, in our own time, can move the world to a just and lasting peace.

9 : The Test Ban Treaty Signed

TREATY ROOM, THE WHITE HOUSE
WASHINGTON, D.C.
OCTOBER 7, 1963*

In its first two decades, the Age of Nuclear Energy has been full of fear, yet never empty of hope. Today the fear is a little less and the hope a little greater. For the first time we have been able to reach an agreement which can limit the dangers of this age.

---

* This was one of the shining occasions of the Kennedy Administration. Early in September the Senate had released the report of its Foreign Relations Committee, after twelve days of hearings, upon the treaty limiting tests of nuclear weapons. The committee agreed by a vote of 16 to 1 that the treaty could safely be approved, because the United States held a superior position in the "number and variety" of

The agreement itself is limited, but its message of hope has been heard and understood not only by the peoples of the three originating nations but by the peoples and governments of the hundred other countries that have signed. This treaty is the first fruit of labors in which multitudes have shared—citizens, legislators, statesmen, diplomats and soldiers, too.

Soberly and unremittingly this nation, but never this nation alone, has sought the doorway to effective disarmament into a world where peace is secure. Today we have a beginning, and it is right for us to acknowledge all whose work across the years has helped make this beginning possible.

What the future will bring, no one of us can know. This first fruit of hope may or may not be followed by larger harvests. Even this limited treaty, great as it is with promise, can survive only if it has from others the determined support in letter and in spirit which I hereby pledge in behalf of the United States.

If this treaty fails, it will not be our doing, and even if it fails, we shall not regret that we have made this clear and honorable national commitment to the cause of man's survival. For under this treaty we can and must still keep our vigil in defense of freedom.

But this treaty need not fail. This small step toward safety can be followed by others longer and less limited, if also harder in the taking. With our courage and understanding enlarged by this achievement, let us press onward in quest of man's essential desire for peace.

---

its nuclear weapons, and that it ought to be approved because it offered "the prospect of a gradual lessening of tensions, of a start toward the progressive elimination of nuclear war." In the subsequent Senate debate, Majority Leader Mike Mansfield had the assistance of Leverett Saltonstall, chairman of the Conference of Republican Senators, in marshaling supporters of the treaty. One leading Republican Senator, Barry Goldwater of Arizona, prominently opposed it, and so did two Democrats, John Stennis of Mississippi and Richard E. Russell of Georgia. But champions of the treaty easily had the better of the debate; public opinion was clearly for ratification; and in the end, on September 22, the opponents were overwhelmed by a vote of 80 to 19. The country was with President Kennedy in his appeal for "courage and understanding."—A. N.

As President of the United States and with the advice and consent of the Senate, I now sign the instruments of ratification of this treaty.

10 : The Meaning of the Test Ban Treaty

UNIVERSITY OF MAINE
ORONO, MAINE
OCTOBER 19, 1963

One year ago this coming week, the United States and the world were gripped with a somber prospect of a military confrontation between the two great nuclear powers. The American people have good reason to recall with pride their conduct throughout that harrowing week. For they neither dissolved in panic nor rushed headlong into reckless belligerence. Well aware of the risks of resistance, they nevertheless refused to tolerate the Soviets' attempt to place nuclear weapons in this hemisphere, but recognized at the same time that our preparations for the use of force necessarily require a simultaneous search for fair and peaceful solutions. . . .

A year ago it would have been easy to assume that all-out war was inevitable, that any agreement with the Soviets was impossible, and that an unlimited arms race was unavoidable. Today it is equally easy for some to assume that the Cold War is over, that all outstanding issues between the Soviets and our country can be quickly and satisfactorily settled, and that we shall now have, in the words of the Psalmist, an "abundance of peace so long as the moon endureth."

The fact of the matter is, of course, that neither view is correct. We have, it is true, made some progress on a long journey. We have achieved new opportunities which we cannot afford to waste. We have concluded with the Soviets a few limited, enforceable agreements or arrangements of mutual benefit to both sides and to the world.

But a change in the atmosphere and in emphasis is not a reversal of purpose. Mr. Khrushchev himself has said that there can be no coexistence in the field of ideology. In addition, there are still major areas of tension and conflict, from Berlin to Cuba to Southeast Asia. The United States and the Soviet Union still have wholly different concepts of the world, its freedom, its future. We still have wholly different views on the so-called wars of liberation and the use of subversion. And so long as these basic differences continue, they cannot and should not be concealed. They set limits to the possibilities of agreements; and they will give rise to further crises, large and small, in the months and years ahead, both in the areas of direct confrontation—Germany and the Caribbean—and in areas where events beyond our control could involve us both—areas such as Africa and Asia and the Middle East.

In times such as these, therefore, there is nothing inconsistent in signing an atmospheric nuclear test ban, on the one hand, and testing underground on the other; about being willing to sell to the Soviets our surplus wheat while refusing to sell strategic items; about probing their interest in a joint lunar landing while making a major effort to master this new environment; or about exploring the possibilities of disarmament while maintaining our stockpile of arms. For all of these moves, and all of these elements of American policy and Allied policy toward the Soviet Union, are directed at a single, comprehensive goal—namely, convincing the Soviet leaders that it is dangerous for them to engage in direct or indirect aggression, futile for them to attempt to impose their will and their system on other unwilling people, and beneficial to them, as well as to the world, to join in the achievement of a genuine and enforceable peace.

Historians report that in 1914, with most of the world already plunged in war, Prince Bülow, the former German Chancellor, said to the then Chancellor Bethmann-Hollweg, "How did it all happen?" And Bethmann-Hollweg replied, "Ah, if only one knew." My fellow Americans, if this planet is ever ravaged by nuclear war, if 300 million Americans, Russians and Europeans are wiped out by a sixty-minute nuclear exchange, if the pitiable survivors of that devastation can then endure the ensuing fire, poison, chaos and catastrophe, I do not want one of those survivors to ask another, "How did it all happen?" and to receive the incredible reply, "Ah, if only one knew."

Therefore, while maintaining our readiness for war, let us exhaust every avenue for peace. Let us always make clear our willingness to talk, if talk will help, and our readiness to fight, if fight we must. Let us resolve to be the masters, not the victims, of our history, controlling our own destiny without giving way to blind suspicion and emotion. . . .

III

POINTS

OF INTERNATIONAL

DANGER

11 : The Vital Importance of West Berlin

PRESIDENT'S RESIDENCE
HYANNIS PORT, MASSACHUSETTS
NOVEMBER 25, 1961*

. . . May I just make one brief response? All Berlin was put under four-power authority by the agreements at Potsdam. East Berlin, which was under the immediate authority of the Soviet Union, has now been turned over to East Germany in violation of those agreements. It is no longer effectively under four-power control. And now the Soviet Union seeks to place Soviet troops in West Berlin. It does not suggest that the troops of the other three powers be placed in East Berlin. In other words, the Soviet Union now seeks to share in the control of West Berlin. That is the first point that is in question.

The second is this question of the rights of access in crossing East Germany. As I gather it, you would give the East German authorities —you say East German Government—the power to interfere with that traffic. It is stated that they would not do so, but we have no assurances in Mr. Ulbricht's statements, which vary from week to week. In my opinion, if such an agreement is signed, if our rights on the communication lines between the West and West Berlin, which are now governed by the Soviet Union, are turned over to the East German authorities, and if the East Germans should inter-

---

* This interview with Aleksei Adzhubei, the editor of *Izvestia*, who brought a Russian interpreter, Mr. Georgi Bolshikov, editor of *USSR Magazine*, took place in the President's Hyannis Port, Massachusetts, home. Mr. Kennedy had just returned from a speaking trip to the Pacific Coast and was in Hyannis Port for Thanksgiving with his family. Mr. Adzhubei, who is a son-in-law of Khrushchev, published the interview in *Izvestia* on November 29, and it was at once reprinted over much of the world.—A. N.

fere with that right of access, for one reason or another, then this would provide for heightened tension, the Soviet Union might come to the support of East Germany, and we would find ourselves, instead of having settled this now, once more face to face.

The reason why we have been reluctant to recognize East Germany as a sovereign power is that we do not recognize the division of Germany. In our opinion the German people wish to have one united country. If the Soviet Union had lost the war, the Soviet people themselves would object to a line being drawn through Moscow and the entire country. If we had been defeated in war, we wouldn't like to have a line drawn down the Mississippi River. The Germans want to be united. I think it should be possible to provide for that under conditions which will protect the interests of all concerned. But the Soviet Union believes that it is more in its interest to keep Germany divided.

Now the question is, given that decision, can we provide for the protection of our rights in West Berlin, which were agreed to in 1945 by the Soviet Union, so that this is not a continuing crisis? In attempting to work out a solution of the problems which came about as a result of World War II, we don't want to increase the chances of World War III. All we wish to do is maintain a very limited—and they are a very limited—number of troops of the three powers in West Berlin and to have, for example, an international administration on the Autobahn so that goods and people can move freely in and out. Then we can have peace in this area for years. . . .

West Germany now has only nine divisions, which is a fraction of the Soviet forces. Nine divisions. It has no nuclear weapons of its own. It has a very small Air Force, almost no Navy—I think perhaps two or three submarines. So it is not a military threat. Its nine divisions are under the international control of NATO, and subject to the command of the NATO organization, which is made up of fifteen countries of Europe, which altogether have, in West Germany now, about twenty-two or twenty-three divisions—about the same number as the Soviet divisions in East Germany. . . .

12 : Matsu and Quemoy: The Basic American Position

NEWS CONFERENCE
JUNE 27, 1962*

The situation in the area of the Taiwan Straits is a matter of serious concern to this government. Very large movements of Chinese Communist forces into this area have taken place. The purpose of these moves is not clear. It seems important in these circumstances that the position of the United States Government be clearly understood.

Our basic position has always been that we are opposed to the use of force in this area. In the earlier years, President Eisenhower made repeated efforts to secure the agreement of Communist China to the mutual renunciation of the use of force in the Taiwan area, and our support for this policy continues.

One possibility is that there might be aggressive action against the offshore islands of Matsu and Quemoy. In that event, the policy of this country will be that established seven years ago under the Formosa Resolution. The United States will take the action necessary to assure the defense of Formosa and the Pescadores. In the last crisis in the Taiwan area in 1958, President Eisenhower made it clear that the United States would not remain inactive in the face of any aggressive action against the offshore islands which might threaten Formosa.

In my own discussion of this issue in the campaign of 1960, I made it quite clear that I was in agreement with President Eisenhower's position on this matter. I stated this position very plainly, for example, on October 16, 1960, and I quote: "The position of the

---

* The critical economic position of mainland China in 1962 sent waves of refugees in May and June to Hong Kong and Taiwan or Formosa, and unrest in China produced a renewal of tension in the Taiwan Straits.—A. N.

administration has been that we would defend Quemoy and Matsu if there were an attack which was part of an attack on Formosa and the Pescadores. I don't want the Chinese Communists to be under any misapprehension. I support the administration's policy toward Quemoy and Matsu over the last five years."

Under this policy, sustained continuously by the United States Government since 1954, it is clear that any threat to the offshore islands must be judged in relation to its wider meaning for the safety of Formosa and the peace of the area.

Exactly what action would be necessary in the event of any such act of force would depend on the situation as it developed. But there must be no doubt that our policy, specifically including our readiness to take necessary action in the face of force, remains just what it has been on this matter since 1955. It is important to have it understood that on this point the United States speaks with one voice. But I repeat that the purposes of the United States in this area are peaceful and defensive.

13 : American Surveillance

NEWS CONFERENCE
SEPTEMBER 13, 1962*

There has been a great deal of talk on the situation in Cuba in recent days both in the Communist camp and in our own, and I would like to take this opportunity to set the matter in perspective.

In the first place, it is Mr. Castro and his supporters who are in trouble. In the last year, his regime has been increasingly isolated

---

* Ever since Castro's statement to the Organization of American States on December 2, 1961, that "I am a Marxist-Leninist and will be one until the day I die," public sentiment in the United States had hardened against him. By this date his acceptance of Soviet support and

from this hemisphere. His name no longer inspires the same fear or following in other Latin-American countries. He has been condemned by the OAS, excluded from the Inter-American Defense Board and kept out of the Free Trade Association. By his own monumental economic mismanagement, supplemented by our refusal to trade with him, his economy has crumbled, and his pledges for economic progress have been discarded, along with his pledges for political freedom. His industries are stagnating; his harvests are declining; his own followers are beginning to see that their revolution has been betrayed.

So it is not surprising that in a frantic effort to bolster his regime he should try to arouse the Cuban people by charges of an imminent American invasion, and commit himself still further to a Soviet takeover in the hope of preventing his own collapse.

Ever since Communism moved into Cuba in 1958, Soviet technical and military personnel have moved steadily onto the island in increasing numbers at the invitation of the Cuban Government.

Now that movement has been increased. It is under our most careful surveillance. But I will repeat the conclusion that I reported last week, that these new shipments do not constitute a serious threat to any other part of this hemisphere.

If the United States ever should find it necessary to take military action against Communism in Cuba, all of Castro's Communist-supplied weapons and technicians would not change the result or significantly extend the time required to achieve that result.

However, unilateral military intervention on the part of the United States cannot currently be either required or justified, and it is regrettable that loose talk about such action in this country might serve to give a thin color of legitimacy to the Communist pretense that such a threat exists. But let me make this clear once again: If at any

---

weapons had aroused apprehension and deep resentment. A clamor for stern action arose in some quarters. But the President now asked for calmness: "I would hope that the future record will show that the only people talking about a war or an invasion at this time are the Communist spokesmen in Moscow and Havana."—A. N.

time the Communist build-up in Cuba were to endanger or interfere with our security in any way, including our base at Guantánamo, our passage to the Panama Canal, our missile and space activities at Cape Canaveral, or the lives of American citizens in this country, or if Cuba should ever attempt to export its aggressive purposes by force or the threat of force against any nation in this hemisphere, or become an offensive military base of significant capacity for the Soviet Union, then this country will do whatever must be done to protect its own security and that of its allies.

We shall be alert, too, and fully capable of dealing swiftly with any such development. As President and Commander in Chief I have full authority now to take such action, and I have asked the Congress to authorize me to call up reserve forces should this or any other crisis make it necessary.

In the meantime we intend to do everything within our power to prevent such a threat from coming into existence. Our friends in Latin America must realize the consequences such developments hold out for their own peace and freedom, and we shall be making further proposals to them. Our friends in NATO must realize the implications of their ships engaging in the Cuban trade.

We shall continue to work with Cuban refugee leaders who are dedicated, as we are, to that nation's future return to freedom. We shall continue to keep the American people and the Congress fully informed. We shall increase our surveillance of the whole Caribbean area. We shall neither initiate nor permit aggression in this hemisphere.

14 : Cuba Quarantined and Khrushchev Challenged

TELEVISION ADDRESS TO THE PEOPLE
THE WHITE HOUSE
WASHINGTON, D.C.
OCTOBER 22, 1962*

This government, as promised, has maintained the closest surveillance of the Soviet military build-up on the island of Cuba. Within the past week, unmistakable evidence has established the fact that a series of offensive missile sites is now in preparation on that imprisoned island. The purpose of these bases can be none other than to provide a nuclear strike capability against the Western Hemisphere.

Upon receiving the first preliminary hard information of this nature last Tuesday morning at nine A.M., I directed that our surveillance be stepped up. And having now confirmed and completed our evalu-

---

* During the late summer and early autumn of 1962 the attention not only of the United States but of the world was centered upon Cuba. The dictator Castro maintained his truculent attitude; Soviet arms and technologists were being thrown into the island; it was plain that emplacements from which missiles could be launched were being erected, though Russian spokesmen, including Foreign Minister Andrei A. Gromyko, declared they were purely defensive. Refugees warned American authorities that dangerous preparations were being made, and the demand in certain quarters for armed intervention became louder. But the President felt that he had to wait for full evidence that offensive weapons were being installed. While he waited, increasing tension formed a background for what was to be the most dramatic and dangerous confrontation of the United States and Soviet Russia in the now long history of the Cold War. Congress had given the President full authority to take whatever action respecting Cuba he deemed necessary.

In mid-October the crisis began to come to a head. Photographs made

ation of the evidence and our decision on a course of action, this government feels obliged to report this new crisis to you in fullest detail.

The characteristics of these new missile sites indicate two distinct types of installations. Several of them include medium range ballistic missiles, capable of carrying a nuclear warhead for a distance of more than one thousand nautical miles. Each of these missiles, in short, is capable of striking Washington, D.C., the Panama Canal, Cape Canaveral, Mexico City or any other city in the Southeastern part of the United States, in Central America or in the Caribbean area.

Additional sites not yet completed appear to be designed for intermediate range ballistic missiles, capable of traveling more than twice as far, and thus capable of striking most of the major cities in the Western Hemisphere, ranging as far north as Hudson's Bay, Canada, and as far south as Lima, Peru. In addition, jet bombers, capable of carrying nuclear weapons, are now being uncrated and assembled in Cuba, while the necessary air bases are being prepared.

This urgent transformation of Cuba into an important strategic base, by the presence of these large, long-range and clearly offensive weapons of sudden mass destruction, constitutes an explicit threat to the peace and security of all the Americas, in flagrant and deliberate defiance of the Rio pact of 1947, the traditions of this nation and hemisphere, the Joint Resolution of the Eighty-seventh Congress, the Charter of the United Nations and my own public warnings to the Soviets on September 4 and 13. This action also contradicts the re-

---

by American reconnaissance planes showed clearly that sites for missile-launching weapons, aimed at the United States, were being built. The President and his principal advisers in and outside the Cabinet worked out a careful plan of action. As they worked, Soviet Foreign Minister Gromyko, unaware of the evidence on the President's desk, formally asserted that the weapons being given Cuba were not at all offensive. The President kept silence through Sunday, October 21. Then on Monday evening, in a television address whose solemnity matched the gravity of the situation, he told the nation what he had learned and what steps he was taking.—A. N.

peated assurances of Soviet spokesmen, both publicly and privately delivered, that the arms build-up in Cuba would retain its original defensive character, and that the Soviet Union had no need or desire to station strategic missiles on the territory of any other nation.

The size of this undertaking makes clear that it has been planned for some months. Yet only last month, after I had made clear the distinction between any introduction of ground-to-ground missiles and the existence of defensive antiaircraft missiles, the Soviet Government publicly stated on September 11 that—and I quote—"The armaments and military equipment sent to Cuba are designed exclusively for defensive purposes," and—and I quote the Soviet Government—"There is no need for the Soviet Government to shift its weapons for a retaliatory blow to any other country, for instance Cuba," and that—and I quote the government—"The Soviet Union has such powerful rockets to carry these nuclear warheads that there is no need to search for sites for them beyond the boundaries of the Soviet Union." That statement was false.

Only last Tuesday, as evidence of this rapid offensive build-up was already in my hand, Soviet Foreign Minister Gromyko told me in my office that he was instructed to make it clear once again, as he said his government had already done, that Soviet assistance to Cuba —and I quote—"pursued solely the purpose of contributing to the defense capabilities of Cuba," that—and I quote him—"training by Soviet specialists of Cuban nationals in handling defensive armaments was by no means offensive," and that "if it were otherwise," Mr. Gromyko went on, "the Soviet Government would never become involved in rendering such assistance." That statement also was false.

Neither the United States of America nor the world community of nations can tolerate deliberate deception and offensive threats on the part of any nation, large or small. We no longer live in a world where only the actual firing of weapons represents a sufficient challenge to a nation's security to constitute maximum peril. Nuclear weapons are so destructive and ballistic missiles are so swift that any substantially increased possibility of their use or any sudden change in their deployment may well be regarded as a definite threat to peace.

For many years both the Soviet Union and the United States, recognizing this fact, have deployed strategic nuclear weapons with great care, never upsetting the precarious status quo which insured that these weapons would not be used in the absence of some vital challenge. Our own strategic missiles have never been transferred to the territory of any other nation, under a cloak of secrecy and deception; and our history, unlike that of the Soviets since the end of World War II, demonstrates that we have no desire to dominate or conquer any other nation or impose our system upon its people. Nevertheless, American citizens have become adjusted to living daily in the bull's-eye of Soviet missiles located inside the U.S.S.R. or in submarines.

In that sense, missiles in Cuba add to an already clear and present danger, although it should be noted the nations of Latin America have never previously been subjected to a potential nuclear threat.

But this secret, swift and extraordinary build-up of Communist missiles, in an area well known to have a special and historical relationship to the United States and the nations of the Western Hemisphere, in violation of Soviet assurances and in defiance of American and hemispheric policy—this sudden, clandestine decision to station strategic weapons for the first time outside of Soviet soil is a deliberately provocative and unjustified change in the status quo which cannot be accepted by this country, if our courage and our commitments are ever to be trusted again by either friend or foe.

The 1930's taught us a clear lesson: aggressive conduct, if allowed to grow unchecked and unchallenged, ultimately leads to war. This nation is opposed to war. We are also true to our word. Our unswerving objective, therefore, must be to prevent the use of these missiles against this or any other country, and to secure their withdrawal or elimination from the Western Hemisphere.

Our policy has been one of patience and restraint, as befits a peaceful and powerful nation, which leads a world-wide alliance. We have been determined not to be diverted from our central concerns by mere irritants and fanatics. But now further action is required, and it is under way; and these actions may only be the beginning. We will not prematurely or unnecessarily risk the costs of world-wide nuclear war in which even the fruits of victory would be ashes in our mouth, but neither will we shrink from that risk at any time it must be faced.

Acting, therefore, in the defense of our own security and of the entire Western Hemisphere, and under the authority entrusted to me by the Constitution as endorsed by the Resolution of the Congress, I have directed that the following initial steps be taken immediately:

First, to halt this offensive build-up, a strict quarantine on all offensive military equipment under shipment to Cuba is being initiated. All ships of any kind bound for Cuba from whatever nation or port will, if found to contain cargoes of offensive weapons, be turned back. This quarantine will be extended, if needed, to other types of cargo and carriers. We are not at this time, however, denying the necessities of life as the Soviets attempted to do in their Berlin blockade of 1948.

Second, I have directed the continued and increased close surveillance of Cuba and its military build-up. The Foreign Ministers of the OAS, in their communiqué of October 6, rejected secrecy on such matters in this hemisphere. Should these offensive military preparations continue, thus increasing the threat to the hemisphere, further action will be justified. I have directed the armed forces to prepare for any eventualities; and I trust that, in the interest of both the Cuban people and the Soviet technicians at the sites, the hazards to all concerned of continuing this threat will be recognized.

Third, it shall be the policy of this nation to regard any nuclear missile launched from Cuba against any nation in the Western Hemisphere as an attack by the Soviet Union on the United States, requiring a full retaliatory response upon the Soviet Union.

Fourth, as a necessary military precaution, I have reinforced our base at Guantánamo, evacuated today the dependents of our personnel there and ordered additional military units to be on a stand-by alert basis.

Fifth, we are calling tonight for an immediate meeting of the Organ of Consultation under the Organization of American States, to consider this threat to hemispheric security and to invoke Articles 6 and 8 of the Rio Treaty in support of all necessary action. The United Nations Charter allows for regional security arrangements, and the nations of this hemisphere decided long ago against the military presence of outside powers. Our other allies around the world have also been alerted.

Sixth, under the Charter of the United Nations, we are asking tonight that an emergency meeting of the Security Council be convoked without delay to take action against this latest Soviet threat to world peace. Our resolution will call for the prompt dismantling and withdrawal of all offensive weapons in Cuba, under the supervision of UN observers, before the quarantine can be lifted.

Seventh and finally, I call upon Chairman Khrushchev to halt and eliminate this clandestine, reckless and provocative threat to world peace and to stable relations between our two nations. I call upon him further to abandon this course of world domination, and to join in an historic effort to end the perilous arms race and transform the history of man. He has an opportunity now to move the world back from the abyss of destruction, by returning to his government's own words that it had no need to station missiles outside its own territory and withdrawing these weapons from Cuba, by refraining from any action which will widen or deepen the present crisis, and then by participating in a search for peaceful and permanent solutions.

This nation is prepared to present its case against the Soviet threat to peace, and our own proposals for a peaceful world, at any time and in any forum—in the OAS, in the United Nations or in any other meeting that could be useful—without limiting our freedom of action. We have in the past made strenuous efforts to limit the spread of nuclear weapons. We have proposed the elimination of all arms and military bases in a fair and effective disarmament treaty. We are prepared to discuss new proposals for the removal of tensions on both sides, including the possibilities of a genuinely independent Cuba, free to determine its own destiny. We have no wish to war with the Soviet Union, for we are a peaceful people who desire to live in peace with all other peoples.

But it is difficult to settle or even discuss these problems in an atmosphere of intimidation. That is why this latest Soviet threat, or any other threat which is made either independently or in response to our actions this week, must and will be met with determination. Any hostile move anywhere in the world against the safety and freedom of peoples to whom we are committed, including in particular the brave people of West Berlin, will be met by whatever action is needed.

Finally, I want to say a few words to the captive people of Cuba, to whom this speech is being directly carried by special radio facilities. I speak to you as a friend, as one who knows of your deep attachment to your fatherland, as one who shares your aspirations for liberty and justice for all. And I have watched and the American people have watched with deep sorrow how your nationalist revolution was betrayed, and how your fatherland fell under foreign domination. Now your leaders are no longer Cuban leaders inspired by Cuban ideals. They are puppets and agents of an international conspiracy which has turned Cuba against your friends and neighbors in the Americas, and turned it into the first Latin-American country to become a target for nuclear war—the first Latin-American country to have these weapons on its soil.

These new weapons are not in your interest. They contribute nothing to your peace and well-being. They can only undermine it. But this country has no wish to cause you to suffer or to impose any system upon you. We know that your lives and land are being used as pawns by those who deny you freedom.

Many times in the past, the Cuban people have risen to throw out tyrants who destroyed your liberty. And I have no doubt that most Cubans today look forward to the time when they will be truly free—free from foreign domination, free to choose their own leaders, free to select their own system, free to own their own land, free to speak and write and worship without fear or degradation. And then shall Cuba be welcomed back to the society of free nations and to the associations of this hemisphere.

My fellow citizens: Let no one doubt that this is a difficult and dangerous effort on which we have set out. No one can foresee precisely what course it will take or what costs or casualties will be incurred. Many months of sacrifice and self-discipline lie ahead, months in which both our patience and our will will be tested, months in which many threats and denunciations will keep us aware of our dangers. But the greatest danger of all would be to do nothing.

The path we have chosen for the present is full of hazards, as all paths are, but it is the one most consistent with our character and courage as a nation and our commitments around the world. The cost of freedom is always high, but Americans have always paid it.

And one path we shall never choose, and that is the path of surrender or submission.

Our goal is not the victory of might, but the vindication of right; not peace at the expense of freedom, but both peace *and* freedom, here in this hemisphere, and, we hope, around the world. God willing, that goal will be achieved.

15 : The Bombers Are Withdrawn

NEWS CONFERENCE
NOVEMBER 20, 1962 *

I have today been informed by Chairman Khrushchev that all of the Il-28 bombers now in Cuba will be withdrawn in thirty days. He also agrees that these planes can be observed and counted as they leave. Inasmuch as this goes a long way toward reducing the danger which faced this hemisphere four weeks ago, I have this afternoon instructed the Secretary of Defense to lift our naval quarantine.

In view of this action, I want to take this opportunity to bring the American people up to date on the Cuban crisis and to review the progress made thus far in fulfilling the understandings between Soviet Chairman Khrushchev and myself as set forth in our letters of October 27 and 28.

---

* Fortunately for the world, Khrushchev retreated. A Soviet convoy moving toward Cuba, presumably with weapons, while the President delivered his address, changed the course of some of its ships. Within a week Khrushchev promised to dismantle the missile bases and carry the missiles back to the Soviet Union. The United States pressed for the removal of Russian long-range bombers, and here too the Soviet Premier yielded. In December American airplanes sighted forty-two Il-28 bombers, presumed to be the entire Russian contingent, on ships departing from Cuba.—A. N.

Chairman Khrushchev, it will be recalled, agreed to remove from Cuba all weapons systems capable of offensive use, to halt the further introduction of such weapons into Cuba, and to permit appropriate United Nations observation and supervision to insure the carrying out and continuation of these commitments. We on our part agreed that once these adequate arrangements for verification had been established, we would remove our naval quarantine and give assurances against invasion of Cuba.

The evidence to date indicates that all known offensive missile sites in Cuba have been dismantled. The missiles and their associated equipment have been loaded on Soviet ships. And our inspection at sea of these departing ships has confirmed that the number of missiles reported by the Soviet Union as having been brought into Cuba, which closely corresponded to our own information, has now been removed. In addition, the Soviet Government has stated that all nuclear weapons have been withdrawn from Cuba and no offensive weapons will be reintroduced.

Nevertheless, important parts of the understanding of October 27 and 28 remain to be carried out. The Cuban Government has not yet permitted the United Nations to verify whether all offensive weapons have been removed, and no lasting safeguards have yet been established against the future introduction of offensive weapons back into Cuba.

Consequently, if the Western Hemisphere is to continue to be protected against offensive weapons, this government has no choice but to pursue its own means of checking on military activities in Cuba. The importance of our continued vigilance is underlined by our identification in recent days of a number of Soviet ground combat units in Cuba, although we are informed that these and other Soviet units were associated with the protection of offensive weapons systems, and will also be withdrawn in due course.

I repeat, we would like nothing better than adequate international arrangements for the task of inspection and verification in Cuba, and we are prepared to continue our efforts to achieve such arrangements. Until that is done, difficult problems remain. As for our part, if all offensive weapons systems are removed from Cuba and kept out of the hemisphere in the future, under adequate verification and safeguards, and if Cuba is not used for the export of aggressive Communist purposes, there will be peace in the Caribbean. And as I said in September, "We shall neither initiate nor permit aggression in this hemisphere."

We will not, of course, abandon the political, economic and other efforts of this hemisphere to halt subversion from Cuba nor our purpose and hope that the Cuban people shall someday be truly free. But these policies are very different from any intent to launch a military invasion of the island.

May I add this final thought. In this week of Thanksgiving, there is much for which we can be grateful as we look back to where we stood only four weeks ago. The unity of this hemisphere, the support of our allies and the calm determination of the American people— these qualities may be tested many more times in this decade, but we have increased reason to be confident that they will continue to serve the cause of freedom with distinction in the years to come.

16 : "Ich Bin Ein Berliner"

RUDOLPH WILDE PLATZ
BERLIN, GERMANY
JUNE 26, 1963*

Two thousand years ago the proudest boast was "Civitas Romanus sum." Today, in the world of freedom, the proudest boast is "Ich bin ein Berliner."

There are many people in the world who really don't understand, or say they don't, what is the great issue between the free world

---

* This was probably the most memorable utterance of President Kennedy in his visit to Europe in the early summer of 1963. His declaration, in the presence of Mayor Willy Brandt, that "Ich bin ein Berliner" touched and heartened the people of West Germany as no other statement could have done. From that moment he had a place in

and the Communist world. Let them come to Berlin. There are some who say that Communism is the wave of the future. Let them come to Berlin. And there are some who say in Europe and elsewhere we can work with the Communists. Let them come to Berlin. And there are even a few who say that it is true that Communism is an evil system, but it permits us to make economic progress. "Lasst sie nach Berlin kommen."

Freedom has many difficulties and democracy is not perfect, but we have never had to put a wall up to keep our people in, to prevent them from leaving us. I want to say, on behalf of my countrymen, who live many miles away on the other side of the Atlantic, who are far distant from you, that they take the greatest pride that they have been able to share with you, even from a distance, the story of the last eighteen years. I know of no town, no city, that has been besieged for eighteen years that still lives with the vitality and the force, and the hope and the determination of the city of West Berlin. While the wall is the most obvious and vivid demonstration of the failures of the Communist system, for all the world to see, we take no satisfaction in it, for it is an offense not only against history but an offense against humanity, separating families, dividing husbands and wives and brothers and sisters, and dividing a people who wish to be joined together.

What is true of this city is true of Germany—real, lasting peace in Europe can never be assured as long as one German out of four is denied the elementary right of free men, and that is to make a free choice. In eighteen years of peace and good faith, this generation of Germans has earned the right to be free, including the right to unite their families and their nation in lasting peace with good will to all

---

the affections of the free Germans that inspired striking manifestations of grief following his assassination. Numerous political leaders and editors had opposed his journey to Europe on the ground that the uneasy foreign situation and the slow progress of Congress with his legislative program made his absence from the country undesirable. But it was later conceded that his trip was a success, with more rewards than penalties; and this was perhaps its most successful moment, though his reception in Ireland gave him special pleasure.—A. N.

people. You live in a defended island of freedom, but your life is part of the main. So let me ask you, as I close, to lift your eyes beyond the dangers of today to the hopes of tomorrow, beyond the freedom merely of this city of Berlin, or your country of Germany, to the advance of freedom everywhere, beyond the wall to the day of peace with justice, beyond yourselves and ourselves to all mankind. Freedom is indivisible, and when one man is enslaved, all are not free. When all are free, then we can look forward to that day when this city will be joined as one—and this country, and this great continent of Europe—in a peaceful and hopeful glow. When that day finally comes, as it will, the people of West Berlin can take sober satisfaction in the fact that they were in the front lines for almost two decades.

All free men, wherever they may live, are citizens of Berlin, and, therefore, as a free man, I take pride in the words "Ich bin ein Berliner."

IV

INTERDEPENDENCE

17 : Trade as a Strengthener of Free Nations

CONFERENCE ON TRADE POLICY
WASHINGTON, D.C.
MAY 17, 1962*

... When I submitted to the Congress the Trade Expansion Act of 1962, I called it "the expression of a nation, not of any single faction or section." That that is true is indicated by the fine messages of President Hoover and President Eisenhower and President Truman and by the support that has been given by Vice President Nixon and Alf Landon and others, who recognize this as a national challenge and opportunity, and not one that belongs to any party.

The trade of a nation expresses in a very concrete way its aims and its aspirations. When the people of Boston in 1773 threw cargoes of tea into the harbor, the American Revolution was in effect under way, symbolized by this revolution against a tariff—a tariff which meant taxation without representation. When our nation turned, in the nineteenth century, to its own protective tariffs as an aid to industrial development, they symbolized a policy of noninvolvement and of isolation, of detachment, from the affairs of the world. When protectionism, in spite of the efforts of President Hoover, reached its zenith in the Smoot-Hawley Tariff, it reflected a national lack of

---

* The President had explained in his second State of the Union Message to Congress the imperative reasons for passing a new five-year Trade Expansion Act. Not only was the reciprocal trade legislation which Cordell Hull had first initiated expiring; a bold new approach to international trade was needed. Now that Western Europe had recovered economic strength and the Common Market had grown powerful, it was more important than ever for the United States to "forge across the Atlantic a trading partnership." The President made a strong insertion in this "trade" speech to give direct support to the Atlantic Alliance at a time when it was being challenged by France's De Gaulle.—A. N.

confidence and growth. And then, in 1934, under the leadership of
Cordell Hull, the United States started on the long road back both
from protectionism and isolationism.

As the reciprocal trade program was renewed and refined through
eleven acts of Congress, under the successive leaderships of President
Roosevelt, President Truman and President Eisenhower, it became
more and more an expression of America's free world leadership—a
symbol of America's aim to encourage free nations to grow together,
through trade and travel, through a common defense, through aiding
the development of poorer nations, and through an increasing exchange of capital and culture.

And now the time has come for a new chapter in American trade
policy, a chapter that symbolizes our new great aspirations: for
greater growth at home, greater progress around the world and, above
all, the emergence of a greater Atlantic Partnership.

In recent days some doubts have been heard about the reality of
this concept of Atlantic Partnership. Fears have been expressed on
this side of the Atlantic that the United States may be excluded
from the councils and the markets of Europe. And fears have been
expressed on the other side of the Atlantic that the United States
may someday abandon its commitment to European security.

But I want to emphasize tonight, to all the peoples of the Western
Alliance, that I strongly believe that such fears are folly. The United
States cannot withdraw from Europe, unless and until Europe should
wish us gone. We cannot distinguish its defenses from our own. We
cannot diminish our contributions to Western security or abdicate
the responsibilities of power. And it is a fact of history that responsibility and influence—in all areas, political, military and economic
—ultimately rise and fall together. No nation can long bear the
heaviest burdens of responsibility without sharing in the progress and
decisions, just as no nation can assert for long its influence without
accepting its share of these burdens. And our policies in Europe today
are founded on one deep conviction: that the threat to Western
Europe and freedom is basically indivisible, as is the Western deterrent to that threat.

The United States, therefore, is committed to the defense of
Europe, by history as well as by choice. We have no wish to join,

much less to dominate, the European Community. We have no intention of interfering in its internal affairs. But neither do we hope or plan to please all our European allies, who do not always agree with each other, on every topic of discussion, or to base those decisions which affect the long-run state of the common security on the short-term state of our popularity in the various capitals of Europe.

Let us remember that we are working with allies, with equals, and both our allies and ourselves have a responsibility to speak frankly as well as constructively on all issues affecting the West. If the alliance were to stand still, if we were to pursue a policy of merely patching over the status quo with the lowest common denominator of generalities, no doubt all disagreements could be avoided or postponed. But dissent does not mean disunity, and disagreement can surely be healthy, so long as we avoid, on both sides of the Atlantic, any ill-tempered or ill-conceived remarks which may encourage those who hope to divide and conquer.

We cannot and do not take any European ally for granted, and I hope no one in Europe would take us for granted either. Our willingness to bear our full share of Western defenses is deeply felt, but it is not automatic. American public opinion has turned away from isolation, but its faith must not be shattered. Our commitment, let it be remembered, is to a common united defense, in which every member of the Western Community plays a full and responsible role, to the limit of his capability and in reliance on the strength of others; and it is that commitment which will be fulfilled. As long as the United States is staking its own national security on the defense of Europe, contributing today 425,000 men at an annual cost— in the balance of payments, and therefore in dollars, and therefore potentially in gold—of $1.6 billion to Europe, and calling up 160,000 men, at a budgetary cost of $3.5 billion since last July, in a far greater effort than that of any other country in response to last summer's crisis, we will continue to participate in the great decisions affecting war and peace in that area. A coherent policy cannot call for both our military presence and our diplomatic absence.

I am confident that Atlantic unity represents the true course of history, that Europe and the United States have not joined forces for more than a decade to be divided now by limited visions and suspicions. The direction of our destiny is toward community and confidence, and the United States is determined to fulfill that destiny.

Far from resenting the rise of a united Europe, this country welcomes it—a new Europe of equals instead of rivals, a new Europe, born of common ideals, instead of the old Europe, torn by national and personal animosities. We look forward to its increased role, as a full and equal partner, in both the burdens and the opportunities of aid, trade, finance, diplomacy and defense. We look forward to the strengthening of world peace that would result from a European Community in which no member could either dominate or endanger the others. And surely, may I add, each member would find in the fabric of European unity and Atlantic Partnership an opportunity for achievement, for grandeur and for a voice in its own destiny far greater than it would find in the more traditional and vulnerable fabrics of disunity and mutual distrust.

The debate now raging in Europe echoes on a grand scale the debates which took place in this country between 1783 and 1789. Small states are sometimes fearful of big ones. Big states are suspicious for historical reasons of one another. Some statesmen cling to traditional forms; others clamor for new ones. And every eye is on the hostile powers who are never far away. All this reminds us of our own organic deliberations.

But whatever the final resolution of today's debates, Western unity is not an end in itself. Collective security and deterrence are not enough. The time and the opportunity that they afford us are not worth the risk and the effort they require if we do not use them for constructive ends. If there is to be a new Atlantic Partnership, it must be a partnership of strong, not weak, economies; of growing, not declining, societies. And the great attraction of trade expansion for the United States is not only its contribution to a grand design of Atlantic Partnership, but its practical benefits to our own economy as well.

For today we wish to step up our growth; and trade expansion, by increasing exports as well as imports, and providing new outlets and new jobs, will help expand that growth.

We wish to avoid inflation; and trade expansion, by inspiring

American business to modernize for competition abroad, and by introducing new import competition here, will help to prevent that inflation.

We wish to improve our balance of payments; and trade expansion, by increasing our export surplus, will enable us to correct this deficit without imposing new restrictions or reneging on our security pledges.

We wish to increase investment at home; and trade expansion, by putting American businessmen on an equal footing with their European counterparts in terms of access to the Common Market, will help make it unnecessary for our industries to build new plants behind the Common Market wall instead of here at home.

We wish to increase the American standard of living; and trade expansion, by enlarging the supply of goods from abroad and stretching the consumer's dollar further, will help every American family.

We have prospered mightily during this period of the reciprocal trade program. Our exports, a meager $2 billion a year during the three years before the enactment of the first Trade Agreements Act in 1934, have increased tenfold to some $20 billion. Every American is richer because of this great effort.

And yet, until recently—and this remains one of our most serious problems today in the Congress—most Americans were largely unaware of the benefits of foreign trade. Many can "see" an import, but very few could "see" an export. While both labor and management in other nations, such as Britain and Japan, recognize that they must trade or die, we have for a long time remained, in both labor and management, largely unconcerned.

Today I believe all this is changing, but it is not, obviously, changing fast enough. American businessmen are determined to share in the phenomenal growth of the Common Market, but we want every American businessman to be looking all around the world for a place in which he can participate successfully in private investment. The Japanese economy as well is growing at the spectacular rate of 8 percent a year or more. Over the past fifty years Americans have sold in Japan $1.5 billion more than we have bought from Japan.

In short, this trade expansion program can benefit us all. I don't say that there won't be some changes in our economy which will require adjustment. But we will be producing more of what we produce best, and others will be producing more of what they produce best. There will be new employment in our growth industries— and this will come mostly in our high-wage industries, which are our most competitive abroad—and less new employment in some others. But these shifts go on every week in our lives, in this country, as the result of domestic competition. At the very most, the number of workers who will have to change jobs as a result of this new trade policy will not in a whole year equal the number of workers who have to change jobs every three weeks because of competitive changes here at home. And yet for these workers we are planning special assistance. . . .

18 : The Doctrine of National Independence

INDEPENDENCE HALL
PHILADELPHIA, PENNSYLVANIA
JULY 4, 1962*

It is a high honor for any citizen of the great Republic to speak at this Hall of Independence on this day of Independence. To speak as President of the United States, to the chief executives of our fifty states, is both an opportunity and an obligation. The necessity for comity between the national government and the several states is an indelible lesson of our history.

———————————————————————

* The President had demonstrated his sympathy with well-regulated national feeling in state visits (with Mrs. Kennedy) to Colombia and Venezuela in 1961. When he delivered this speech, he had just returned from a state visit to Mexico City, where he was greeted by cheering crowds of more than a million people. Later this month he was to tell Brazilian students in Washington that his primary concern with other nations was not in their economic systems but in their political freedoms.—A. N.

Because our system is designed to encourage both differences and dissent, because its checks and balances are designed to preserve the rights of the individual and the locality against pre-eminent central authority, you and I both recognize how dependent we are, one upon the other, for the successful operation of our unique and happy form of government. Our system and our freedom permit the legislative to be pitted upon occasions against the executive, the state against the federal government, the city against the countryside, party against party, interest against interest, all in competition or in contention one with another. Our task—your task in the State House and my task in the White House—is to weave from all these tangled threads a fabric of law and progress. Others may confine themselves to debate, discussion and that ultimate luxury, free advice. Our responsibility is one of decision, for to govern is to choose.

Thus in a very real sense you and I are the executors of the testament handed down by those who gathered in this historic hall 186 years ago today. For they gathered to affix their names to a document which was above all else a document not of rhetoric, but of bold decision. It was, it is true, a document of protest, but protests had been made before. It set forth their grievances with eloquence, but such eloquence had been heard before. But what distinguished this paper from all the others was the final, irrevocable decision that it took to assert the independence of free states in place of colonies and to commit to that goal their lives, their fortunes and their sacred honor.

Today, 186 years later, that Declaration, whose yellowing parchment and fading, almost illegible lines I saw in the past week in the National Archives in Washington, is still a revolutionary document. To read it today is to hear a trumpet call. For that Declaration unleashed not merely a revolution against the British, but a revolution in human affairs. Its authors were highly conscious of its world-wide implications, and George Washington declared that liberty and self-government were, in his words, "finally staked on the experiment entrusted to the hands of the American people."

This prophecy has been borne out for 186 years. This doctrine of national independence has shaken the globe, and it remains the most powerful force anywhere in the world today. There are those struggling to eke out a bare existence in a barren land who have never heard of free enterprise, but who cherish the idea of independence. There are those who are grappling with overpowering problems of illiteracy and ill health, and who are ill-equipped to hold free elections, but they are determined to hold fast to their national independence. Even those unwilling or unable to take part in any struggle between East and West are strongly on the side of their own national independence. If there is a single issue in the world today which divides the world, it is independence—the independence of Berlin or Laos or Vietnam, the longing for independence behind the Iron Curtain, the peaceful transition to independence in those newly emerging areas whose troubles some hope to exploit.

The theory of independence, as old as man himself, was not invented in this hall, but it was in this hall that the theory became a practice, that the word went out to all the world that "the God who gave us life gave us liberty at the same time."

And today this nation, conceived in revolution, nurtured in liberty, matured in independence, has no intention of abdicating its leadership in that world-wide movement for independence to any nation or society committed to systematic human suppression.

As apt and applicable as this historic Declaration of Independence is today, we would do well to honor that other historic document drafted in this hall, the Constitution of the United States, for it stressed not independence but interdependence, not the individual liberty of one but the indivisible liberty of all.

In most of the old colonial world the struggle for independence is coming to an end. Even in areas behind the Curtain, that which Jefferson called "the disease of liberty" still appears to be infectious. With the passing of ancient empires, today less than 2 percent of the world's population lives in territories officially termed "dependent." As this effort for independence, inspired by the spirit of the American Declaration of Independence, now approaches a successful close, a great new effort for independence is transforming the world about us. And the spirit of that new effort is the same spirit which gave birth to the American Constitution.

That spirit is today most clearly seen across the Atlantic Ocean.

The nations of Western Europe, long divided by feuds more bitter than any which existed among the thirteen colonies, are joining together, seeking, as our forefathers sought, to find freedom in diversity and unity in strength.

The United States looks on this vast new enterprise with hope and admiration. We do not regard a strong and united Europe as a rival but as a partner. To aid its progress has been the basic objective of our foreign policy for seventeen years. We believe that a united Europe will be capable of playing a greater role in the common defense, of responding more generously to the needs of poorer nations, of joining with the United States and others in lowering trade barriers, resolving problems of currency and commodities, and developing coordinated policies in all other economic, diplomatic and political areas. We see in such a Europe a partner with whom we could deal on a basis of full equality in all the great and burdensome tasks of building and defending a community of free nations.

It would be premature at this time to do more than to indicate the high regard with which we view the formation of this partnership. The first order of business is for our European friends to go forward in forming the more perfect union which will someday make this partnership possible.

A great new edifice is not built overnight. It was eleven years from the Declaration of Independence to the writing of the Constitution. The construction of workable federal institutions required still another generation. The greatest works of our nation's founders lay not in documents and declarations, but in creative, determined action. The building of the new house of Europe has followed this same practical and purposeful course. Building the Atlantic Partnership will not be cheaply or easily finished.

But I will say here and now on this day of Independence that the United States will be ready for a Declaration of Interdependence, that we will be prepared to discuss with a United Europe the ways and means of forming a concrete Atlantic Partnership, a mutually beneficial partnership between the new union now emerging in Europe and the old American union founded here 175 years ago.

All this will not be completed in a year, but let the world know it is our goal.

In urging the adoption of the United States Constitution, Alexander Hamilton told his fellow New Yorkers to "think continentally." Today Americans must learn to think intercontinentally.

Acting on our own by ourselves, we cannot establish justice throughout the world. We cannot insure its domestic tranquillity, or provide for its common defense, or promote its general welfare, or secure the blessings of liberty to ourselves and our posterity. But joined with other free nations, we can do all this and more. We can assist the developing nations to throw off the yoke of poverty. We can balance our world-wide trade and payments at the highest possible level of growth. We can mount a deterrent powerful enough to deter any aggression, and ultimately we can help achieve a world of law and free choice, banishing the world of war and coercion.

For the Atlantic Partnership of which I speak would not look inward only, preoccupied with its own welfare and advancement. It must look outward to cooperate with all nations in meeting their common concern. It would serve as a nucleus for the eventual union of all free men, those who are now free and those who are avowing that someday they will be free.

On Washington's birthday in 1861, standing right there, President-Elect Abraham Lincoln spoke at this hall on his way to the nation's capital. And he paid a brief and eloquent tribute to the men who wrote, and fought for, and who died for, the Declaration of Independence. Its essence, he said, was its promise not only of liberty "to the people of this country, but hope to the world . . . [hope] that in due time the weights should be lifted from the shoulders of all men, and that *all* should have an equal chance."

On this fourth day of July, 1962, we who are gathered at this same hall, entrusted with the fate and future of our states and nation, declare now our vow to do our part to lift the weights from the shoulders of all, to join other men and nations in preserving both peace and freedom, and to regard any threat to the peace or freedom of one as a threat to the peace and freedom of all. "And for the support of this Declaration, with a firm reliance on the Protection of Divine Providence, we mutually pledge to each other our lives, our Fortunes, and our sacred Honor."

19 : Partnership with Germany and a United Europe

ASSEMBLY HALL OF PAULSKIRCHE
FRANKFURT, GERMANY
JUNE 25, 1963*

. . . As one who has known the satisfaction of the legislator's life, I am particularly pleased that so many members of your *Bundestag* and *Bundesrat* are present today, for the vitality of your legislature has been a major factor in your demonstration of a working democracy, a democracy world-wide in its influence. In your company also are several of the authors of the Federal Constitution who have been able through their own political service to give a new and lasting validity to the aims of the Frankfurt Assembly.

One hundred and fifteen years ago a most learned Parliament was convened in this historic hall. Its goal was a united German Federation. Its members were poets and professors, lawyers and philosophers, doctors and clergymen, freely elected in all parts of the land. No nation applauded its endeavors as warmly as my own. No assembly ever strove more ardently to put perfection into practice. And though in the end it failed, no other building in Germany deserves more the title of "cradle of German democracy."

But can there be such a title? In my own home city of Boston, Faneuil Hall, once the meeting place of the authors of the American Revolution, has long been known as the "cradle of American Liberty." But when, in 1852, the Hungarian patriot Kossuth addressed

---

* During his rapid visit to Europe, the President delivered important speeches in West Germany, Italy and Ireland, and talked with Prime Minister Macmillan in Great Britain. He was anxious to drive home what he had said in his second State of the Union Message, that the emergence of the new Europe would be matched by the emergence of new ties between Europe and America.—A. N.

an audience there, he criticized its name. "It is," he said, "a great name, but there is something in it which saddens my heart. You should not say 'American liberty.' You should say 'liberty in America.' Liberty should not be either American or European; it should just be 'liberty.'"

Kossuth was right. For unless liberty flourishes in all lands, it cannot flourish in one. Conceived in one hall, it must be carried out in many. Thus the seeds of the American Revolution had been brought earlier from Europe, and they later took root around the world. And the German Revolution of 1848 transmitted ideas and idealists to America and to other lands. Today, in 1963, democracy and liberty are more international than ever before. And the spirit of the Frankfurt Assembly, like the spirit of Faneuil Hall, must live in many hearts and nations if it is to live at all.

For we live in an age of interdependence as well as independence, an age of internationalism as well as nationalism. In 1948 many countries were indifferent to the goals of the Frankfurt Assembly. It was, they said, a German problem. Today there are no exclusively German problems, or American problems, or even European problems. There are world problems, and our two countries and continents are inextricably bound together in the tasks of peace as well as war.

We are partners for peace, not in a narrow bilateral context but in a framework of Atlantic Partnership. The ocean divides us less than the Mediterranean divided the ancient world of Greece and Rome. Our Constitution is old and yours is young, and our culture is young and yours is old, but in our commitment we can and must speak and act with but one voice. Our roles are distinct but complementary, and our goals are the same: peace and freedom for all men, for all time, in a world of abundance, in a world of justice.

That is why our nations are working together to strengthen NATO, to expand trade, to assist the developing countries, to align our monetary policies and to build the Atlantic Community. I would not diminish the miracle of West Germany's economic achievements. But the true German miracle has been your rejection of the past for the future—your reconciliation with France, your participation in the building of Europe, your leading role in NATO and your growing support for constructive undertakings throughout the world.

Your economic institutions, your constitutional guarantees, your confidence in civilian authority are all harmonious with the ideals of older democracies. And they form a firm pillar of the democratic European community.

But Goethe tells us in his greatest poem that Faust lost the liberty of his soul when he said to the passing moment, "Stay, thou art so fair." And our liberty, too, is endangered if we pause for the passing moment, if we rest on our achievements, if we resist the pace of progress. For time and the world do not stand still. Change is the law of life. And those who look only to the past are certain to miss the future.

The future of the West lies in Atlantic Partnership—a system of cooperation, interdependence and harmony whose peoples can jointly meet their burdens and opportunities throughout the world. Some say that is only a dream, but I do not agree. A generation of achievement—the Marshall Plan, NATO, the Schuman Plan and the Common Market—urges us up the path to greater unity.

There will be difficulties and delays. There will be doubts and discouragement. There will be differences of approach and opinion. But we have the will and the means to serve three related goals: the heritage of our countries, the unity of our continents and the interdependence of the Western Alliance.

Some say that the United States will neither hold to these purposes nor abide by its pledges, that we will revert to a narrow nationalism. But such doubts fly in the face of history. For eighteen years the United States has stood its watch for freedom all around the world. The firmness of American will and the effectiveness of American strength have been shown, in support of free men and free governments, in Asia, in Africa, in the Americas and, above all, here in Europe. We have undertaken, and sustained in honor, relations of mutual trust and obligation with more than forty allies. We are proud of this record, which more than answers all doubts. But, in addition, these proven commitments to the common freedom and safety are assured, in the future as in the past, by one great fundamental fact—that they are deeply rooted in America's own self-interest. Our commitment to Europe is indispensable, in our interest as well as yours.

It is not in our interest to try to dominate the European councils of decision. If that were our objective, we would prefer to see Europe divided and weak, enabling the United States to deal with each fragment individually. Instead, we look forward to a Europe united and strong, speaking with a common voice, acting with a common will, a world power capable of meeting world problems as a full and equal partner.

This is in the interest of us all. For war in Europe, as we learned twice in forty years, destroys peace in America. A threat to the freedom of Europe is a threat to the freedom of America. That is why no administration in Washington can fail to respond to such a threat, not merely from goodwill but from necessity. And that is why we look forward to a united Europe in an Atlantic Partnership, an entity of interdependent parts, sharing equally both burdens and decisions, and linked together in the tasks of defense and the arts of peace.

This is no fantasy. It will be achieved by concrete steps to solve the problems that face us all, military, economic and political. Partnership is not a posture but a process, a continuous process that grows stronger each year as we devote ourselves to common tasks.

The first task of the Atlantic Community was to assure its common defense. That defense was and still is indivisible. The United States will risk its cities to defend yours because we need your freedom to protect ours. Hundreds of thousands of our soldiers serve with yours on this continent, as tangible evidence of that pledge. Those who would doubt our pledge or deny this indivisibility, those who would separate Europe from America or split one ally from another, would only give aid and comfort to the men who make themselves our adversaries and welcome any Western disarray. . . .

Second, our partnership is not military alone. Economic unity is also imperative, not only among the nations of Europe but across the wide Atlantic. Indeed, economic cooperation is needed throughout the entire free world. By opening our markets to the developing countries of Africa, Asia and Latin America, by contributing our capital and our skills, by stabilizing basic prices, we can help assure them of a favorable climate for freedom and growth. This is an Atlantic responsibility. For the Atlantic nations themselves helped to awaken these peoples. Our merchants and traders plowed up their soils, and their societies as well, in search of minerals and oil and rubber and coffee. Now we must help them gain full membership in the twentieth century, closing the gap between rich and poor.

Another great economic challenge is the coming round of trade negotiations. Those deliberations are much more important than a technical discussion of trade and commerce. They are an opportunity to build common industrial and agricultural policies across the Atlantic. They are an opportunity to open up new sources of demand to give new impetus to growth, and make more jobs and prosperity, for our expanding populations. They are an opportunity to recognize the trading needs and aspirations of other free countries, including Japan.

In short, these negotiations are a test of our unity. While each nation must naturally look out for its own interests, each nation must also look out for the common interest: the need for greater markets on both sides of the Atlantic, the need to reduce the imbalance between developed and underdeveloped nations, and the need to stimulate the Atlantic economy to higher levels of production rather than to stifle it by higher levels of protection.

We must not return to the 1930's when we exported to each other our own stagnation. We must not return to the discredited view that trade favors some nations at the expense of others. Let no one think that the United States, with only a fraction of its economy dependent on trade and only a small part of that with Western Europe, is seeking trade expansion in order to dump our goods on this Continent. Trade expansion will help us all. The experience of the Common Market, like the experience of the German *Zollverein*, shows an increased rise in business activity and general prosperity resulting for all participants in such trade agreements, with no member profiting at the expense of another. As they say on my own Cape Cod, a rising tide lifts all the boats. And a partnership, by definition, serves both partners, without domination or unfair advantage. Together we have been partners in adversity; let us also be partners in prosperity.

Beyond development and trade is monetary policy. Here again our interests run together. Indeed, there is no field in which the wider interest of all more clearly outweighs the narrow interest of one. We have lived by that principle, as bankers to freedom, for a generation. Now that other nations, including West Germany, have found new economic strength, it is time for common efforts here, too. The great free nations of the world must take control of our monetary problems if those problems are not to take control of us.

Third and finally, our partnership depends on common political purpose. Against the hazards of division and lassitude, no lesser force will serve. History tells us that disunity and relaxation are the great internal dangers of an alliance. Thucydides reported that the Peloponnesians and their allies were mighty in battle but handicapped by their policy-making body, in which, he related, "each presses its own ends . . . which generally results in no action at all . . . they devote more time to the prosecution of their own purposes than to the consideration of the general welfare—each supposes that no harm will come of his own neglect, that it is the business of another to do this or that; and so, as each separately entertains the same illusion, the common cause imperceptibly decays."

Is that also to be the story of the Grand Alliance? Welded in a moment of imminent danger, will it disintegrate in complacency, with each member pressing its own ends to the neglect of the common cause? This must not be the case. Our old dangers are not gone beyond return, and any division among us would bring them back in doubled strength.

Our defenses are now strong, but they must be made stronger. Our economic goals are now clear, but we must get on with their performance. And the greatest of our necessities, the most notable of our omissions, is progress toward unity of political purpose.

For we live in a world in which our own united strength and will must be our first reliance. As I have said before, and will say again, we work toward the day when there may be real peace between us and the Communists. We will not be second in that effort. But that day is not yet here.

We in the United States and Canada are 200 million, and here on the European side of the Atlantic Alliance are nearly 300 million more. The strength and unity of this half billion human beings are, and will continue to be, the anchor of all freedom, for all nations. Let us from time to time pledge ourselves again to the common purposes.

But let us go on, from words to actions, to intensify our efforts for still greater unity among us, to build new associations and institutions on those already established. Lofty words cannot construct an alliance or maintain it; only concrete deeds can do that.

The great present task of construction is here on this continent where the effort for a unified free Europe is under way. It is not for Americans to prescribe to Europeans how this effort should be carried forward. Nor do I believe that there is any one right course or any single final pattern. It is Europeans who are building Europe.

Yet the reunion of Europe, as Europeans shape it, bringing a permanent end to the civil wars that have repeatedly racked the world, will continue to have the determined support of the United States. For that reunion is a necessary step in strengthening the community of freedom. It would strengthen our alliance for its defense. And it would be in our national interest as well as yours.

It is only a fully cohesive Europe that can protect us all against fragmentation of the alliance. Only such a Europe will permit full reciprocity of treatment across the ocean, in facing the Atlantic agenda. With only such a Europe can we have a full give-and-take between equals, an equal sharing of responsibilities and an equal level of sacrifice. I repeat again, so that there may be no misunderstanding, the choice of paths to the unity of Europe is a choice which Europe must make. But as you continue this great effort, undeterred by either difficulty or delay, you should know that this new European greatness will be not an object of fear, but a source of strength, for the United States of America.

There are other political tasks before us. We must all learn to practice more completely the art of consultation on matters stretching well beyond immediate military and economic questions. Together, for example, we must explore the possibilities of leashing the tensions of the Cold War and reducing the dangers of the arms race. Together we must work to strengthen the spirit of those Europeans who are now not free, to re-establish their old ties to freedom and the West, so that their desire for liberty and their sense of nationhood and their sense of belonging to the Western Community will survive for future expression. We ask those who would be our adversaries to understand that in our relations with them we will not bargain one nation's interest against another's and that the commitment to the cause of freedom is common to us all.

All of us in the West must be faithful to our conviction that peace in Europe can never be complete until everywhere in Europe—and that includes Germany—men can choose, in peace and freedom, how their countries shall be governed, and choose, without threat to any neighbor, reunification with their countrymen.

I preach no easy liberation and I make no empty promises; but my countrymen, since our country was founded, believe strongly in the proposition that all men shall be free and all free men shall have this right of choice.

As we look steadily eastward in the hope and purpose of new freedom, we must also look, and ever more closely, to our transatlantic ties. The Atlantic Community will not soon become a single, overarching superstate. But practical steps toward stronger common purpose are well within our means. As we widen our common effort in defense, and our threefold cooperation in economics, we shall inevitably strengthen our political ties as well. Just as your current efforts for unity in Europe will produce a stronger voice in the dialogue between us, so in America our current battle for the liberty and prosperity of all citizens can only deepen the meaning of our common historic purposes. In the far future there may be a new great union for us all. But for the present, there is plenty for all to do in building new and enduring connections.

In short, the words of Thucydides are a warning, not a prediction. We have it in us, as eighteen years have shown, to build our defenses, to strengthen our economies and to tighten our political bonds, both in good weather and in bad. We can move forward with the confidence that is born of success and the skill that is born of experience. And as we move, let us take heart from the certainty that we are united not only by danger and necessity, but by hope and purpose as well.

For we know now that freedom is more than the rejection of tyranny, that prosperity is more than an escape from want, that partnership is more than a sharing of power. These are all, above all, great human adventures. They must have meaning and conviction and purpose; and because they do, in your country now and in mine, in all the nations of the alliance, we are called to a great new mission.

It is not a mission of self-defense alone, for that is a means, not an end. It is not a mission of arbitrary power, for we reject the idea that one nation should dominate another. The mission is to create a new social order, founded on liberty and justice, in which men are the masters of their fate, in which states are the servants of their citizens and in which all men and women can share a better life for themselves and their children. That is the object of our common policy.

To realize this vision, we must seek, above all, a world of peace; a world in which peoples dwell together in mutual respect and work together in mutual regard; a world where peace is not a mere interlude between wars, but an incentive to the creative energies of humanity. We will not find such a peace today, or even tomorrow. The obstacles to hope are large and menacing. Yet the goal of a peaceful world must, today and tomorrow, shape our decisions and inspire our purposes.

So we are all idealists. We are all visionaries. Let it not be said of this Atlantic generation that we left ideals and visions to the past, nor purpose and determination to our adversaries. We have come too far, we have sacrificed too much, to disdain the future now. And we shall ever remember what Goethe told us—that the "highest wisdom, the best that mankind ever knew" was the realization that "he only earns his freedom and existence who daily conquers them anew."

20 : The Defense of West Berlin and West Germany

FREE UNIVERSITY
WEST BERLIN, GERMANY
JUNE 26, 1963*

. . . Prince Bismarck once said that one-third of the students of German universities broke down from overwork, another third broke down from dissipation, and the other third ruled Germany. I do not know which third of the student body is here today, but I am confident that I am talking to the future rulers of this country, and also of other free countries, stretching around the world, who have come to this center of freedom in order to understand what the world struggle is all about. . . .

This school is not interested in turning out merely corporation

---

* It was important that President Kennedy should reaffirm the commitment of the United States to the freedom of West Berlin; a commitment shared with Great Britain and France. West Germany was on the brink of a change of regime. In mid-October Chancellor Adenauer, after a tenure of fourteen years, would give way to Ludwig Erhard. Adenauer had persistently refused to consider such steps toward a relaxation of tensions between Russia and the West as the conclusion of a non-aggression pact between the NATO powers and the Warsaw Treaty powers, or an agreement by which the Soviet Union would place military observers west of the Iron Curtain while the democracies would station observers east of the line. The old Chancellor was determined not to accept any agreement that might seem to imply acceptance of a divided Germany—or result in the withdrawal of American troops across thousands of miles of ocean, while the Communists could still hold tactical positions just east of the overland invasion routes. Erhard was expected to take a more flexible position, but it would be easier for him to do so, giving Western diplomacy more room for maneuver, if the American Government underlined its purpose to labor for a united Berlin in a United Germany, both made whole by free self-determination.—A. N.

lawyers or skilled accountants. What it is interested in—and this must be true of every university—is in turning out citizens of the world, men who comprehend the difficult, sensitive tasks that lie before us as free men and women, and men who are willing to commit their energies to the advancement of a free society. That is why you are here, and that is why this school was founded, and all of us benefit from it.

It is a fact that in my own country the American Revolution and the society developed thereafter were built by some of the most distinguished scholars in the history of the United States, who were, at the same time, among our foremost politicians. They did not believe that knowledge was merely for the study, but they thought it was for the marketplace as well; and Madison and Jefferson and Franklin and all the others who built the United States, who built our Constitution and built it on a sound framework, I believe set an example for us all. And what was true of my country has been true of your country, and the countries of Western Europe. . . .

Goethe, whose home city I visited yesterday, believed that education and culture were the answer to international strife. "With sufficient learning," he wrote, "a scholar forgets national hatreds, stands above nations, and feels the well-being or troubles of a neighboring people as if they happened to his own." That is the kind of scholar that this university is training.

In the fifteen turbulent years since this institution was founded, dedicated to the motto "Truth, Justice and Liberty," much has changed. The university enrollment has increased sevenfold, and related colleges have been founded. West Berlin has been blockaded, threatened, harassed; but it continues to grow in industry and culture and size, and in the hearts of free men. Germany has changed. Western Europe and, indeed, the entire world have changed, but this university has maintained its fidelity to these three ideals: truth, justice and liberty. I choose, therefore, to discuss the future of this city briefly in the context of these three obligations.

Speaking a short time ago in the center of the city, I reaffirmed my country's commitment to West Berlin's freedom and restated our confidence in its people and their courage. The shield of the military commitment with which we, in association with two other great powers, guard the freedom of West Berlin will not be lowered or put aside so long as its presence is needed; but behind that shield it is not enough to mark time, to adhere to a status quo, while awaiting a change for the better. In a situation fraught with challenge—and the last four years in the world have seen the most extraordinary challenges, the significance of which we cannot even grasp today, for only when history and time have passed shall we realize the significant events that happened at the end of the fifties and the beginning of the sixties—in a situation fraught with change and challenge, in an era of this kind, every resident of West Berlin has a duty to consider where he is, where his city is going and how best it can get there. The scholar, the teacher, the intellectual have a higher duty than any of the others, for society has trained you to think as well as do. This community has committed itself to that objective, and you have a special obligation to think and to help forge the future of this city in terms of truth and justice and liberty.

First, what does truth require? It requires us to face the facts as they are, not to involve ourselves in self-deception; to refuse to think merely in slogans. If we are to work for the future of the city, let us deal with the realities as they actually are, not as they might have been, and not as we wish they were. Reunification, I believe, will someday be a reality. The lessons of history support that belief, especially the history of the world in the last eighteen years. The strongest force in the world today has been the strength of the state, of the idea of nationalism of a people; and in Africa and in Latin America and in Asia, all around the globe, new countries have sprung into existence determined to maintain their freedom. This has been one of the strongest forces on the side of freedom.

And it is a source of satisfaction to me that so many countries of Western Europe recognized this and chose to move with this great tide, and that therefore that tide has served us and not our adversaries. But we all know that a police state regime has been imposed on the Eastern Sector of this city and country. The peaceful reunification of Berlin and Germany will, therefore, not be either quick or easy. We must first bring others to see their own true interests better than they do today. What will count in the long run are the realities of Western strength, the realities of Western commitment, the realities of Germany as a nation and a people, without regard to artificial boundaries of barbed wire. Those are the realities upon which we rely and on which history will move, and others too would do well to recognize them.

Second, what does justice require? In the end, it requires liberty. And I will come to that. But in the meantime justice requires us to do what we can do in this transition period, to improve the lot and maintain the hopes of those on the other side. It is important that the people on the quiet streets in the East be kept in touch with Western society. Through all the contacts and communication that can be established, through all the trade that Western security permits, above all whether they see much or little of the West, what they see must be so bright as to contradict the daily drumbeat of distortion from the East. You have no higher opportunity, therefore, than to stay here in West Berlin, to contribute your talents and skills to its life, to show your neighbors democracy at work, a growing and productive city offering freedom and a better life for all. You are helping now by your studies and by your devotion to freedom, and you therefore earn the admiration of your fellow students from wherever they come.

Today I have had a chance to see all of this myself. I have seen housing and factories and office buildings, and commerce and a vigorous academic and scientific life here in this community. I have seen the people of this city, and I think that all of us who have come here know that the morale of this city is high, that the standard of living is high, the faith in the future is high, and that this is not merely an isolated outpost cut off from the world, cut off from the West. Students come here from many countries, and I hope more will come, especially from Africa and Asia. Those of you who may return from study here to other parts of Western Europe will still be helping to forge a society which most of those across the wall yearn to join. The Federal Republic of Germany, as all of us know from our visit better than ever, has created a free and dynamic economy from the disasters of defeat and a bulwark of freedom from the ruins of tyranny.

West Berlin and West Germany have dedicated and demonstrated their commitment to the liberty of the human mind, to the welfare of the community and to peace among nations. They offer social and economic security and progress for their citizens; and all this has been accomplished—and this is the important point—not only because of their economic plant and capacity, but because of their commitment to democracy, because economic well-being and democracy must go hand in hand.

And, finally, what does liberty require? The answer is clear: a united Berlin in a united Germany, united by self-determination and living in peace. This right of free choice is no special privilege claimed by the Germans alone. It is an elemental requirement of human justice. So this is our goal, and it is a goal which may be attainable most readily in the context of the reconstitution of the larger Europe on both sides of the harsh line which now divides it. This idea is not new in the postwar West. Secretary Marshall, soon after he delivered his famous speech at Harvard University urging aid to the reconstruction of Europe, was asked what areas his proposal might cover, and he replied that he was "taking the commonly accepted geography of Europe—west of Asia." His offer of help and friendship was rejected, but it is not too early to think once again in terms of all of Europe, for the winds of change are blowing across the Curtain as well as the rest of the world.

The cause of human rights and dignity, some two centuries after its birth in Europe and the United States, is still moving men and nations with ever-increasing momentum. The Negro citizens of my own country have strengthened their demand for equality of opportunity. And the American people and the American Government are going to respond. The pace of decolonization has quickened in Africa. The people of the developing nations have intensified their pursuit of economic and social justice. The people of Eastern Europe, even after eighteen years of oppression, are not immune to change. The truth does not die. The desire for liberty cannot be fully suppressed. The people of the Soviet Union, even after forty-five years of party dictatorship, feel the forces of historical evolution. The harsh precepts of Stalinism are officially recognized as bankrupt. Economic and political variation and dissent are appearing, for example, in Poland, Rumania and the Soviet Union itself. The growing emphasis on scientific and industrial achievement has been accompanied by increased education and by intellectual ferment. Indeed, the very nature of the modern technological society requires human initiative and the diversity of free minds. So history itself runs against the Marxist dogma, not toward it.

Nor are such systems equipped to deal with the organization of modern agriculture and the diverse energy of the modern consumer in a developed society. In short, these dogmatic police states are an anachronism. Like the division of Germany and of Europe, it is against the tide of history. The new Europe of the West, dynamic, diverse and democratic, must exert an ever-increasing attraction to the people of the East; and when the possibilities of reconciliation appear, we in the West will make it clear that we are not hostile to any people or system, providing they choose their own destiny without interfering with the free choice of others. There will be wounds to heal and suspicions to be eased on both sides. The difference in living standards will have to be reduced by leveling up, not down. Fair and effective agreements to end the arms race must be reached. These changes will not come today or tomorrow. But our efforts for a real settlement must continue undiminished.

As I said this morning, I am not impressed by the opportunities open to popular fronts throughout the world. I do not believe that any democrat can successfully ride that tiger. But I do believe in the necessity of great powers working together to preserve the human race, or otherwise we can be destroyed. This process can only be helped by the growing unity of the West, and we must all work toward that unity, for in unity there is strength—and that is why I travel to this continent, and speak for the unity of this continent —and any division or weakness only makes our task more difficult. Nor can the West ever negotiate a peaceful reunification of Germany from a divided and uncertain and competitive base. In short, only if they see over a period of time that we are strong and united, that we are vigilant and determined, are others likely to abandon their course of armed aggression or subversion. Only then will genuine, mutually acceptable proposals to reduce hostility have a chance to succeed. . . .

21 : American Ties with Ireland

JOINT SESSION OF THE DAIL AND SEANAD EIREANN
LEINSTER HOUSE
DUBLIN, IRELAND
JUNE 28, 1963*

The thirteenth day of September, 1862, will be a day long remembered in American history. At Fredericksburg, Maryland, thousands of men fought and died on one of the bloodiest battlefields of the American Civil War. One of the most brilliant stories of that day was written by a band of twelve hundred men who went into battle wearing a green sprig in their hats. They bore a proud heritage and a special courage, given to those who had long fought for the cause of freedom. I am referring, of course, to the Irish Brigade. General Robert E. Lee, the great military leader of the Southern Confederate forces, said of this group of men after the battle, "The gallant stand which this bold brigade made on the heights of Fredericksburg is well known. Never were men so brave. They ennobled their race by their splendid gallantry on that desperate occasion. Their brilliant though hopeless assaults on our lines excited the hearty applause of our officers and soldiers."

---

* It was from County Wexford, a part of Leinster in southeastern Ireland, that the Kennedys had come; a shire of Danish name, but whose records run back beyond the Danish occupation. Pugin had designed the Roman Catholic cathedral at Enniscorthy, Cromwell had conquered the district, and the United Irishmen had made it a seat of revolt in 1798. His visit to the ancestral area and reunion with family connections gave President Kennedy more personal satisfaction than any other part of his brief European tour in the early summer of 1963. He followed this visit to the old family home by an address to the Irish Parliament, which gave him a fervent welcome. Few of his speeches better reflect his abiding interest in history.—A. N.

Of the twelve hundred men who took part in that assault, 280 survived the battle. The Irish Brigade was led into battle on that occasion by Brigadier General Thomas F. Meagher, who had participated in the unsuccessful Irish uprising of 1848, was captured by the British and sent in a prison ship to Australia, from whence he finally came to America. In the fall of 1862, after serving with distinction and gallantry in some of the toughest fighting of this most bloody struggle, the Irish Brigade was presented with a new set of flags. In the city ceremony, the city chamberlain gave them the motto "The Union, Our Country, and Ireland Forever." Their old ones having been torn to shreds by bullets in previous battles, Captain Richard McGee took possession of these flags on September 2 in New York City and arrived with them at the Battle of Fredericksburg and carried them in the battle. Today, in recognition of what these gallant Irishmen and what millions of other Irish have done for my country, and through the generosity of the Fighting 69th, I would like to present one of these flags to the people of Ireland.

As you can see, gentlemen, the battle honors of the brigade include Fredericksburg, Chancellorsville, Yorktown, Fair Oaks, Gaines's Mill, Allen's Farm, Savage's Station, White Oak Bridge, Glendale, Malvern Hills, Antietam, Gettysburg and Bristoe's Station.

I am deeply honored to be your guest in the free Parliament of a free Ireland. If this nation had achieved its present political and economic stature a century or so ago, my great-grandfather might never have left New Ross, and I might, if fortunate, be sitting down there with you. Of course, if your own President had never left Brooklyn, he might be standing up here instead of me.

This elegant building, as you know, was once the property of the Fitzgerald family, but I have not come here to claim it. Of all the new relations I have discovered on this trip, I regret to say that no one has yet found any link between me and a great Irish patriot, Lord Edward Fitzgerald. Lord Edward, however, did not like to stay here in his family home because, as he wrote his mother, "Leinster House does not inspire the brightest ideas." That was a long time ago, however.

It has also been said by some that a few of the features of this stately mansion served to inspire similar features in the White House in Washington. Whether this is true or not, I know that the White House was designed by James Hoban, a noted Irish-American architect, and I have no doubt that he believed by incorporating several features of the Dublin style he would make it more homelike for any President of Irish descent. It was a long wait, but I appreciate his efforts.

There is also an unconfirmed rumor that Hoban was never fully paid for his work on the White House. If this proves to be true, I will speak to our Secretary of the Treasury about it, although I hear this body is not particularly interested in the subject of revenues.

I am proud to be the first American President to visit Ireland during his term of office, proud to be addressing this distinguished assembly and proud of the welcome you have given me. My presence and your welcome, however, only symbolize the many and the enduring links which have bound the Irish and the Americans since the earliest days.

Benjamin Franklin, the envoy of the American Revolution, who was also born in Boston, was received by the Irish Parliament in 1772. It was neither independent nor free from discrimination at the time, but Franklin reported its members "disposed to be friends of America." "By joining our interest with theirs," he said, "a more equitable treatment . . . might be obtained for both nations."

Our interests have been joined ever since. Franklin sent leaflets to Irish Freedom Fighters. O'Connell was influenced by Washington, and Emmet influenced Lincoln. Irish volunteers played so predominant a role in the American Army that Lord Mountjoy lamented in the British Parliament, "We have lost America through the Irish." John Barry, whose statue was honored yesterday, and whose sword is in my office, was only one who fought for liberty in America to set an example for liberty in Ireland. Yesterday was the 117th anniversary of the birth of Charles Stewart Parnell, whose grandfather fought under Barry and whose mother was born in America, and who, at the age of thirty-four, was invited to address the American Congress on the cause of Irish freedom. "I have seen since I have been in this country," he said, "so many tokens of the good wishes of the American people toward Ireland. . . ." And today, eighty-three

years later, I can say to you that I have seen in this country so many
tokens of good wishes of the Irish people toward America.

And so it is that our two nations, divided by distance, have been
united by history. No people ever believed more deeply in the cause
of Irish freedom than the people of the United States. And no country contributed more to building my own than your sons and daughters. They came to our shores in a mixture of hope and agony, and
I would not underrate the difficulties of their course once they arrived in the United States. They left behind hearts, fields and a nation
yearning to be free. It is no wonder that James Joyce described the
Atlantic as a bowl of bitter tears, and an earlier poet wrote, "They
are going, going, going, and we cannot bid them stay."

But today this is no longer the country of hunger and famine
that those immigrants left behind. It is not rich and its progress
is not yet complete, but it is, according to statistics, one of the
best-fed countries in the world. Nor is it any longer a country of
persecution, political or religious. It is a free country, and that is
why any American feels at home.

There are those who regard this history of past strife and exile
as better forgotten, but to use the phrase of Yeats, "Let us not
casually reduce that great past to a trouble of fools, for we need not
feel the bitterness of the past to discover its meaning for the present and the future."

And it is the present and the future of Ireland that today hold
so much promise to my nation as well as to yours, and, indeed, to
all mankind, for the Ireland of 1963, one of the youngest of nations
and the oldest of civilizations, has discovered that the achievement
of nationhood is not an end, but a beginning. In the years since independence, you have undergone a new and peaceful revolution,
an economic and industrial revolution, transforming the face of this
land, while still holding to the old spiritual and cultural values.
You have modernized your economy, harnessed your rivers, diversified your industry, liberalized your trade, electrified your farms,
accelerated your rate of growth and improved the living standard
of your people.

Other nations of the world in whom Ireland has long invested
her people and her children are now investing their capital as well

as their vacations here in Ireland. This revolution is not yet over, nor will it be, I am sure, until a fully modern Irish economy fully shares in world prosperity. But prosperity is not enough.

Eighty-three years ago, Henry Grattan, demanding the more independent Irish Parliament that would always bear his name, denounced those who were satisfied merely by new grants of economic opportunity. "A country," he said, "enlightened as Ireland, chartered as Ireland, armed as Ireland, and injured as Ireland, will be satisfied with nothing less than liberty." And today, I am certain, free Ireland, a full-fledged member of the world community, where some are not yet free and where some counsel an acceptance of tyranny —free Ireland will not be satisfied with anything less than liberty.

I am glad, therefore, that Ireland is moving in the mainstream of current world events. For I sincerely believe that your future is as promising as your past is proud, and that your destiny lies not as a peaceful island in a sea of troubles, but as a maker and shaper of world peace.

For self-determination can no longer mean isolation; and the achievement of national independence today means withdrawal from the old status only to return to the world scene with a new one. New nations can build with their former governing powers the same kind of fruitful relationship that Ireland has established with Great Britain—a relationship founded on equality and mutual interests. And no nation, large or small, can be indifferent to the fate of others, near or far. Modern economics, weaponry and communications have made us realize more than ever that we are one human family and this one planet is our home.

"The world is large," wrote John Boyle O'Reilly,

The world is large when its weary leagues two loving hearts divide,
But the world is small when your enemy is loose on the other side.

The world is even smaller today, though the enemy of John Boyle O'Reilly is no longer a hostile power. Indeed, across the gulfs and barriers that now divide us, we must remember that there are no permanent enemies. Hostility today is a fact, but it is not a ruling law. The supreme reality of our time is our indivisibility as children of God and our common vulnerability on this planet.

Some may say that all this means little to Ireland. In an age when "history moves with the tramp of earthquake feet," in an age when a handful of men and nations have the power to devastate mankind, in an age when the needs of the developing nations are so staggering that even the richest lands often groan with the burden of assistance, in such an age, it may be asked, how can a nation as small as Ireland play much of a role on the world stage?

I would remind those who ask that question, including those in other small countries, of these words of one of the great orators of the English language:

All the world owes much to the little "five feet high" nations. The greatest art of the world was the work of little nations. The most enduring literature of the world came from little nations. The heroic deeds that thrill humanity through generations were the deeds of little nations fighting for their freedom. And, oh, yes, the salvation of mankind came through a little nation.

Ireland has already set an example and a standard for other small nations to follow. This has never been a rich or powerful country, and yet since earliest times its influence on the world has been rich and powerful. No larger nation did more to keep Christianity and Western culture alive in their darkest centuries. No larger nation did more to spark the cause of independence in America, indeed, around the world. And no larger nation has ever provided the world with more literary and artistic genius.

This is an extraordinary country. George Bernard Shaw, speaking as an Irishman, summed up an approach to life. "Other peoples," he said, "see things and say, 'Why?' . . . But I dream things that never were, and I say, 'Why not?' "

It is that quality of the Irish, the remarkable combination of hope, confidence and imagination, that is needed more than ever today. The problems of the world cannot possibly be solved by skeptics or cynics whose horizons are limited by the obvious realities. We need men who can dream of things that never were and ask, "Why not?" It matters not how small a nation is that seeks world peace and freedom, for, to paraphrase a citizen of my country, "The humblest nation of all the world, when clad in the armor of a righteous cause, is stronger than all the hosts of Error."

Ireland is clad in the cause of national and human liberty with peace. To the extent that the peace is disturbed by conflict between the former colonial powers and the new and developing nations, Ireland's role is unique. For every new nation knows that Ireland was the first of the small nations in the twentieth century to win its struggle for independence, and that the Irish have traditionally sent their doctors and technicians and soldiers and priests to help other lands to keep their liberty alive. At the same time, Ireland is part of Europe, associated with the Council of Europe, progressing in the context of Europe, and a prospective member of an expanded European Common Market. Thus Ireland has excellent relations with both the new and the old, the confidence of both sides and an opportunity to act where the actions of greater powers might be looked upon with suspicion.

The central issue of freedom, however, is between those who believe in self-determination and those in the East who would impose on others the harsh and oppressive Communist system; and here your nation wisely rejects the role of a go-between or a mediator. Ireland pursues an independent course in foreign policy, but it is not neutral between liberty and tyranny and never will be.

For knowing the meaning of foreign domination, Ireland is the example and inspiration to those enduring endless years of oppression. It was fitting and appropriate that this nation played a leading role in censuring the suppression of the Hungarian Revolution, for how many times was Ireland's quest for freedom suppressed, only to have that quest renewed by the succeeding generation? Those who suffer beyond that wall I saw on Wednesday in Berlin must not despair of their future. Let them remember the constancy, the faith, the endurance and the final success of the Irish. And let them remember, as I heard sung by your sons and daughters yesterday in Wexford, the words,

The boys of Wexford, who fought with heart and hand,
To burst in twain the galling chain and free our native land.

The major forum for your nation's greater role in world affairs is that of protector of the weak and voice of the small, the United Nations. From Cork to the Congo, from Galway to the Gaza Strip, from this legislative assembly to the United Nations, Ireland is sending its most talented men to do the world's most important work—the work of peace.

In a sense, this export of talent is in keeping with an historic Irish role. But you no longer go as exiles and emigrants, but for the service of your country and, indeed, of all men. Like the Irish missionaries of medieval days, like the wild geese after the Battle of the Boyne, you are not content to sit by your fireside while others are in need of your help. Nor are you content with the recollections of the past when you face the responsibilities of the present.

Twenty-six sons of Ireland have died in the Congo; many others have been wounded. I pay tribute to them and to all of you for your commitment and dedication to world order. And their sacrifice reminds us all that we must not falter now.

The United Nations must be fully and fairly financed. Its peace-keeping machinery must be strengthened. Its institutions must be developed until someday, and perhaps some distant day, a world of law is achieved.

Ireland's influence in the United Nations is far greater than your relative size. You have not hesitated to take the lead on such sensitive issues as the Kashmir dispute, and you sponsored that most vital resolution, adopted by the General Assembly, which opposed the spread of nuclear arms to any nation not now possessing them, urging an international agreement with inspection and control, and I pledge to you that the United States of America will do all in its power to achieve such an agreement and fulfill your resolution.

I speak of these matters today not because Ireland is unaware of its role, but I think it important that you know that we know what you have done, and I speak to remind the other small nations that they too can and must help build a world peace. They too, as we all are, are dependent on the United Nations for security, for an equal chance to be heard, for progress toward a world made safe for diversity. The peace-keeping machinery of the United Nations cannot work without the help of the smaller nations, nations whose forces threaten no one and whose forces can thus help create a world in which no nation is threatened.

Great powers have their responsibilities and their burdens, but the smaller nations of the world must fulfill their obligations as well. A great Irish poet once wrote, "I believe profoundly in the future of Ireland, that this is an isle of destiny, that that destiny will be glorious, and that when our hour has come we will have something to give to the world."

My friends, Ireland's hour has come. You have something to give to the world, and that is a future of peace with freedom.

22 : Italy, NATO and European Unity

NATO HEADQUARTERS
NAPLES, ITALY
JULY 2, 1963*

It is fitting that my travels away from home should end in this country and in this city. Italy, wrote Shelley, is the "paradise of exiles"; and in my exile from Washington I have enjoyed this paradise as the last stop in Europe. I shall leave this country with regret. It is also fitting that the final event of this European tour

---

* The problems before NATO at this moment were so numerous and perplexing that the President's speech, though general in terms, had an encouraging effect. One problem was the position of West Germany. In view of her significant contribution of traditional forces to NATO, some Germans felt entitled to nuclear weapons. And De Gaulle of France, in common with others in continental Europe, was apprehensive that the United States might abstain from nuclear retaliation in the event of total war between the West and the Communist powers for fear of a Soviet counterattack on America. De Gaulle wished France to keep the power to use her nuclear weapons independently. American leaders were evolving the idea of a multi-national nuclear force including American ships and men. Mr. Kennedy emphasized the desire of the United States to make NATO count effectively for European defense and European unity.—A. N.

should take place at this NATO headquarters. NATO is one of the best and the earliest examples of cooperation between Western Europe and North America. The NATO Defense Treaty pledges us all to the common defense, to regard an attack upon one as an attack upon all, and to respond with all the force at our command. And that pledge is as strong and unshakable today as it was when it was made.

Finally, it is fitting to take this opportunity to review our findings and feelings after ten days in Western Europe. Specifically, I return to Washington newly confirmed in my convictions regarding eight principal propositions:

First, it is increasingly clear that our Western European allies are committed to the path of progressive democracy, to social justice and to economic reform, attained through the free processes of debate and consent. I sit here again to stress the fact that this is not a matter of domestic policies or politics, but a key to Western freedom and Western solidarity. Nations which agree in applying at home the principles of freedom and justice are better able to work with each other abroad.

Second, it is increasingly clear that our Western European allies are determined to maintain and coordinate their military strength in cooperation with my own nation. In a series of briefings and reviews, I have been impressed less by NATO weaknesses, which are so often discussed, and more by the quality of the men, the officers, their steadily more modern weapons, their command structure and their dedication to freedom and peace. While we can take heart from these accomplishments, we still have much to do. Important improvements and additions are still needed, and this is not the time to slacken our efforts. But if we continue to build up our strength at all levels, we can be increasingly certain that no attack will take place at any level against the territory of any NATO country.

Third, it is increasingly clear that our Western European allies are committed to peace. The purpose of our military strength is peace. The purpose of our partnership is peace. So our negotiations for an end to nuclear tests and our opposition to nuclear dispersal are fully consistent with our attention to defense. These are

all complementary parts of a single strategy for peace. We do not believe that war is unavoidable or that negotiations are inherently undesirable. We do believe that an end to the arms race is in the interest
of all, and that we can move toward that end with injury to none. In
negotiations to achieve peace, as well as in preparations to prevent
war, the West is united, and no ally will abandon the interests of
another to achieve a spurious *détente*. But as we arm to parley, we
will not reject any path or refuse any proposal without examining its
possibilities for peace.

Fourth, it is increasingly clear that our Western European allies
are willing to look outward on the world, not merely inward on
their own needs and demands. The economic institutions and support of Western European unity are founded on the principles of
cooperation, not isolation; on expansion, not restriction. The Common Market was not designed by its founders or supported by the
United States to build walls against other European and Western
countries, or to build walls against the ferment of the developing
nations. These nations need assistance in their struggle for political
and economic independence. They need markets for their products
and capital for their economies. Our allies in Europe, I am confident, will increase their role in this important effort, not only in
lands with which they were previously associated, but in Latin
America and every area of need.

Fifth, it is increasingly clear that nations united in freedom are
better able to build their economies than those that are repressed
by tyranny. In the last ten years, the gross national product of the
NATO countries has risen by some 75 percent. We can do better
than we are doing, but we are doing much better than the party
dictatorships of the East. There was a time when some would say
that this system of admitted dictatorship, for all its political and
social faults, nevertheless seemed to offer a successful economic
system, a swift and certain path to modernization and prosperity.
But it is now apparent that this system is incapable in today's world
of achieving the organization of agriculture, of satisfying consumer
demands and the attainment of lasting prosperity. You need only
compare West Berlin with East Berlin, West Germany with East
Germany, Western Europe with Eastern Europe. Communism has

sometimes succeeded as a scavenger, but never as a leader. It has never come to power in any country that was not disrupted by war or internal repression, or both. Rejecting reform and diversity in freedom, the Communists cannot reconcile their ambition for domination with other men's ambition for freedom. It is clear that this system is outmoded and doomed to failure.

Sixth, it is increasingly clear that the people of Western Europe are moved by a strong and irresistible desire for unity. Whatever path is chosen, whatever delays or obstacles are encountered, that movement will go forward, and the United States welcomes this movement and the greater strength it insures. We did not assist in the revival of Europe to maintain its dependence upon the United States, nor do we seek to bargain selectively with many and separate voices. We welcome a stronger partner, for today no nation can build its destiny alone. The age of self-sufficient nationalism is over. The age of interdependence is here. The cause of Western European unity is based on logic and common sense. It is based on moral and political truth. It is based on sound military and economic principles, and it moves with the tide of history.

Seventh, it is increasingly clear that the United States and Western Europe are tightly bound by shared goals and mutual respect. On both sides of the Atlantic, trade barriers are being reduced, military cooperation is increasing, and the cause of Atlantic unity is being promoted. There will always be differences among friends, and they should be freely and frankly discussed. But these are differences of means, not ends. They are differences of approach, not spirit. Recognizing these and other problems—monetary payments, foreign assistance, agriculture and the rest—I return to the United States more firmly convinced than ever that common ideals have given us a common destiny, and that the Atlantic partnership is a growing reality.

Eighth, and finally, it is increasingly clear and increasingly understood that the central moving force of our great adventure is enduring mutual trust. I came to Europe to reassert as clearly and persuasively as I could that the American commitment to the freedom of Europe is reliable; not merely because of goodwill, although that is strong; not merely because of a shared heritage, although that is deep and wide; and not at all because we seek to dominate, because we do not. I came to make it clear that this commitment rests upon the inescapable requirements of intelligent self-interest. It is a commitment whose wisdom is confirmed by its absence when two world wars began and by its presence in eighteen years of well-defended peace. The response which this message has evoked from European citizens and the press, and leaders of the Continent, makes it increasingly clear that our commitment and its durability are understood. And at the same time, all that I have seen and heard in these ten crowded days confirms me in the conviction, which I am proud to proclaim to my own countrymen, that the free men and free governments of free Europe are also firm in their commitments to our common cause.

We have been able to trust each other for twenty years, and we are right to go on. One hundred and fifteen years ago this month, Mazzini addressed a mass meeting in Milan with these words: "We are here . . . to build up the unity of the human family so the day may come when it shall represent a single sheepfold with a single shepherd . . . the spirit of God. . . . Beyond the Alps, beyond the sea, are other peoples now," Mazzini said, "striving by different routes to reach the same goals . . . improvement, association, and the foundations of an authority that shall put an end to world anarchy. . . . Unite with them; they will unite with you."

Today Italy, the United States and other free countries are committed to this great end: the development of the human family. In time, the unity of the West can lead to the unity of East and West, until the human family is truly a single sheepfold under God.

23 : World Involvement Is Irreversible

MORMON TABERNACLE
SALT LAKE CITY, UTAH
SEPTEMBER 26, 1963*

. . . Americans have come a long way in accepting in a short time the necessity of world involvement, but the strain of this involvement remains and we find it all over the country. I see it in the letters that come to my desk every day. We find ourselves entangled with apparently unanswerable problems in unpronounceable places. We discover that our enemy in one decade is our ally the next. We find ourselves committed to governments whose actions we cannot often approve, assisting societies with principles very different from our own.

The burdens of maintaining an immense military establishment with one million Americans serving outside our frontiers, of financing a far-flung program of development assistance, of conducting a complex and baffling diplomacy, all weigh heavily upon us and cause some to counsel retreat. The world is full of contradiction and confusion, and our policy seems to have lost the black-and-white clarity of simpler times when we remembered the Maine and went to war. It is little wonder, then, that in this confusion we look back to the old days with nostalgia. It is little wonder that there is a desire in the

---

* This address in the Mormon Tabernacle in Salt Lake City was aimed directly at the ultraconservatives, reactionaries and members of the John Birch Society who longed to take the United States back to the year 1880. The costs of our military establishment abroad, the bill for the successful efforts of the United Nations to restore order in the Congo (the United States in 1961 paid not only its assessment of $32.5 million, but $10 million for Congo reconstruction and $15 million as a voluntary contribution to the UN treasury) and other burdens gave great pain to people with more money than intelligent understanding of the responsibilities of citizenship.—A. N.

country to go back to the time when our nation lived alone. It is little wonder that we increasingly want an end to entangling alliances, an end to all help to foreign countries, a cessation of diplomatic relations with countries or states whose principles we dislike, that we get the United Nations out of the United States and the United States out of the United Nations, and that we retreat to our own hemisphere, or even within our own boundaries, to take refuge behind a wall of force.

This is an understandable effort to recover an old feeling of simplicity, yet in world affairs, as in all other aspects of our lives, the days of the quiet past are gone forever. Science and technology are irreversible. We cannot return to the day of the sailing schooner or the covered wagon, even if we wished, and if this nation is to survive and succeed in the real world of today, we must acknowledge the realities of the world. . . .

24 : The Family of Man

PROTESTANT COUNCIL OF THE CITY OF NEW YORK
NEW YORK, NEW YORK
NOVEMBER 8, 1963*

The *New York Times* two weeks ago, I think, had an article by Mr. Bigart on desperate poverty in several rural counties of eastern Kentucky; schools which were without windows, sometimes with occasional teachers, counties without resources to distribute the surplus food we make available. And what is true in some of the older coal

---

* When Mr. Kennedy made this speech, with the Eighty-eighth Congress in its eleventh month, the foreign aid program was facing heavy opposition. The citizens' committee under General Lucius D. Clay which he had appointed to appraise the work had reported in March, 1963, that foreign aid was "essential to the security of the nation," but had also declared that the United States was "attempting too

mining areas of the United States is very true in our cities, and we see it in some of our statistics, where we have a mental retardation rate of three times that of Sweden, where we have an infant mortality rate higher than half the countries of Europe. We have about eight million boys and girls in this decade who will drop out of school, and a good many of them out of work, and this Council and the religious leaders of the Jewish and Catholic faiths have a great responsibility not only for the moral life of the community but also for the well being of those who have been left behind. . . .

I want to speak tonight very briefly, however, about the Family of Man beyond the United States. Just as the Family of Man is not limited to a single race or religion, neither can it be limited to a single city or country. The Family of Man is more than three billion strong. It lives in more than one hundred nations. Most of its members are not white. Most of them are not Christians. Most of them know nothing about free enterprise or due process of law or the Australian ballot.

If our society is to promote the Family of Man, let us realize the magnitude of our task. This is a sobering assignment, for the Family of Man in the world of today is not faring well.

The members of a family should be at peace with one another, but they are not; and the hostilities are not confined to the great powers of East and West. On the contrary, the United States and the Soviet Union, each fully aware of their mutually destructive powers and their world-wide responsibilities and obligations, have on occasion sought to introduce a greater note of caution in their approach to areas of conflict.

Yet lasting peace between East and West would not bring peace to the Family of Man. Within the last month, the last four weeks, the world has witnessed active or threatened hostilities in a dozen or more disputes independent of the struggle between Communism and the free world—disputes between Africans and Europeans in

---

much for too many." Senator Wayne Morse of Oregon led a battle in the Senate for heavy cuts. The President, who had seen approximately a billion dollars cut from his foreign aid request the previous year, was determined to prevent any new slashes.—A. N.

Angola, between North African neighbors in the Mahgreb, between two Arab states over Yemen, between India and Pakistan, between Indonesia and Malaysia, Cambodia and Vietnam, Ethiopia and Somalia, and there is a long list of others.

In each of these cases of conflict, neither party can afford to divert to these needless hostilities the precious resources that their people require. In almost every case, the parties to these disputes have more in common ethnically and ideologically than do the Soviet Union and the United States—yet they often seem less able and less willing to get together and negotiate. In almost every case, their continuing conflict invites outside intervention and threatens world-wide escalation—yet the major powers are hard put to limit events in these areas.

As I said recently at the United Nations, even little wars are dangerous in this nuclear world. The long labor of peace is an undertaking for every nation, large and small, for every member of the Family of Man. "In this effort none of us can remain unaligned. To this goal none can be uncommitted." If the Family of Man cannot achieve greater unity and harmony, the very planet which serves as its home may find its future in peril.

But there are other troubles besetting the human family. Many of its members live in poverty and misery and despair. More than one out of three, according to the FAO, suffer from malnutrition or undernutrition or both—while more than one in ten live below the breadline. Two out of every five adults on this planet are, according to UNESCO, illiterate. One out of eight suffers from trachoma or lives in an area where malaria is still a clear and present danger. Ten million—nearly as many men, women and children as inhabit this city and Los Angeles combined—still suffer from leprosy; and countless others suffer from yaws or tuberculosis or intestinal parasites.

For the blessings of life have not been distributed evenly to the Family of Man. Life expectancy in this most fortunate of nations has reached the Biblical three score years and ten; but in the less developed nations of Africa, Asia and Latin America, the overwhelming majority of infants cannot expect to live even two score years and five. In those vast continents, more than half the children of primary school age are not in school. More than half the families live in substandard dwellings. More than half the people live on less than $100 a year. Two out of every three adults are illiterate.

The Family of Man can survive differences of race and religion. Contrary to the assertions of Mr. Khrushchev, it can accept differences of ideology, politics and economics. But it cannot survive in the form in which we know it a nuclear war—and neither can it long endure the growing gulf between the rich and the poor.

The rich must help the poor. The industrialized nations must help the developing nations. And the United States, along with its allies, must do better—not worse—by its foreign aid program, which is now being subjected to such intensive debate in the Senate of the United States.

Too often we advance the need of foreign aid only in terms of our economic self-interest. To be sure, foreign aid is in our economic self-interest. It provides more than a half million jobs for workers in every state. It finances a rising share of our exports and builds new and growing export markets. It generates the purchase of military and civilian equipment by other governments in this country. It makes possible the stationing of 3½ million troops along the Communist periphery at a price one-tenth the cost of maintaining a comparable number of American soldiers. And it helps to stave off the kind of chaos or Communist takeover or Communist attack that would surely demand our critical and costly attention. . . .

The Korean conflict alone, forgetting for a moment the thousands of Americans who lost their lives, cost four times as much as our total world-wide aid budget for the current year. But foreign aid is not advanced only out of American economic self-interest. The gulf between rich and poor which divides the Family of Man is an invitation to agitators, subversives, and aggressors. It encourages the ambitions of those who desire to dominate the world, which threatens the peace and freedom of us all.

"Never has there been any question in my mind," President Eisenhower said recently, "as to the necessity of a program of economic and military aid to keep the free nations of the world from being overrun by the Communists. It is that simple."

This is not a partisan matter. For seventeen years, through three administrations, this program has been supported by Presidents and leaders of both parties. It is being supported today in the Congress by those in leadership on both sides of the aisle who recognize the urgency of this program in the achievement of peace and freedom. Yet there are still those who are unable or unwilling to accept these simple facts—who find it politically convenient to denounce foreign aid on the one hand and in the same sentence to denounce the Communist menace. I do not say that there have been no mistakes in AID administration. I do not say it has purchased for us lasting popularity or servile satellites.

I do say it is one essential instrument in the creation of a better, more peaceful world. I do say that it has substituted strength for weakness all over the globe, encouraging nations struggling to be free to stand on their own two feet—and I do not say merely because others may not bear their share of the burden that it is any excuse for the United States not to meet its responsibility. To those who say it has been a failure, how can we measure success—by the economic viability of fourteen nations in Western Europe, Japan, Spain, Lebanon, where our economic aid, after having completed its task, has ended; by the refusal of a single one of the more than fifty new members of the United Nations to go the Communist route; by the reduction of malaria in India, for example, from 75 million cases to 2,000, by the 18,000 classrooms and four million textbooks bringing learning to Latin America under the infant Alliance for Progress.

Nearly two years ago my wife and I visited Bogotá, Colombia, where a vast new Alliance for Progress housing project was just getting under way. Earlier this year I received a letter from the first resident of this 1,200-new-home development. "Now," he wrote, "we have dignity and liberty."

Dignity and liberty—these words are the foundation, as they have been since 1947, of the mutual security program. For the dignity and liberty of all free men, of a world of diversity where the balance of power is clearly on the side of free nations, is essential to the security of the United States. And to weaken and water down the pending program, to confuse and confine its flexibility with rigid restrictions and rejections, will not only harm our economy; it will hamper our security. It will waste our present investment and it will, above all, forfeit our obligations to our fellow man, obligations that stem from our wealth and strength, from our devotion to freedom and from our membership in the Family of Man.

I think we can meet those obligations. I think we can afford to fulfill these commitments around the world when 90 percent of them are used to purchase goods and services here in the United States, including, for example, one-third of this nation's total fertilizer exports, one-fourth of our iron and steel exports around the world, one-third of our locomotive exports. A cut of $1 billion in our total foreign aid program may save $100 million in our balance of payments—but it costs us $900 million in exports.

I think the American people are willing to shoulder this burden. Contrary to repeated warnings, prophecies and expressions of hope, in the seventeen years since the Marshall Plan began, I know of no single officeholder who was ever defeated because he supported this program, and the burden is less today than ever before. Despite the fact that this year's AID request is about $1 billion less than the average request of the last fifteen years, many members of Congress today complain that 4 percent of our budget is too much to devote to foreign aid. Yet in 1951 that program amounted to nearly 20 percent of our budget—20 percent in 1951, and 4 percent today. They refuse today to vote more than $4 billion to this effort—yet in 1951, when this country was not nearly as well off, the Congress voted $8 billion to the same cause. They are fearful today of the effects of sending to other people seven-tenths of 1 percent of our Gross National Product—but in 1951 we devoted nearly four times that proportion to this purpose, and concentrated in a very limited area, unlike today when our obligations stretch around the globe . . .

This Congress has already reduced this year's aid budget $600 million below the amount recommended by the Clay Committee. Is this nation stating it cannot afford to spend an additional $600 million to help the developing nations of the world become strong and free and independent—an amount less than this country's annual outlay for lipstick, face cream and chewing gum? Are we saying that we cannot help nineteen needy neighbors in Latin America and do as much for the nineteen as the Communist bloc is doing for the island of Cuba alone?

Some say that they are tiring of this task. We are tired of world problems and their complexities. We are tired of hearing those who receive our aid disagree with us. But are we tired of living in a free world? Do we expect that world overnight to be like the United States? Are we going to stop now merely because we have not produced complete success?

I do not believe our adversaries are tired, and I cannot believe that the United States of America in 1963 is fatigued.

Surely the Americans of the 1960's can do half as well as the Americans of the 1950's. Surely we are not going to throw away our hopes and means for peaceful progress in an outburst of irritation and frustration. I do not want it said of us what T. S. Eliot said of others some years ago: "These were a decent people. Their only monument: the asphalt road and a thousand lost golf balls."

I think we can do better than that.

My fellow Americans, I hope we will be guided by our interests. I hope we will recognize that the struggle is by no means over; that it is essential that we not only maintain our effort but that we also persevere; that we not only endure, in Mr. Faulkner's words, but also prevail. It is essential, in short, that the word go forth from the United States to all who are concerned about the future of the Family of Man that we are not weary in well-doing. And I am confident, if we maintain the pace, we shall in due season reap the kind of world we deserve and deserve the kind of world we shall have.

≈§ V

LATIN AMERICA
AND THE ALLIANCE
FOR PROGRESS

25 : "The Cooperative Effort of Our Great Free Nations"

SAN CARLOS PALACE
BOGOTÁ, COLOMBIA
DECEMBER 17, 1961*

. . . In 1934, one of the greatest of my predecessors, President Franklin Roosevelt, was the first President of the United States to visit this country. He came in pursuit of a new policy, the policy of the Good Neighbor. This policy, based on the ideas of Bolívar and San Martín and Santander, recognized the common interests of the American states, denied that any nation in this hemisphere had the right to im-

---

* When the charter of the Alliance for Progress was signed by participants in the Inter-American Conference at Punta del Este in Uruguay in the summer of 1961, Secretary of the Treasury Dillon saluted it in exuberant terms. On this foundation, he said, "will rise a new hemisphere where human freedom flourishes in lands of hope and progress." President Kennedy now gave a new statement of the hope of the United States that a broad socio-economic revolution, democratic in character, could be begun in Latin America. The task was of staggering magnitude, for the 210,000,000 people of the Latin nations involved, increasing at 3 percent a year, were lamentably deficient in education, in housing, in medical facilities, in roads, and in sound industrial enterprises. American assistance was generously provided. Chile, for example, was offered $214,000,000 in Alliance funds and materials in 1962, or nearly $28 for every inhabitant. The response given to the American challenge by some countries, including Argentina and Brazil, was extremely disappointing. But nearly 400 useful projects were gotten under way in the next two years in more than a score of lands. Although the difficulties of the program had clearly been underestimated, perhaps in time—a long, long time—the new hemisphere of which Dillon spoke *would* arise.—A. N.

pose its will on any other nation, and called for a great cooperative effort to strengthen the spirit of human liberty here in the Americas.

I am here today, the second American President to visit Colombia, in that same spirit. For our generation also has a new policy—*la Alianza para el Progreso*. Today again, that policy calls for a joint effort to protect and extend the values of our civilization, going beyond the Good Neighbor policy to a great unified attack on the problems of our age. Today again, we deny the right of any state to impose its will upon any other. And today again, these new policies are based upon the vision and the imagination of the great statesmen of Latin America.

In 1960, your distinguished President, Dr. Lleras Camargo, addressed the United States Congress of which I was a member. He spoke of the need for the American states to work together to conquer the evils of poverty and injustice. He called for participation by the United States. And, later in the same visit, he said—and I quote him —that "It is necessary to make a supreme effort in each country, with the cooperation of all the others, to prevent Western civilization from being threatened within the very stronghold that has defended it."

Those warnings of your President have been heard. The cooperative effort of our great free nations has begun. Help has already begun. And the stronghold of our civilization, the individual dignity of the individual, free man, has begun to strengthen the bulwarks of freedom. . . .

Bolívar, in a letter written when he was in exile, and the cause of liberty seemed dim, wrote: "The veil has been torn asunder. We have already seen the light and it is not our desire to be thrust back into the darkness." In our time the veil again has been torn asunder. The millions of our people who have lived in hopeless poverty, patiently suffering hunger, social injustice and ignorance, have now glimpsed the hope of a better and more abundant life for themselves and their children. And they do not intend to be thrust back into darkness.

La Alianza para el Progreso is designed to transform this hope into a reality. It calls for a vast and immediate effort on the part of all the Americas to satisfy the basic needs of our people for work and land, and homes and schools. It expects within the next ten years, the Decade of Development, to be well on the way toward satisfying these basic needs.

Much has already been done since *la Alianza para el Progreso* was announced on March 13. And today at Techo I saw some of the results of this effort. There President Lleras and I, in the presence of the families of hundreds of workers, dedicated a housing project in which more than eighty thousand people will, for the first time, know what it will be like to live in a home in which they would want to raise their children. We also dedicated one of eighteen schools, in which thirty thousand children, the most valuable asset of this hemisphere, will be given their opportunity to study and to learn, and to build their lives.

And along with the social progress symbolized by the Techo project will also come an intensive effort to develop and industrialize the economies of Latin America, reducing dependence on raw materials and steadily narrowing the relative gap between the wealthy industrialized countries and the republics of Latin America.

Thus *la Alianza para el Progreso* is a program which is revolutionary in its dimensions. It calls for staggering efforts by us all and unprecedented changes by us all. It raises far-reaching aspirations and demands difficult sacrifices. And although we have already done much in a short time, we must do much more and act much more swiftly in the months to come. For on the success of the Alliance, on our success in this hemisphere, depends the future of that human dignity and national independence for which our forebears in every country of the hemisphere struggled.

26 : "A Task for a Decade"

SPECIAL MESSAGE TO CONGRESS
WASHINGTON, D.C.
MARCH 12, 1962

The Charter of Punta del Este, which last August established the Alliance for Progress, is the framework of goals and conditions for what has been called "a peaceful revolution on a hemispheric scale."

That revolution had begun before the Charter was drawn. It will continue after its goals are reached. If its goals are not achieved, the revolution will continue, but its methods and results will be tragically different. History has removed for governments the margin of safety between the peaceful revolution and the violent revolution. The luxury of a leisurely interval is no longer available.

These were the facts recognized at Punta del Este. These were the facts that dictated the terms of the Charter. And these are the facts which require our participation in this massive cooperative effort.

To give this program the special recognition and additional resources which it requires, I therefore propose an authorization of $3 billion for the Alliance for Progress for the next four years. Of the $3 billion, an authorization and appropriation of $600 million is being requested for 1963, with up to $100 million to be used for grants and the balance of $500 million or more for development loans. This authorization will be separate from and supplementary to the $6 billion already authorized for loans for development for 1963 through 1966, which will remain available for use throughout the world.

During the year beginning last March over $1 billion has been committed in Latin America by the United States in support of the Alliance, fulfilling the pledge we made at the first Punta del Este meeting, and launching in a very real way for this hemisphere a dramatic Decade of Development. But even with this impressive support, the destiny of the Alliance lies largely in the hands of the countries themselves. For even large amounts of external aid can do no more than provide the margin which enables each country through its own determination and action to achieve lasting success.

The United States recognizes that it takes time to develop careful programs for national development and the administrative capacity necessary to carry out such a program, to go beyond the enactment of land reform measures and actually transfer the land and make the most productive use of it, to pass new tax laws and then achieve their acceptance and enforcement. It is heartening, therefore, that the changes called for by the Alliance for Progress have been the central issue in several Latin-American elections, demonstrating that its effects will be deep and real. Under the Organization of American States, nine outstanding economists and development advisers have begun to assist countries in critically reviewing their plans. Three Latin-American countries have already completed and submitted for review their plans for the more effective mobilization of their resources toward national development. The others are creating and strengthening their mechanisms for development planning. A number of Latin-American countries have already taken significant steps toward land or tax reform; and throughout the region there is a new ferment of activity, centered on improvements in education, in rural development, in public administration and on other essential institutional measures required to give a sound basis for economic growth.

But more important still is the changed attitudes of peoples and governments already noticeable in Latin America. The Alliance has fired the imagination and kindled the hopes of millions of our good neighbors. Their drive toward modernization is gaining momentum as it unleashes the energies of these millions; and the United States is becoming increasingly identified in the minds of the people with the goal they move toward: a better life with freedom. Our hand, extended in help, is being accepted without loss of dignity.

But the Alliance is barely under way. It is a task for a decade, not for a year. It requires further changes in outlook and policy by all American states. New institutions will need to be formed. New plans, if they are to be serious, will have to assume a life other than on paper. . . .

27 : How Much Real Progress in Latin America?

NEWS CONFERENCE
DECEMBER 12, 1962 *

QUESTION: Mr. President, this also has to do with the Alliance for Progress. Aside from the good intentions expressed by various governments in Latin America, how much real advance has been made in the area of economic, social and political reform, and, number two, is there any procedure by which those reforms can be evaluated here or in OAS?

THE PRESIDENT: Well, as you know, there is a procedure under the Alliance for Progress, the so-called Wise Men, who have been analyzing and approving the various steps that we take under the Alliance, without attempting in any way to be exclusive. I know that a good many reforms have been made in Venezuela, in Colombia. In fact, in Chile we have been discussing, and the President has described, some of the agrarian and tax reforms that Chile is now undertaking, which give us greater promise for the future.

So I think, even though, as I said in my toast yesterday, the problems of Latin America are staggering—lack of resources and over-dependence on one or two commodities—these governments in many

---

* The President spoke at this conference of the difficulties of Brazil, which had not carried out anti-inflation measures promised in 1961, when the republic got new loans. "I think the situation is most painful to the Brazilians themselves," he said, "with inflation of 50 percent . . . within a year." He added: "There is nothing, really, that the United States can do that can possibly benefit the people of Brazil if you have a situation so unstable as the fiscal and monetary situation within Brazil." This colloquy followed.—A. N.

cases are making a very determined effort under staggering difficulties. We had a visit from the President of Honduras the other day. Fifty-six percent of the people of Honduras are illiterate. These are terribly difficult problems. I don't think we should be impatient with failure; we should not desist because we have not solved all the problems overnight.

In the case of Chile, as the President has pointed out, they depend, as many other Latin-American countries do, on one or two commodities for their foreign exchange. The prices of these commodities in the case of nearly every country of Latin America have dropped in the last three or four years. The price of raw material exports of Colombia, as I pointed out in another press conference, has dropped more than our aid has given them. Brazil depended on coffee and coffee has dropped, though we hope the coffee agreement will make some difference.

So I am disturbed, but I think we ought to realize that we are dealing with the most staggering problems.

28 : Central America and the Development of Progressive Societies

NEWS CONFERENCE
MARCH 21, 1963

Last night I returned from a three-day meeting in San José, Costa Rica, with the presidents of five Central American republics and Panama. This was a most useful meeting. For the first time a President of the United States journeyed to Central America and conferred with all the leaders of this vital area, which, in terms of history, geography, common interest and common goals, is as closely allied with the United States as any area in the world. We agreed to continue our efforts under the Alliance for Progress to build and strengthen the machinery for economic cooperation with and among the nations of Central America and Panama, including the creation of a unified economic community in Central America. And we also agreed on the necessity for measures to halt the flow of agents, money, arms and propaganda from Cuba to Central America.

Every nation present was determined that we would both protect ourselves against immediate danger and go forward with the great work of constructing dynamic, progressive societies, immune to the false promises of Communism. This is the fourth Latin-American country which I have visited. Here, as in all the others, we found a spontaneous outpouring of friendship and affection for the United States; and here, as in all the others, we saw impressive evidence of the work now being done under the Alliance for Progress.

Each trip makes it clear that Latin Americans, by an overwhelming majority, are ready to work, to sacrifice, to fight if necessary, to maintain their own freedom, and to build societies which serve the welfare of all their people. They lack only the full measure of resources necessary to build a hemisphere where all can be secure and free. They know that they bear the fundamental responsibility for their own welfare and progress, but the receptions we have received in Costa Rica, in Mexico, in Venezuela and in Colombia demonstrate that they also know that we in the United States today have a deep concern for their problems, a common dedication to their aspirations and a faithful commitment to help them in their efforts. For all these reasons, I returned from San José with increased confidence that we will continue to live in a hemisphere of independent, firm and faithful friends.

29 : "Harsh Facts of Poverty and Social Injustice"

INTER-AMERICAN PRESS ASSOCIATION
MIAMI BEACH, FLORIDA
NOVEMBER 18, 1963*

It is on the Alliance for Progress that we base our common hope for the future.

That hope is for a hemisphere where every man has enough to eat and a chance to work, where every child can learn and every family can find decent shelter. It is for a hemisphere where every man, from the American Negro to the Indian of the Altiplano, can be liberated from the bonds of social injustice, free to pursue his own talents as far as they will take him, allowed to participate in the fruits of progress.

It is a hope for a hemisphere of nations, each confident in the strength of its own independence, devoted to the liberty of its citizens and joined with all the nations of the West in an association based on national strength and a common dedication to freedom. For we all share a common heritage. And if the idea of Atlantic Community is to have its full meaning, it must include the nations of Latin America.

The fulfillment of these hopes is not an easy task. It is important

---

* This meeting took place just as the annual review of the Alliance for Progress had ended in São Paulo. It took place when this annual report showed that Brazil and Argentina were making the slowest growth of all the South American nations. Yet in both troubled nations the governments seemed to be taking a surly attitude toward the Alliance and the United States. President João Goulart of Brazil asked for a solid front of the Latin nations against the highly industrialized nations. President Arturo Illia of Argentina was leading a movement for the expropriation of American oil companies' property, after these corporations had invested more than $200 billion in production facilities in the Argentine. The President's frank address therefore commanded more than usual interest.—A. N.

that the people of the United States, on whom much responsibility rests, realize how enormous that task is.

They can see its dimensions in the fact that Latin America is the fastest-growing continent in the world. Its population has increased 10 percent over the past ten years. Its almost 200 million people will be 400 million by the 1980's.

They can see its dimensions in the fact that tens of millions of their neighbors to the south exist in poverty with annual incomes of less than $100; that life expectancy in almost half the countries of Latin America is less than fifty years; that half the children have no schools to attend, that almost half the adults cannot read or write; that tens of millions of city dwellers live in unbearable slums; that millions more in rural areas suffer from easily curable diseases without hope of treatment; that in vast areas men and women are crippled by hunger while we possess the scientific tools necessary to grow all the food we need.

These problems, the hard reality of life in much of Latin America, will not be solved simply by complaints about Castro, by blaming all problems on Communism or generals or nationalism.

The harsh facts of poverty and social injustice will not yield merely to promises and goodwill. The task we have set ourselves in the Alliance for Progress—the development of an entire continent—is a far greater task than any we have ever undertaken. It will require difficult and painful labor over a long period of time.

Despite the enormity of these problems and our heavy responsibility, the people of the United States have been asked to sacrifice relatively little. Less than one percent of our federal budget is allocated to assist half a hemisphere. It is the people of Latin America who must undergo the agonizing process of reshaping institutions, not the people of the United States. It is the people of Latin America who must draw up development programs and mobilize their total resources to finance those programs, not the people of the United States. It is the people of Latin America whose cities and farms, homes and halls of government will bear the shock wave of rapid change and progress, not the people of the United States. It is the people of Latin America who will have to modify the traditions of centuries, not the people of the United States. Certainly we in the

United States cannot fail to do so little when so much is at stake for so many.

The last two and a half years have been a time of trial and experiment. We have labored to build a structure of cooperation and common effort for years to come. No nation in the Americas can deny that much more must be done to strengthen and speed our efforts, that there have been setbacks and disappointments.

That is why we intend to support strongly the leadership of the new Inter-American Committee for the Alliance for Progress; and why we are working to clear away unnecessary obstacles to the swift and imaginative administration of United States contributions.

But necessary concentration on obstacles and improvements should not obscure the fact that the *Alianza para el Progreso* has also made important progress. We have created new machinery of inter-American cooperation. The United States has committed $2.3 billion to the *Alianza* and the Latin-American nations have committed billions more. In many countries there have been new efforts at land reforms and tax reforms, education and agriculture.

The basic issues of progress and reform, long ignored, have become the battleground of the political forces of the hemisphere. And on the economic front, last year ten of the nineteen Latin-American nations exceeded the per capita growth goal of 2.5 percent established by the Charter of Punta del Este.

Nor can the failure of some to meet the goals of the Charter be blamed wholly on the shortcomings of the Alliance.

No amount of external resources, no stabilization of commodity prices, no new inter-American institutions can bring progress to nations which do not have political stability and determined leadership. No series of hemispheric agreements or elaborate machinery can help those who lack internal discipline, who are unwilling to make sacrifices and renounce privileges. No one who sends his money abroad, who is unwilling to invest in the future of his own country, can blame others for the deluge which threatens to overwhelm him.

For the *Alianza para el Progreso* is not an external aid program. It is more than a cooperative effort to finance development plans. It is a battle for the progress and freedom of nations. And it must be fought on every front of national interest and need.

First is the front of social justice. It is impossible to have real progress as long as millions are shut out from opportunity and others forgiven obligations. In my own country we have prepared legislation and mobilized government to insure to American Negroes, and all other minorities, access to the benefits of American society.

Others also must do the same for the landless *campesino*, for the underprivileged slum dweller, the oppressed Indian. Privilege is not easily yielded up. But until the interests of a few yield to the needs of the nation, the promise of progress and modernization will remain an empty mockery for millions of our citizens.

The second front is the front of economic welfare: the principle that every American has the right to a decent life for himself and a better life for his children. This means we must continue to perfect national development plans, to improve financing machinery and institutions. It means every nation must be willing to make sacrifices and mobilize its own resources for development. It also means that the United States must live up to its full commitment to provide continuing help. I have pledged the full energies of my government to insure that that commitment will be met.

In pursuit of economic welfare the Alliance does not dictate to any nation how it must organize its economic life. Every country is free to shape its economic institutions in accordance with its own national needs and will. However, just as no country can tell another how it must order its economy, no nation should act within its own borders so as to violate the rights of others under accepted principles of international law.

Private enterprise also has an important place in the Alliance for Progress. There is not enough available public capital, either in the United States or in Latin America, to carry development forward at the pace that is demanded. Yet the net flow of foreign capital alone was almost $250 million less this year than last—a third as much as the entire request to the United States Congress for assistance funds.

If encouraged, private investment, responsive to the needs, the laws and the interests of the nation, can cooperate with public activity to provide the vital margin of success; as it did in the development of all the nations of the West, including my own.

If we are to have the growth essential to the requirements of our people in this hemisphere, then an atmosphere must be developed and maintained that will encourage the flow of capital in response to opportunity. Today that capital is moving into growth here in the United States and Western Europe. Together we must provide the environment that will encourage its flow to Latin America.

Third is the front of political democracy and stability. This is at the core of our hopes for the future.

There can be no progress if people have no faith in tomorrow. That faith is undermined when men seek the reins of power, ignoring the restraints of constitutional procedures. They may even do so out of a sincere desire to benefit their own country. But democratic government demands that those in opposition accept the defects of to-day and work toward remedying them within the machinery of peaceful change. Otherwise, in return for momentary satisfaction, we tear apart the fabric and the hope of lasting democracy.

VI

RACE RELATIONS

AND

CIVIL RIGHTS

30 : James Meredith and the University of Mississippi

TELEVISION ADDRESS TO THE PEOPLE
THE WHITE HOUSE
WASHINGTON, D.C.
SEPTEMBER 30, 1962*

The orders of the court in the case of Meredith versus Fair are beginning to be carried out. Mr. James Meredith is now in residence on the campus of the University of Mississippi.

This has been accomplished thus far without the use of National Guard or other troops. And it is to be hoped that the law enforcement officers of the State of Mississippi and the federal marshals will continue to be sufficient in the future.

All students, members of the faculty and public officials in both Mississippi and the nation will be able, it is hoped, to return to their normal activities with full confidence in the integrity of American law.

This is as it should be, for our nation is founded on the principle that observance of the law is the eternal safeguard of liberty and de-

---

*Governor Ross Barnett of Mississippi had appeared in person at Oxford, seat of the State University, to deny James H. Meredith admission to the institution; this on September 25, 1962. Meredith, a singularly cool, well-behaved, earnest young man, and a veteran of the Korean War, had duly satisfied all the entrance requirements but one —he had not been born with a white skin. On Sunday night, September 30, with the backing of the Federal Circuit Court of Appeals, the Department of Justice and the President, he appeared on the campus to assert his rights. Simultaneously, the President made this national television appeal for peaceful submission to the Constitution, the law and the courts. Unfortunately, the provocative stand taken by Barnett and others resulted in bloodshed. Segregationists, including townspeople,

fiance of the law is the surest road to tyranny. The law which we obey includes the final rulings of the courts, as well as the enactments of our legislative bodies. Even among law-abiding men few laws are universally loved, but they are uniformly respected and not resisted.

Americans are free to disagree with the law, but not to disobey it. For in a government of laws and not of men, no man, however prominent and powerful, and no mob, however unruly or boisterous, is entitled to defy a court of law. If this country should ever reach the point where any man or group of men by force or threat of force could long defy the commands of our court and our Constitution, then no law would stand free from doubt, no judge would be sure of his writ, and no citizen would be safe from his neighbors.

In this case, in which the United States Government was not until recently involved, Mr. Meredith brought a private suit in federal court against those who were excluding him from the university. A series of federal courts all the way to the Supreme Court repeatedly ordered Mr. Meredith's admission to the university. When those orders were defied, and those who sought to implement them threatened with arrest and violence, the United States Court of Appeals, consisting of Chief Judge Tuttle of Georgia, Judge Hutcheson of Texas, Judge Rives of Alabama, Judge Jones of Florida, Judge Brown of Texas, Judge Wisdom of Louisiana, Judge Girwin of Alabama and Judge Bell of Georgia, made clear the fact that the enforcement of its order had become an obligation of the United States Government.

---

men from the countryside and some students, began a riot that Sunday evening which extended into Monday, October 1. A French correspondent and a local citizen were killed by shots of unknown origin; others were hurt. According to impartial observers, the state police did nothing to check the disorder and finally left the scene while fighting continued. The President thereupon used federal troops, and National Guardsmen sworn into federal service, to take control of the situation. Meredith began attending his classes under the protection of federal marshals, and the Federal Court of Appeals presently directed that criminal contempt proceedings be opened against Barnett for his obstruction of court orders. The segregationist rioting shocked the world, but the President's firm stand earned general praise.—A. N.

JAMES MEREDITH : 169

Even though this government had not originally been a party to the case, my responsibility as President was therefore inescapable. I accept it. My obligation under the Constitution and statutes of the United States was and is to implement the orders of the court with whatever means are necessary, and with as little force and civil disorder as the circumstances permit.

It was for this reason that I federalized the Mississippi National Guard as the most appropriate instrument should any be needed to preserve law and order while United States marshals carried out the orders of the court and prepared to back them up with whatever other civil or military enforcement might have been required.

I deeply regret the fact that any action by the Executive Branch was necessary in this case, but all other avenues and alternatives, including persuasion and conciliation, had been tried and exhausted. Had the police powers of Mississippi been used to support the orders of the court, instead of deliberately and unlawfully blocking them, had the University of Mississippi fulfilled its standard of excellence by quietly admitting this applicant in conformity with what so many other Southern state universities have done for so many years, a peaceable and sensible solution would have been possible without any federal intervention.

I recognize that the present period of transition and adjustment in our nation's Southland is a hard one for many people. Neither Mississippi nor any other Southern state deserves to be charged with all the accumulated wrongs of the last hundred years of race relations. To the extent that there has been failure, the responsibility for that failure must be shared by us all, by every state, by every citizen.

Mississippi and her university, moreover, are noted for their courage, for their contribution of talent and thought to the affairs of this nation. This is the state of Lucius Lamar and many others who have placed the national good ahead of sectional interest. This is the state which had four Medal of Honor winners in the Korean War alone. In fact, the Guard unit federalized this morning, early, is part of the 155th Infantry, one of the ten oldest regiments in the Union and one of the most decorated for sacrifice and bravery in six wars. In Mississippi in 1945 Jake Lindsey was honored by an unusual joint session of the Congress.

I close therefore with this appeal to the students of the university, the people who are most concerned.

You have a great tradition to uphold, a tradition of honor and courage, won on the field of battle and on the gridiron as well as the university campus. You have a new opportunity to show that you are men of patriotism and integrity. For the most effective means of upholding the law is not the state policeman or the marshals or the National Guard. It is you. It lies in your courage to accept those laws with which you disagree as well as those with which you agree. The eyes of the nation and all the world are upon you and upon all of us, and the honor of your university and state are in the balance. I am certain the great majority of the students will uphold that honor.

There is, in short, no reason why the books on this case cannot now be quickly and quietly closed in the manner directed by the court. Let us preserve both the law and the peace, and then, healing those wounds that are within, we can turn to the greater crises that are without, and stand united as one people in our pledge to man's freedom.

31 : The End of Federal Discrimination in Housing

NEWS CONFERENCE
NOVEMBER 20, 1962*

I would also like to announce that I have today signed an Executive Order directing federal departments and agencies to take every proper and legal action to prevent discrimination in the sale or lease of hous-

---

* The President's order here announced did not touch housing erected with the usual private financing, and did not cover housing already constructed with federal assistance. It was nevertheless of great value to Negroes and was received with warm gratification. Such steps

ing facilities owned or operated by the federal government, housing constructed or sold as a result of loans or grants to be made by the federal government or by loans to be insured or guaranteed by the federal government, and housing to be made available through the development or redevelopment of property under federal slum clearance or urban renewal programs.

With regard to existing housing facilities constructed or purchased as a result of direct loans or grants from the federal government, or under federal guarantees, or as a result of the Urban Renewal Program, I have directed the Housing Agency and other appropriate agencies to use their good offices to promote and encourage the abandonment of discriminatory practices that may now exist.

In order to assist the departments and agencies in implementing this policy, and to coordinate their efforts, I have established the President's Committee on Equal Opportunity in Housing. It is neither proper nor equitable that Americans should be denied the benefits of housing owned by the federal government or financed through federal assistance on the basis of their race, color, creed or national origin.

Our national policy is equal opportunity for all, and the federal government will continue to take such legal and proper steps as it may to achieve the realization of this goal.

---

were the more appreciated because the President failed in his effort to persuade Congress to establish a Department of Urban Affairs, with Cabinet rank. Negroes were now a powerful urban element, and the President had announced that he would make Robert C. Weaver the Secretary of the Department.—A. N.

32 : The Ballot, Education, Fair Employment and Other Rights

SPECIAL MESSAGE TO CONGRESS
WASHINGTON, D.C.
FEBRUARY 28, 1963*

"Our Constitution is color-blind," wrote Mr. Justice Harlan before the turn of the century, "and neither knows nor tolerates classes among citizens." But the practices of the country do not always conform to the principles of the Constitution. And this message is intended to examine how far we have come in achieving first-class citizenship for all citizens regardless of color, how far we have yet to go, and what further tasks remain to be carried out—by the Executive and Legislative Branches of the federal government, as well as by state and local governments and private citizens and organizations.

One hundred years ago the Emancipation Proclamation was signed by a President who believed in the equal worth and opportunity of

---

* Throughout the country the struggle of the Negroes for equal rights showed a rising fervor and in parts of the South provoked conflict. Two organizations, the Congress of Racial Equality (CORE) and the National Association for the Advancement of Colored People (NAACP), led the movement, but other groups, like the National Urban League, helped. In 1961 the "Freedom Riders," using nonviolent methods even when met with violence, did much to break down segregation in interstate buses and stations. Negroes took vigorous measures to compel restaurants, cafeterias and department stores to serve food to all patrons on equal terms. They made earnest efforts all over the country to promote the desegregation of public schools, and were able to note that by the end of 1962 more than a quarter of a million Negro children were attending schools in states which had previously drawn a color line. A drive to register Negroes as voters resulted in violence in 1962 in Georgia and

every human being. That Proclamation was only a first step, a step which its author unhappily did not live to follow up, a step which some of its critics dismissed as an action which "frees the slave but ignores the Negro." Through these long one hundred years, while slavery has vanished, progress for the Negro has been too often blocked and delayed. Equality before the law has not always meant equal treatment and opportunity. And the harmful, wasteful and wrongful results of racial discrimination and segregation still appear in virtually every aspect of national life, in virtually every part of the nation. . . .

The right to vote in a free American election is the most powerful and precious right in the world, and it must not be denied on the ground of race or color. It is a potent key to achieving other rights of citizens. For American history, both recent and past, clearly reveals that the power of the ballot has enabled those who achieve it to win other achievements as well, to gain a full voice in the affairs of their state and nation, and to see their interests represented in the governmental bodies which affect their future. In a free society those with the power to govern are necessarily responsive to those with the right to vote.

In enacting the 1957 and 1960 Civil Rights Acts, Congress provided the Department of Justice with basic tools for protecting the

---

Mississippi, but it too made progress. The militant temper of the race, the determination which made great bodies of plain men and women brook arrest, fines and imprisonment, and the leadership shown by such men as the Rev. Martin Luther King, Jr., demonstrated that a true revolution was under way; and the administration was glad to support it.

The Kennedy administration appointed a long list of able Negroes to high office. It made George L. L. Weaver Assistant Secretary of Labor; Robert C. Weaver head of the Housing and Home Finance Agency; Thurgood Marshall a judge on the bench of the Second Circuit Court of Appeals; Carl Rowan Deputy Assistant Secretary of State; and Andrew Hatcher a press secretary to the President. In the summer of 1962 the annual convention of the NAACP, a body which heartily approved of the steps the President had taken, called upon him for "bold and diligent leadership" in the work yet to be done.—A. N.

right to vote, and this administration has not hesitated to use those tools. Legal action is brought only after voluntary efforts fail; and, in scores of instances, local officials, at the request of the Department of Justice, have voluntarily made voting records available or abandoned discriminatory registration, discriminatory voting practices or segregated balloting.

Where voluntary local compliance has not been forthcoming, the Department of Justice has approximately quadrupled the previous level of its legal effort—investigating coercion, inspecting records, initiating lawsuits, enjoining intimidation and taking whatever follow-up action is necessary to forbid further interference or discrimination. As a result, thousands of Negro citizens are registering and voting for the first time, many of them in counties where no Negro had ever voted before. The Department of Justice will continue to take whatever action is required to secure the right to vote for all Americans.

Experience has shown, however, that these highly useful acts of the Eighty-fifth and Eighty-sixth Congresses suffer from two major defects. One is the usual long and difficult delay which occurs between the filing of a lawsuit and its ultimate conclusion. In one recent case, for example, nineteen months elapsed between the filing of the suit and the judgment of the court. In another, an action brought in July, 1961, has not yet come to trial. The legal maxim "Justice delayed is justice denied" is dramatically applicable in these cases.

Too often those who attempt to assert their constitutional rights are intimidated. Prospective registrants are fired. Registration workers are arrested. In some instances, churches in which registration meetings are held have been burned. In one case where Negro tenant farmers chose to exercise their right to vote, it was necessary for the Justice Department to seek injunctions to halt their eviction and for the Department of Agriculture to help feed them from surplus stocks. Under these circumstances, continued delay in the granting of the franchise, particularly in counties where there is mass racial disfranchisement, permits the intent of the Congress to be openly flouted.

Federal executive action in such cases, no matter how speedy and how drastic, can never fully correct such abuses of power. It is necessary, instead, to free the forces of our democratic system within these areas by promptly insuring the franchise to all citizens, making it possible for their elected officials to be truly responsive to all their constituents.

The second and somewhat overlapping gap in these statutes is their failure to deal specifically with the most common forms of abuse of discretion on the part of local election officials who do not treat all applicants uniformly.

Objections were raised last year to the proposed literacy test bill, which attempted to speed up the enforcement of the right to vote by removing one important area of discretion from registration officials who used that discretion to exclude Negroes. Preventing that bill from coming to a vote did not make any less real the prevalence in many counties of the use of literacy and other voter qualification tests to discriminate against prospective Negro voters, contrary to the requirements of the Fourteenth and Fifteenth Amendments, and adding to the delays and difficulties encountered in securing the franchise for those denied it.

An indication of the magnitude of the over-all problem, as well as the need for speedy action, is a recent five-state survey disclosing over two hundred counties in which fewer than 15 percent of the Negroes of voting age are registered to vote. This cannot continue. I am, therefore, recommending legislation to deal with this problem of judicial delay and administrative abuse. . . .

Nearly nine years have elapsed since the Supreme Court ruled that state laws requiring or permitting segregated schools violate the Constitution. That decision represented both good law and good judgment; it was both legally and morally right. Since that time it has become increasingly clear that neither violence nor legalistic evasions will be tolerated as a means of thwarting court-ordered desegregation, that closed schools are not an answer, and that responsible communities are able to handle the desegregation process in a calm and sensible manner. This is as it should be, for, as I stated to the nation at the time of the Mississippi violence last September:

"Our nation is founded on the principle that observance of the law is the eternal safeguard of liberty and defiance of the law is the surest road to tyranny. The law which we obey includes the final rulings of the courts, as well as the enactments of our legislative bodies. Even among law-abiding men few laws are universally loved, but they are uniformly respected and not resisted.

"Americans are free to disagree with the law, but not to disobey it. For in a government of laws and not of men, no man, however prominent and powerful, and no mob, however unruly or boisterous, is entitled to defy a court of law. If this country should ever reach the point where any man or group of men by force or threat of force could long defy the commands of our court and our Constitution, then no law would stand free from doubt, no judge would be sure of his writ, and no citizen would be safe from his neighbors."

The shameful violence which accompanied but did not prevent the end of segregation at the University of Mississippi was an exception. State-supported universities in Georgia and South Carolina met this test in recent years with calm and maturity, as did the state-supported universities of Virginia, North Carolina, Florida, Texas, Louisiana, Tennessee, Arkansas and Kentucky in earlier years. In addition, progress toward the desegregation of education at all levels has made other notable and peaceful strides, including the following forward moves in the last two years alone:

Desegregation plans have been put into effect peacefully in the public schools of Atlanta, Dallas, New Orleans, Memphis and elsewhere, with over sixty school districts desegregated last year, frequently with the help of federal persuasion and consultation, and in every case without incident or disorder.

Teacher training institutes financed under the National Defense Education Act are no longer held in colleges which refuse to accept students without regard to race, and this has resulted in a number of institutions opening their doors to Negro applicants voluntarily. I recommend, therefore, a program of federal technical and financial assistance to aid school districts in the process of desegregation in compliance with the Constitution. . . .

The Commission on Civil Rights, established by the Civil Rights Act of 1957, has been in operation for more than five years, and is scheduled to expire on November 30, 1963. During this time it has fulfilled its statutory mandate. . . . The Commission's reports and recommendations have provided the basis for remedial action both by

Congress and the Executive Branch. . . . But the Commission is now in a position to provide even more useful service to the nation. As more communities evidence a willingness to face frankly their problems of racial discrimination, there is an increasing need for expert guidance and assistance in devising workable programs for civil rights progress. . . .

I recommend, therefore, that the Congress authorize the Civil Rights Commission to serve as a national civil rights clearing house providing information, advice and technical assistance to any requesting agency, private or public; that in order to fulfill these new responsibilities, the Commission be authorized to concentrate its activities upon those problems within the scope of its statute which most need attention; and that the life of the Commission be extended for a term of at least four more years.

Racial discrimination in employment is especially injurious both to its victims and to the national economy. It results in a great waste of human resources and creates serious community problems. It is, moreover, inconsistent with the democratic principle that no man should be denied employment commensurate with his abilities because of his race or creed or ancestry.

The President's Committee on Equal Employment Opportunity, reconstituted by Executive Order in early 1961, has, under the leadership of the Vice President, taken significant steps to eliminate racial discrimination by those who do business with the government. Hundreds of companies, covering seventeen million jobs, have agreed to stringent nondiscriminatory provisions now standard in all government contracts. One hundred four industrial concerns, including the nation's major employers, have in addition signed agreements calling for an affirmative attack on discrimination in employment; and 117 labor unions, representing about 85 percent of the membership of the AFL-CIO, have signed similar agreements with the Committee.

Comprehensive compliance machinery has been instituted to enforce these agreements. The Committee has received over thirteen hundred complaints in two years, more than in the entire seven and one-half years of the Committee's prior existence, and has achieved corrective action on 72 percent of the cases handled—a heartening and unprecedented record. Significant results have been achieved in placing Negroes with contractors who previously employed whites only, and in the elevation of Negroes to a far higher proportion of professional, technical and supervisory jobs. Let me repeat my assurances that these provisions in government contracts and the voluntary nondiscrimination agreements will be carefully monitored and strictly enforced.

In addition, the federal government, as an employer, has continued to pursue a policy of nondiscrimination in its employment and promotion programs. . . .

No act is more contrary to the spirit of our democracy and Constitution, or more rightfully resented by a Negro citizen who seeks only equal treatment, than the barring of that citizen from restaurants, hotels, theaters, recreational areas and other public accommodations and facilities.

Wherever possible, this administration has dealt sternly with such acts. In 1961 the Justice Department and the Interstate Commerce Commission successfully took action to bring an end to discrimination in rail and bus facilities. In 1962 the fifteen airports still maintaining segregated facilities were persuaded to change their practices, thirteen voluntarily and two others after the Department of Justice brought legal action. As a result of these steps, systematic segregation in interstate transportation has virtually ceased to exist. No doubt isolated instances of discrimination in transportation terminals, restaurants, rest rooms and other facilities will continue to crop up, but any such discrimination will be dealt with promptly.

In addition, restaurants and public facilities in buildings leased by the federal government have been opened up to all federal employees in areas where previously they had been segregated. The General Services Administration no longer contracts for the lease of space in office buildings unless such facilities are available to all federal employees without regard to race. This move has taken place without fanfare and practically without incident; and full equality of facilities will continue to be made available to all federal employees in every state.

National parks, forests and other recreation areas, and the District of Columbia Stadium, are open to all without regard to race. Meetings sponsored by the federal government or addressed by federal appointees are held in hotels and halls which do not practice discrimination or segregation. The Department of Justice has asked the Supreme Court to reverse the convictions of Negroes arrested for seeking to use public accommodations, and took action both through the courts and the use of federal marshals to protect those who were testing the desegregation of transportation facilities.

In these and other ways, the federal government will continue to encourage and support action by state and local communities, and by private entrepreneurs, to assure all members of the public equal access to all public accommodations. A country with a "color-blind" Constitution, and with no castes or classes among its citizens, cannot afford to do less.

33 : The Racial Clash in Birmingham

NEWS CONFERENCE
MAY 8, 1963*

I am gratified to note the progress in the efforts by white and Negro citizens to end an ugly situation in Birmingham, Alabama. I have made it clear since assuming the Presidency that I would use all available means to protect human rights and uphold the law of the land. Through mediation and persuasion and, where that effort has failed, through lawsuits and court actions, we have attempted to meet our responsibilities in this most difficult field where federal court orders have been circumvented, ignored or violated. We have committed

---

* For some days early in May, 1963, Birmingham, Alabama, was the scene of turmoil which shocked the nation and the world. Negroes, by carefully organized and well-behaved processions, in which children marched, protested against the inequalities and indignities to which they were subjected; the authorities used police dogs and fire hoses to break up these demonstrations.—A. N.

all of the power of the federal government to insure respect and obedience of court decisions and the law of the land.

In the City of Birmingham the Department of Justice some time ago instituted an investigation into voting discrimination. It supported in the Supreme Court an attack on the city's segregation ordinances. We have, in addition, been watching the present controversy, to detect any violation of the federal civil rights or other statutes. In the absence of such violation or any other federal jurisdiction, our efforts have been focused on getting both sides together to settle in a peaceful fashion the very real abuses too long inflicted on the Negro citizens of that community.

Assistant Attorney General Burke Marshall, representing the Attorney General and myself on the scene, has made every possible effort to halt a spectacle which was seriously damaging the reputation of both Birmingham and the country. Today, as the result of responsible efforts on the part of both white and Negro leaders over the last seventy-two hours, the business community of Birmingham has responded in a constructive and commendable fashion and pledged that substantial steps would begin to meet the justifiable needs of the Negro community.

Negro leaders have announced suspension of their demonstrations, and when the newly elected mayor, who has indicated his desire to resolve these problems, takes office, the City of Birmingham has committed itself wholeheartedly to continuing progress in this area.

While much remains to be settled before the situation can be termed satisfactory, we can hope that tensions will ease, and that this case history, which has so far only narrowly avoided widespread violence and fatalities, will remind every state, every community and every citizen how urgent it is that all bars to equal opportunity and treatment be removed as promptly as possible.

34 : The Moral Issue of Equal Rights for All Colors

TELEVISION ADDRESS TO THE PEOPLE
THE WHITE HOUSE
WASHINGTON, D.C.
JUNE 11, 1963

This afternoon, following a series of threats and defiant statements, the presence of Alabama National Guardsmen was required at the University of Alabama to carry out the final and unequivocal order of the United States District Court of the Northern District of Alabama. That order called for the admission of two clearly qualified young Alabama residents who happened to have been born Negro.

That they were admitted peacefully on the campus is due in good measure to the conduct of the students of the University of Alabama, who met their responsibilities in a constructive way.

I hope that every American, regardless of where he lives, will stop and examine his conscience about this and other related incidents. This nation was founded by men of many nations and backgrounds. It was founded on the principle that all men are created equal, and that the rights of every man are diminished when the rights of one man are threatened.

Today we are committed to a world-wide struggle to promote and protect the rights of all who wish to be free, and when Americans are sent to Vietnam or West Berlin, we do not ask for whites only. It ought to be possible, therefore, for American students of any color to attend any public institution they select without having to be backed up by troops.

It ought to be possible for American consumers of any color to receive equal service in places of public accommodation, such as hotels and restaurants and theaters and retail stores, without being forced to resort to demonstrations in the street, and it ought to be possible for American citizens of any color to register and to vote in a free election without interference or fear of reprisal.

It ought to be possible, in short, for every American to enjoy the privileges of being American without regard to his race or his color. In short, every American ought to have the right to be treated as he would wish to be treated, as one would wish his children to be treated. But this is not the case.

The Negro baby born in America today, regardless of the section of the nation in which he is born, has about one-half as much chance of completing high school as a white baby born in the same place on the same day, one-third as much chance of completing college, one-third as much chance of becoming a professional man, twice as much chance of becoming unemployed, about one-seventh as much chance of earning $10,000 a year, a life expectancy which is seven years shorter, and the prospects of earning only half as much.

This is not a sectional issue. Difficulties over segregation and discrimination exist in every city, in every state of the Union, producing in many cities a rising tide of discontent that threatens the public safety. Nor is this a partisan issue in a time of domestic crisis. Men of goodwill and generosity should be able to unite regardless of party or politics. This is not even a legal or legislative issue alone. It is better to settle these matters in the courts than on the streets, and new laws are needed at every level, but law alone cannot make men see right.

We are confronted primarily with a moral issue. It is as old as the Scriptures and is as clear as the American Constitution.

The heart of the question is whether all Americans are to be afforded equal rights and equal opportunities, whether we are going to treat our fellow Americans as we want to be treated. If an American, because his skin is dark, cannot eat lunch in a restaurant open to the public, if he cannot send his children to the best public school available, if he cannot vote for the public officials who represent him, if, in short, he cannot enjoy the full and free life which all of us want, then who among us would be content to have the color of his skin changed and stand in his place? Who among us would then be content with the counsels of patience and delay?

One hundred years of delay have passed since President Lincoln freed the slaves, yet their heirs, their grandsons, are not fully free. They are not yet freed from the bonds of injustice. They are not yet freed from social and economic oppression, and this nation, for all its hopes and all its boasts, will not be fully free until all its citizens are free. . . .

We preach freedom around the world, and we mean it, and we cherish our freedom here at home; but are we to say to the world and, much more importantly, to each other that this is a land of the free except for the Negroes; that we have no second-class citizens except Negroes; that we have no class or caste system, no ghettos, no master race except with respect to Negroes? . . .

It is not enough to pin the blame on others, to say this is a problem of one section of the country or another, or deplore the facts that we face. A great change is at hand, and our task, our obligation, is to make that revolution, that change, peaceful and constructive for all.

Those who do nothing are inviting shame as well as violence. Those who act boldly are recognizing right as well as reality.

Next week I shall ask the Congress of the United States to act, to make a commitment it has not fully made in this century to the proposition that race has no place in American life or law. The federal judiciary has upheld that proposition in a series of forthright cases. The Executive Branch has adopted that proposition in the conduct of its affairs, including the employment of federal personnel, the use of federal facilities and the sale of federally financed housing.

But there are other necessary measures which only the Congress can provide, and they must be provided at this session. The old code of equity law under which we live commands for every wrong a remedy, but in too many communities, in too many parts of the country, wrongs are inflicted on Negro citizens for which there are no remedies at law. Unless the Congress acts, their only remedy is in the street.

I am, therefore, asking the Congress to enact legislation giving all Americans the right to be served in facilities which are open to the public—hotels, restaurants, theaters, retail stores and similar establishments.

This seems to me to be an elementary right. Its denial is an arbitrary indignity that no American in 1963 should have to endure, but many do.

I have recently met with scores of business leaders, urging them to take voluntary action to end this discrimination, and I have been encouraged by their response, and in the last two weeks over seventy-five cities have seen progress made in desegregating these kinds of facilities. But many are unwilling to act alone, and for this reason nationwide legislation is needed if we are to move this problem from the streets to the courts.

I am also asking Congress to authorize the federal government to participate more fully in lawsuits designed to end segregation in public education. We have succeeded in persuading many districts to desegregate voluntarily. Dozens have admitted Negroes without violence. Today a Negro is attending a state-supported institution in every one of our fifty states, but the pace is very slow. . . .

My fellow Americans, this is a problem which faces us all, in every city of the North as well as the South. Today there are Negroes unemployed, two or three times as many compared to whites, inadequate in education, moving into the large cities, unable to find work, young people particularly out of work, without hope, denied equal rights, denied the opportunity to eat at a restaurant or lunch counter or go to a movie theater, denied the right to a decent education, denied the right to attend a state university even though qualified. It seems to me that these are matters which concern us all, not merely Presidents or Congressmen or Governors, but every citizen of the United States.

This is one country. It has become one country because all of us and all the people who came here had an equal chance to develop their talents.

We cannot say to 10 percent of the population that they can't have that right; that their children can't have the chance to develop whatever talents they have; that the only way that they are going to get their rights is to go into the streets and demonstrate. I think we owe them and we owe ourselves a better country than that.

Therefore, I am asking for your help in making it easier for us to move ahead and to provide the kind of equality of treatment which we would want ourselves; to give a chance to every child to be educated to the limit of his talents. . . .

35 : Southern Progress in School Desegregation

NEWS CONFERENCE
SEPTEMBER 12, 1963

I would like to say something about what has happened in the schools in the last few days. In the past two weeks, schools in 150 Southern cities have been desegregated. There may have been some difficulties, but to the great credit of the vast majority of the citizens and public officials of these communities, this transition has been made with understanding and respect for the law. The task was not easy. The emotions underlying segregation have persisted for generations, and in many instances leaders in these communities have had to overcome their own personal attitudes as well as the ingrained social attitudes of the communities. In some instances the obstacles were greater, even to the point of physical interference. Nevertheless, as we have seen, what prevailed in these cities through the South finally was not emotion but respect for law. The courage and responsibility of those community leaders in those places provide a meaningful lesson not only for the children in those cities but for the children all over the country.

&§ VII

THE NATION'S ECONOMY: BUSINESS, AGRICULTURE, TAXES AND THE ROLE OF GOVERNMENT

36 : The Chaos of American Transportation

SPECIAL MESSAGE TO CONGRESS
WASHINGTON, D.C.
APRIL 4, 1962*

. . . An efficient and dynamic transportation system is vital to our domestic economic growth, productivity and progress. Affecting the cost of every commodity we consume or export, it is equally vital to our ability to compete abroad. It influences both the cost and the flexibility of our defense preparedness, and both the business and recreational opportunities of our citizens. This nation has long enjoyed one of the most highly developed and diversified transportation systems in the world, and this system has helped us to achieve a highly efficient utilization of our manpower and resources.

Transportation is thus an industry which serves, and is affected with, the national interest. Federal laws and policies have expressed the national interest in transportation particularly in the last eighty years—through the promotion and development of transportation facilities, such as highways, airways and waterways; through the regulation of rates and services; and through general governmental policies relating to taxation, procurement, labor and competition. A

---

* No other nation approached the United States in expenditures upon highways. The total outlay by all units of government upon them was estimated in 1961 at nearly $11 billion, and in 1962 at more than $11.3 billion. Federal aid to the states for building and improving highways reached $3.3 billion for the fiscal year 1962–63. But the motor vehicle registration of the country in 1962 came to more than 78.5 million, and in many cities the traffic jams were horrible. Legislation on road use, as the President pointed out to Congress, was largely obsolete. Other problems in the carriage of passengers and freight urgently demanded attention. But Congress was indifferent to the long-range program the President offered.—A. N.

comprehensive program for transportation must consider all these elements of public policy.

During the last session of Congress, action was taken to place our federal-aid highway program on a sounder fiscal basis. Initial steps were taken to improve the operations of our regulatory agencies through reorganization. A beginning was also made toward meeting the needs of our cities for mass transportation. By Executive Order, I recently assigned to the Department of Commerce authority for emergency transportation planning.

But pressing problems are burdening our national transportation system, jeopardizing the progress and security on which we depend. A chaotic patchwork of inconsistent and often obsolete legislation and regulation has evolved from a history of specific actions addressed to specific problems of specific industries at specific times. This patchwork does not fully reflect either the dramatic changes in technology of the past half-century or the parallel changes in the structure of competition. . . .

At present, the transportation of bulk commodities by water carriers is exempt from all rate regulation under the Interstate Commerce Act, including the approval of minimum rates; but this exemption is denied to all other modes of transportation. This is clearly inequitable both to the latter and to shippers, and it is an inequity which should be removed. Extending to all other carriers the exemption from the approval or prescription of minimum rates would permit the forces of competition and equal opportunity to replace cumbersome regulation for these commodities, while protecting the public interest by leaving intact the ICC's control over maximum railroad rates and other safeguards (such as the prohibition against discrimination and requirements on car service and common carrier responsibility). While this would be the preferable way to eliminate the existing inequality, Congress could elect to place all carriers on an equal footing by repealing the existing exemption, although this would result in more, instead of less, regulation and very likely in higher though more stable rates. Whichever alternative is adopted, these commodities are too important a part of carrier traffic to continue to be governed so unequally by federal rate regulation.

An exemption similar to that described above, and now available only to motor carriers and freight forwarders, relates to agricultural and fishery products. This exemption from minimum rates should also be extended to all carriers. Here, too, the ICC should retain control of maximum railroad rates and certain other controls to protect the public interest in those areas where there is no effective truck or water carrier competition to keep rates down.

The combined effect of extending these bulk and agricultural exemptions will be to reduce drastically and equalize fairly the regulation of freight rates in this country. Freed to exercise normal managerial initiative, carriers will be able to rationalize their operations and reduce costs; and shippers should consequently enjoy a wider choice, improved service and lower rates. . . .

I have previously emphasized to the Congress the need for action on the transportation problems resulting from burgeoning urban growth and the changing urban scene.

Higher incomes coupled with the increasing availability of the automobile have enabled more and more American families, particularly younger ones with children, to seek their own homes in suburban areas. Simultaneously, changes and improvements in freight transportation, made possible by the development of modern highways and the trucking industry, have reduced the dependence of manufacturers on central locations near port facilities or railroad terminals. The development of improved production techniques that require spacious, one-story plant layouts has impelled many industries to move to the periphery of urban areas. At the same time the importance of the central city is increasing for trade, financial, governmental and cultural activities.

One result of these changes in location patterns has been a change in the patterns of urban travel. Formerly people traveled mainly along high-density corridors radiating to and from downtown. Today traffic patterns are increasingly diverse. Added to traditional suburb-to-city movements are large crosstown flows which existing mass transportation systems are often not geared to handle. Also, the increasing use of automobiles to meet urban transportation needs has resulted in increasing highway congestion, and this has greatly impeded mass transportation service using those highways.

This drastic revision of travel patterns in many urban areas has seriously impaired the effectiveness and economic viability of public mass transportation, which is geared to the older patterns. A steady decline in patronage and a concomitant rise of unprofitability and financial problems have occurred. This has been particularly true of rail commuter and streetcar services limited to particular routes by fixed roadbeds.

To conserve and enhance values in existing urban areas is essential. But at least as important are steps to promote economic efficiency and livability in areas of future development. In less than twenty years we can expect well over half of our expanded population to be living in forty great urban complexes. Many smaller places will also experience phenomenal growth. The ways that people and goods can be moved in these areas will have a major influence on their structure, on the efficiency of their economy and on the availability of social and cultural opportunities they can offer their citizens. Our national welfare therefore requires the provision of good urban transportation, with the properly balanced use of private vehicles and modern mass transport to help shape as well as serve urban growth.

At my request, the problems of urban transportation have been studied in detail by the Housing and Home Finance Administrator and the Secretary of Commerce. Their field investigations have included some forty metropolitan and other communities, large and small. Their findings support the need for substantial expansion and important changes in the urban mass transportation program authorized in the Housing Act of 1961, as well as revisions in federal highway legislation. They give dramatic emphasis, moreover, to the need for greater local initiative and to the responsibility of the states and municipalities to provide financial support and effective governmental auspices for strengthening and improving urban transportation.

Specifically, I recommend that the Congress authorize the first installment of a long-range program of federal aid to our urban regions for the revitalization and needed expansion of public mass transportation, to be administered by the Housing and Home Finance Agency. I recommend a capital grant authorization of $500 million to be made available over a three-year period, with $100 million to be made available in fiscal 1963. Only a program that offers substantial support and continuity of federal participation can induce our urban regions to organize appropriate administrative arrangements and to meet their share of the costs of fully balanced transportation systems. . . .

Time will be required by most metropolitan areas to organize effectively for the major planning efforts required. Even more time may be needed to create public agencies with adequate powers to develop, finance and administer new or improved public transportation systems. . . .

In recognition of this serious situation, I also recommend that the Congress, for a period of three years only, authorize the Housing Administrator to make emergency grants (a) where there is an urgent need for immediate aid to an existing mass transportation facility or service that might otherwise cease to be available for transportation purposes, (b) where an official long-range program for a coordinated system is being actively prepared, and (c) where the facilities or equipment acquired under the emergency grant can reasonably be expected to be required for the new long-range system. . . .

To permit the state highway departments greater flexibility in the use of federal-aid highway funds to meet urban transportation needs, I further recommend that the federal-aid highway law be amended to permit more extensive use of federal-aid secondary funds for extensions of the secondary system in urban areas. . . .

We should endeavor to . . . gear international transportation investment to the requirements of our peacetime international trade and travel, and provide incentives to users that will channel traffic to those forms of transportation that provide desirable service at the lowest total cost. . . . Determinations must be made as to whether the number and types of ships and aircraft adequate to meet long-range peacetime needs are also adequate to meet probable military emergencies. . . .

I have also recommended a stepped-up research program for developing ways and means of increasing the competitive efficiency of our merchant marine and related industries. . . .

37 : Steel Prices and the Public Interest

NEWS CONFERENCE
APRIL 11, 1962*

Simultaneous and identical actions of United States Steel and other leading steel corporations, increasing steel prices by some six dollars a ton, constitute a wholly unjustifiable and irresponsible defiance of the public interest.

In this serious hour in our nation's history, when we are confronted with grave crises in Berlin and Southeast Asia, when we are devoting our energies to economic recovery and stability, when we are asking

---

* President Kennedy tried hard and with general success, from the beginning of his administration, to hold the line against inflation. He constantly labored to impress upon industrialists the fact that they must keep prices down to penetrate the increasingly resistant markets overseas. In mid-April, 1962, the steel companies and the United Steelworkers of America signed two-year contracts which kept wages stationary except for fringe benefits totaling ten cents an hour. The President hailed this "noninflationary" agreement as a signal contribution to national welfare and the competitive position of America in the world. But immediately thereafter Roger M. Blough, chairman of the board of United States Steel, called on him and without warning announced that the corporation was lifting its prices an average of $6 a ton, or about 3.5 percent. Most other steel producers followed this example. The President was both astonished and incensed. Next day came this press conference and his forceful but reasoned denunciation of "Big Steel." Blough attempted to defy the administration. But it promptly took measures which, combined with the refusal of three producers, Inland Steel, Kaiser Steel and Armco Steel, to raise their prices, broke the will of United States Steel and the others. First Bethlehem Steel and then the rest rescinded their increases. The President had, he hoped, taught industry a lesson in its public responsibilities.—A. N.

Reservists to leave their homes and families for months on end, and servicemen to risk their lives—and four were killed in the last two days in Vietnam—and asking union members to hold down their wage requests; at a time when restraint and sacrifice are being asked of every citizen, the American people will find it hard, as I do, to accept a situation in which a tiny handful of steel executives whose pursuit of private power and profit exceeds their sense of public responsibility can show such utter contempt for the interests of 185 million Americans.

If this rise in the cost of steel is imitated by the rest of the industry, instead of rescinded, it would increase the cost of homes, autos, appliances and most other items for every American family. It would increase the cost of machinery and tools to every American businessman and farmer. It would seriously handicap our efforts to prevent an inflationary spiral from eating up the pensions of our older citizens and our new gains in purchasing power.

It would add, Secretary McNamara informed me this morning, an estimated one billion dollars to the cost of our defenses, at a time when every dollar is needed for national security and other purposes. It would make it more difficult for American goods to compete in foreign markets, more difficult to withstand competition from foreign imports, and thus more difficult to improve our balance-of-payments position and stem the flow of gold. And it is necessary to stem it for our national security if we are going to pay for our security commitments abroad. And it would surely handicap our efforts to induce other industries and unions to adopt responsible price and wage policies.

The facts of the matter are that there is no justification for an increase in the steel prices. The recent settlement between the industry and the union, which does not even take place until July 1, was widely acknowledged to be noninflationary, and the whole purpose and effect of this administration's role, which both parties understood, was to achieve an agreement which would make unnecessary any increase in prices.

Steel output per man is rising so fast that labor costs per ton of steel can actually be expected to decline in the next twelve months. And, in fact, the Acting Commissioner of the Bureau of Labor

Statistics informed me this morning that—and I quote—"Employ-ment costs per unit of steel output in 1961 were essentially the same as they were in 1958."

The cost of major raw materials, steel scrap and coal has also been declining, and for an industry which has been generally operating at less than two-thirds of capacity, its profit rate has been normal and can be expected to rise sharply this year in view of the reduction in idle capacity. Their lot has been easier than that of a hundred thou-sand steel workers thrown out of work in the last three years. The industry's cash dividends have exceeded $600 million in each of the last five years, and earnings in the first quarter of this year were esti-mated in the February 28 *Wall Street Journal* to be among the highest in history.

In short, at a time when they could be exploring how more efficiency and better prices could be obtained, reducing prices in this industry in recognition of lower costs, their unusually good labor contract, their foreign competition and their increase in production and profits which are coming this year, a few gigantic corporations have decided to increase prices in ruthless disregard of their public responsibilities.

The Steelworkers Union can be proud that it abided by its respon-sibilities in this agreement, and this government also has responsibil-ities, which we intend to meet.

38 : Steel: Profits, Modernization and Investment

NEWS CONFERENCE
APRIL 18, 1962

I believe it would be appropriate to say a few words to follow up last week's events concerning steel prices. First, let me make it clear that this administration harbors no ill will against any individual, any industry, corporation or segment of the American economy. Our goals of economic growth and price stability are dependent upon the success of both business corporations and labor, and there can be no room on either side in this country at this time for any feelings of hostility or vindictiveness.

When a mistake has been retracted and the public interest preserved, nothing is to be gained from further public recriminations.

Second, while our chief concern last week was to prevent an inflationary spiral, we were not then and are not now unmindful of the steel industry's needs for profits, modernization and investment capital. I believe, in fact, that this administration and the leaders of steel and other American industries are in basic agreement on far more objectives than we are in disagreement.

We agree on the necessity of increased investment, in modern plant and equipment. We agree on the necessity of improving our industry's ability to compete with the products of other nations. We agree on the necessity of achieving an economic recovery and growth that will make the fullest possible use of idle capacity. We agree on the necessity of preventing an inflationary spiral that will lead to harmful restrictions on credit and consumption, and we agree on the necessity of preserving the nation's confidence in free, private, collective bargaining and price decisions, holding the role of government to the minimum level needed to protect the public interest.

In the pursuit of these objectives, we have fostered a responsible wage policy aimed at holding increases within the confines of productivity gains. We have encouraged monetary policies aimed at making borrowed capital available at reasonable cost; prepared a new transportation policy aimed at providing increased freedom of competition at lower costs; proposed a new trade expansion bill to gain for our industries increased access to foreign markets; proposed an 8 percent income tax credit to reward investment in new equipment and machinery and proceeded to modernize administratively the Treasury Department's guidelines on the depreciable lives of capital assets; and, finally, taken a host of other legislative and administrative actions to foster the kind of economic recovery which will improve both profits and incentives to invest.

I believe that the anticipated profits this year for industry in general and steel in particular indicate that these policies are meeting with some measure of success; and it is a fact that the last quarter of last year, and I think the first quarter of this year, will see the highest profits in the history of this country, and the highest number of people working, and the highest productivity.

39 : Attitude Toward Business

U.S. CHAMBER OF COMMERCE
WASHINGTON, D.C.
APRIL 30, 1962*

It is easy to charge an administration is antibusiness, but it is more difficult to show how an administration, composed, we hope, of rational men, can possibly feel they can survive without business, or how the nation can survive unless the government and business and all other groups in our country are exerting their best efforts in an atmosphere of understanding and, I hope, cooperation.

We have worked to establish the responsible view that we take of our role in the economy, and I do not think the record of our decisions, taken in totality, has been one to suggest that we are not responsive to the problems of business. I will point to our efforts in the field of inflation, to the balance of payments, to the transportation policy, for example, recently enunciated, as tenders of this concern. I expect to be able to point soon to more realistic income tax guidelines on the depreciable lives of business assets, and to the 8 percent tax credit for investment in equipment and machinery, which has been proposed and is now being considered by the Senate.

---

* As the Chamber had been founded in the April before Woodrow Wilson's election, this meeting marked its fiftieth anniversary. "To the extent that you want to protect your profit margins," the President told the members, "our interests are identical, for after all we in the national government have a large stake in your profits. To the extent that you raise your prices to make these profits, our interests at home and abroad stand in delicate balance."—A. N.

I do not regard the vigorous enforcement of the antitrust laws, for example, to be antibusiness. These statutes, most of which have a long historic past antedating the life of the Chamber of Commerce, are based on the basic premise that a private enterprise system must be truly competitive if it is to realize its full potential. And it is natural in these important basic industries, in which one or two companies may control over 50 percent of the total national production, that the government should be concerned that the realities of competition exist, as well as their appearance. But this is in the interest of business, and you know quite well that nearly every action taken by this government, and by previous administrations, in the field of antitrust actions, or actions by the Federal Trade Commission, have been based upon complaints brought by businessmen themselves. This is in the interests, therefore, of business, as well as of the general public.

When I talk of the public interest in these matters, I am not using a rhetorical phrase. It costs the United States $3 billion a year to maintain our troops and our defense establishment and security commitments abroad. If the balance of trade is not sufficiently in our favor to finance this burden, we have two alternatives: one, to lose gold, as we have been doing; and two, to begin to withdraw our security commitments.

This is the heart of the issue which has occupied the attention of so many of us in recent months, of our efforts to persuade the steel union to accept a noninflationary wage agreement and to persuade the steel companies to make every effort to maintain price stability.

In the competitive contest for world markets, upon which the balance of payments depends, our record since the end of the Korean War has not been wholly satisfactory, I am sure, to any of us. From the end of the Korean War, our export prices rose about 11 percent, while average export prices in the Common Market held steady. There were significant wage raises during this period, as we know. Indeed our wage levels in the large manufacturing industries rose 30 percent in the United States, but they rose 58 percent in the same period in France and Germany. But their output per man-hour increased sufficiently so that their costs per unit of output rose less than ours. During this period, our gold stocks declined by $5.5 billion, and the short-term dollar claims of foreigners, a potential call on our gold stock, rose by an equal amount, $11 billion in the past few years.

I do not mean to say that we have priced ourselves out of world markets. Our merchandise exports of over $20 billion testify that we have not. And our comparative price performance has improved in the last two or three years. But if we are to stem the gold outflow, which we must by one means or another, eliminate the deficit in our balance of payments and continue, as I believe we must, to discharge our far-flung international obligations, we must avoid inflation, modernize American industry and improve our relative position in the world markets.

Never in the fifty-year history of the Chamber of Commerce has its dedication to a vigorous economy been more in the national and international interest than it is today. This administration, I assure you, shares your concern about the cost-profit squeeze on American business. We want prosperity, and in a free enterprise system there can be no prosperity without profit. We want a growing economy, and there can be no growth without the investment that is inspired and financed by profit. . . .

40 : Myths Respecting American Government

YALE UNIVERSITY
NEW HAVEN, CONNECTICUT
JUNE 11, 1962*

. . . Mythology distracts us everywhere—in government as in business, in politics as in economics, in foreign affairs as in domestic policy. But today I want particularly to consider the myth and reality in our national economy. In recent months many have come to feel,

---

* The President delivered this speech at the Yale University Commencement. A little more than two months later, at his news conference on August 22, a questioner asked whether he was satisfied with the response to his invitation for replacing old myths with fresh ideas

as I do, that the dialogue between the parties—between business and government—is clogged by illusion and platitude and fails to reflect the true realities of contemporary American society.

I speak of these matters here at Yale because of the self-evident truth that a great university is always enlisted against the spread of illusion and on the side of reality. No one has said it more clearly than your President Griswold: "Liberal learning is both a safeguard against false ideas of freedom and a source of true ones." Your role as university men, whatever your calling, will be to increase each new generation's grasp of its new duties.

There are three great areas of our domestic affairs in which, today, there is a danger that illusion may prevent effective action. They are, first, the question of the size and the shape of government's responsibilities; second, the question of public fiscal policy; and, third, the matter of confidence—business confidence or public confidence, or simply confidence in America. I want to talk about all three, and I want to talk about them carefully and dispassionately—and I emphasize that I am concerned here not with political debate, but with finding ways to separate false problems from real ones. . . .

Let us take first the question of the size and shape of government. The myth here is that government is big and bad—and steadily getting bigger and worse. Obviously this myth has some excuse for existence. It is true that in recent history each new administration has spent much more money than its predecessor. Thus President Roosevelt outspent President Hoover and, with allowances for the special case of the Second World War, President Truman outspent President Roosevelt. Just to prove that this was not a partisan matter, President Eisenhower outspent President Truman by the handsome

---

and more accurate thinking. He replied that some progress had been made in dispelling economic fallacies. The hearings by the Joint Economic Committee had been useful, and the discussions of fiscal and monetary policies not only by Americans but by Europeans had been very beneficial. But, he added, "It is quite a long struggle to try to change the thinking which has been driven into us for so many years." A distinguished banker had told him that he had been certain that the fiscal deficit of 1962 would be certain to bring inflation, and the banker had been astonished to find that nothing of the sort happened.—A. N.

figure of $182 billion. It is even possible something of this trend may continue.

But does it follow that big government is growing relatively bigger? It does not, for the fact is for the last fifteen years the federal government—and also the federal debt, and also the federal bureaucracy—has grown less rapidly than the economy as a whole. If we leave defense and space expenditures aside, the federal government since the Second World War has expanded less than any other major sector of our national life—less than industry, less than commerce, less than agriculture, less than higher education, and very much less than the noise about big government.

The truth about big government is the truth about any other great activity: it is complex. Certainly it is true that size brings dangers, but it is also true that size also can bring benefits. Here at Yale, which has contributed so much to our national progress in science and medicine, it may be proper for me to mention one great and little-noticed expansion of government which has brought strength to our whole society: the new role of our federal government as the major patron of research in science and in medicine. Few people realize that in 1961, in support of all university research in science and medicine, three dollars out of every four came from the federal government. I need hardly point out that this has taken place without undue enlargement of government control, that American scientists remain second to none in their independence and in their individualism. . . .

Next, let us turn to the problem of our fiscal policy. Here the myths are legion and the truth hard to find. But let me take as a prime example the problem of the federal budget. We persist in measuring our federal fiscal integrity today by the conventional or administrative budget, with results which would be regarded as absurd in any business firm, in any country of Europe or in any careful assessment of the reality of our national finances. The administrative budget has sound administrative uses. But for wider purposes it is less helpful. It omits our special trust funds; it neglects changes in assets or inventories. It cannot tell a loan from a straight expenditure; and, worst of all, it cannot distinguish between operating expenditures and long-term investments. . . .

Still in the area of fiscal policy, let me say a word about deficits. The myth persists that federal deficits create inflation and budget surpluses prevent it. Yet sizable budget surpluses after the war did not prevent inflation, and persistent deficits for the last several years have not upset our basic price stability. Obviously deficits are sometimes dangerous, and so are surpluses. But honest assessment plainly requires a more sophisticated view than the old and automatic cliché that deficits automatically bring inflation.

There are myths also about our public debt. It is widely supposed that this debt is growing at a dangerously rapid rate. In fact, both the debt per person and the debt as a proportion of our Gross National Product have declined sharply since the Second World War. In absolute terms the national debt increased only 8 percent, while private debt was increasing 305 percent, and the debts of state and local governments increased 378 percent. Moreover, debts, public and private, are neither good nor bad, in and of themselves. Borrowing can lead to overextension and collapse, but it can also lead to expansion and strength. There is no single, simple slogan in this field that we can trust.

Finally, I come to the problem of confidence. Confidence is a matter of myth and also a matter of truth, and this time let me take the truth of the matter first.

It is true—and of high importance—that the prosperity of this country depends on assurance that all major elements within it will live up to their responsibilities. If business were to neglect its obligations to the public; if labor were blind to all public responsibility; above all, if government were to abandon its obvious, and statutory, duty of watchful concern for our economic health—if any of these things should happen, then confidence might well be weakened and danger of stagnation would increase. This is the true issue of confidence.

But there is also the false issue; and its simplest form is the assertion that any and all unfavorable turns of the speculative wheel, however temporary and however plainly speculative in character, are the result of—and I quote—"lack of confidence in the national administration." This, I must tell you, while comforting, is not wholly true. Worse, it obscures the reality, which is also simple. The solid ground of mutual confidence is the necessary partnership of government with all of the sectors of our society in the steady quest for economic progress.

Corporate plans are not based on a political confidence in party leaders, but on an economic confidence in the nation's ability to invest and produce and consume. Business had full confidence in the administrations in power in 1929, 1954, 1958 and 1960, but this was not enough to prevent recession when business lacked full confidence in the economy. What matters is the capacity of the nation as a whole to deal with its economic problems and its opportunities.

The stereotypes I have been discussing distract our attention and divide our effort. These stereotypes do our nation a disservice, not just because they are exhausted and irrelevant, but above all because they are misleading, because they stand in the way of the solution of hard and complicated facts. It is not new that past debates should obscure present realities. But the damage of such a false dialogue is greater today than ever before simply because today the safety of all the world—the very future of freedom—depends as never before upon the sensible and clear-headed management of the domestic affairs of the United States. . . .

41 : Avoiding the Deficit of Stagnation

ECONOMIC CLUB OF NEW YORK
NEW YORK, NEW YORK
DECEMBER 14, 1962

. . . Our true choice is not between tax reduction, on the one hand, and the avoidance of large federal deficits, on the other. It is increasingly clear that no matter what party is in power, so long as our national security needs keep rising, an economy hampered by restrictive tax rates will never produce enough revenues to balance our budget, just as it will never produce enough jobs or enough profits. Surely the lesson of the last decade is that budget deficits are caused not by wild-eyed spenders, but by slow economic growth and periodic recessions, and any new recession would break all deficit records.

In short, it is a paradoxical truth that tax rates are too high today and tax revenues are too low, and the soundest way to raise revenues in the long run is to cut rates now. The experience of a number of European countries has borne this out. This country's own experience with tax reduction in 1954 has borne this out. And the reason is that only full employment can balance the budget and tax reduction can pave the way to full employment. The purpose of cutting taxes now is not to incur a budget deficit, but to achieve the more prosperous, expanding economy which will bring a budget surplus.

I repeat: our practical choice is not between a tax-cut deficit and a budgetary surplus. It is between two kinds of deficits: a chronic deficit of inertia, as the unwanted result of inadequate revenues and a restricted economy, or a temporary deficit of transition, resulting from a tax cut designed to boost the economy, increase tax revenue and achieve—and I believe this can be done—a future budget surplus. The first type of deficit is a sign of waste and weakness. The second reflects an investment in the future.

Nevertheless, as Chairman Mills of the House Ways and Means Committee pointed out this week, the size of the deficit is to be regarded with concern, and tax reduction must be accompanied, in his words, by "increased control of the rises in expenditures." That is precisely the course we intend to follow in 1963.

At the same time that our tax program is presented to the Congress in January, the federal budget for fiscal 1964 will also be presented. Defense and space expenditures will necessarily rise in order to carry out programs which are demanded and are necessary for our own security, and which have largely been authorized by members in both parties of the Congress with overwhelming majorities. Fixed charges on the debt also rise slightly. But I can tell you now that the total of all other expenditures combined will be held approximately at its current level.

This is not an easy task. During the past nine years, domestic civilian expenditures in the national government have risen at an average rate of more than 7.5 percent. State and local government expenditures have risen at an annual rate of 9 percent. Expenditures by the New York State government, for example, have risen in recent years at the rate of roughly 10 percent a year. At a time when government pay scales have necessarily risen—and I take New York just as an example—when our population and pressures are growing and the demand for services and state aid is thus increasing, next year's federal budget, which will hold domestic outlays at their present level, will represent a genuine effort in expenditure control. This budget will reflect among other economies a $750 million reduction in the postal deficit. It will reflect a savings of over $300 million in the storage costs of surplus feed grain stocks—and as result of the feed grain bill of 1961 we will have two-thirds less in storage than we would otherwise have had in January, 1963—and a savings of at least $600 million from the cancellation of obsolescent or unworkable weapons systems. Secretary McNamara is undertaking a cost reduction program expected to save at least $3 billion a year in the Department of Defense, cutting down on duplication and closing down nonessential installations. Other agencies must do the same.

42 : Farmers and Farm Life

SPECIAL MESSAGE TO CONGRESS
WASHINGTON, D.C.
JANUARY 31, 1963*

Proper management of our resources of food and fiber is a key factor in the economic future of the nation. Both fiscal necessity and economic common sense require us to go beyond the gains we have made in the last two years. Our capacity to produce still outruns the growth

---

* No area of national policy was more sensitive or more difficult than the agricultural sector. The farmers, who for generations had suffered great adversities unaided, were anxious to preserve the hard-won protec-

of both domestic and foreign demand for food and fiber. Our abundance must still be harnessed in such a way as to bring supply and demand more nearly into balance. And the benefits of our agricultural progress still need to be translated into improved income to farm families, lower prices to consumers for food and fiber, expanded exports, and reduced expenditures for price support programs.

Nevertheless, the past two years have seen substantial improvement in farm income, a substantial decrease in government holdings of agricultural products, and a substantial reduction in costs to the taxpayer for carrying farm surpluses, without increasing the consumer's burden.

Net farm income at the end of 1962 was $1.8 billion a year more than it was in 1960. Gross farm income is $3.5 billion higher. Average net income per farm has risen 21 percent, from $3,044 to $3,690, the highest level in our history. The increase in farm income has generated added business for rural industries and farm communities, putting millions of dollars into Main Street cash registers and adding at least 200,000 jobs to the national economy. At the same time, government stockpiles of surplus grain have been reduced by 929 million bushels from their 1961 peak. And, finally, over this same two-year period, the proportion of consumer income required to purchase food has declined to the lowest ratio in history—19 percent of take-home pay.

These successes have been made possible by a series of Congressional and Executive actions undertaken in the last two years. The principles underlying these actions are further pursued in the recommendations contained in this message.

---

tions they had first received under Franklin D. Roosevelt; urban dwellers, however, regarded the high costs of the national program, and the heavy waste in handling crop surpluses, with a jaundiced eye. No President had succeeded in dealing with the agricultural situation to the general satisfaction of the country. The message here given embraces all of Mr. Kennedy's main proposals except those relating to the expanded utilization of our farm abundance for the benefit of needy people at home and abroad.—A. N.

The success of those principles also calls for an affirmative vote in the forthcoming wheat referendum, to be held under the permanent legislation enacted by the Congress last year. If two-thirds of the wheat producers vote this spring to approve the bushel marketing program authorized by that law, the present income of our wheat farms will be protected and the overhanging surpluses of wheat will be further reduced. Failure to approve the wheat program will leave the wheat farmer without either supply management or effective price supports—at the mercy of unlimited production and unprotected prices. I do not believe that anyone who clearly understands the choice would prefer a return to the depression conditions that preceded the initiation of price supports a generation ago. New legislation for wheat is neither necessary nor feasible this year.

Exports of farm commodities reached a record $5.1 billion in the fiscal year 1962. Dollar markets abroad for the products of our farms have been expanded to a total of $3.5 billion, and thus constitute a significant factor in our balance of payments.

The American farmer is one of our best foreign exchange earners. It is our firm policy to maintain and expand these exports. We do, however, have a special problem of maintaining access to the European Common Market for some of our important agricultural commodities. This government intends to take every step necessary to protect the full rights due American agricultural exports. We have impressed on our trading partners the vital necessity of a fair agreement as an essential first part of the broad scale negotiations to be undertaken under the Trade Expansion Act of 1962.

The areas of agriculture policy which require action by the Congress this year include the following:

Feed Grains. The emergency and temporary feed grain legislation of 1961 and 1962—which covers this crop year as well—has been successful. It has earned wide bipartisan support. Savings already assured by two years of surplus reduction will amount ultimately to nearly $1 billion. The stocks of corn and grain sorghums, totaling 85 million tons two years ago, and costing nearly $500 million a year for handling and storing charges alone, will be reduced to 57 million tons by the end of this marketing year. They should be further reduced to 45 to 50 million tons by the end of the 1963 crop year. At the same time, this program has contributed significantly to the improvement in farm income.

If new legislation is not enacted this year to consolidate the gains thus far achieved, the feed grain program for 1964, under existing law, would automatically revert to unlimited, excessive production and disastrously low prices. Corn price supports, which will be $1.25 a bushel for 1963, would go down to 80 cents; and even at that level, unrestrained production might well lead to new accumulations of surplus stocks. Prices for hogs, cattle, poultry, dairy and other commodities would fall. It is imperative that action be taken by the Congress this year to avoid these consequences.

The new legislation should take advantage of the knowledge and experience gained under the 1961-62 and 1963 programs. It should be a voluntary program; be flexible enough to meet varying conditions and needs; and be based upon the same basic principles which have proven successful in the last two years.

These objectives can be achieved by authorizing the Secretary of Agriculture to adjust the feed grain program—in the light of the supply and utilization outlook—to obtain the needed reduction in production at the lowest cost consistent with the protection of farm family income. He may select either the 1962 or the 1963 type of feed grain program. Payments will be made to feed grain producers who reduce production below their established base acreage. These payments may be made either in kind or in cash. Their size and the required acreage reduction will be determined on the basis of the outlook just before the crops are planted.

Such feed grain legislation should provide for necessary adaptations to meet changes in weather, new international crises, sudden opportunities or strictures in the European Common Market and other areas of trade, and developments in the economy of the United States as a whole. It would enable farmers to make full use of the permanent wheat program by permitting wheat growers to produce wheat in lieu of feed grains on feed grain bases. The continued and successful operation of voluntary feed grain programs, in conjunction with the new wheat program, should resolve two of our most difficult commodity problems.

Cotton. A healthy, growing cotton industry is vital to the strength and prosperity of our nation. Over a million persons are engaged in producing our cotton crop. Another million and a half are employed in converting the raw cotton into consumer items. Additional millions supply goods and services to this industry. Cotton exports contribute significantly to our balance of payments position.

Our cotton industry—both producers and mills—is confronted with many problems which it alone cannot resolve. Because domestic prices are much higher than those of foreign producers, our cotton mills must pay substantially more for cotton than their off-shore competitors. Domestic cotton textile products are being displaced not only by substitute fibers in consumer products but also by increased cotton imports. Cotton exports are sharply lower.

Loss of markets for United States cotton increases surplus stocks held by the CCC, causes higher and higher government costs, and reduces the cotton farmer's income.

The time has come for us to fashion a sound and enduring national policy for cotton, to enable it to make its maximum contribution to our nation's growth at a minimum of governmental expense. At present, the domestic support level is 31.88 cents a pound. An 8.5 cent export subsidy enables domestic cotton to compete with foreign cotton selling at 24 cents or less. This imposes a substantial handicap upon the domestic mill which must buy American cotton at the support price level, while competing with foreign mills which buy it at the subsidized level.

This handicap could, of course, be overcome by either eliminating the export subsidy or by reducing the support level. But elimination of the subsidy would also eliminate American cotton from the world markets and give impetus to expanding foreign production. The effect such a move would have upon the American cotton farmer, our balance of payments, and our economy prevents this from being an acceptable line of action. Allowing domestic cotton prices to fall low enough to compete with foreign cotton is similarly unacceptable. For the average American farmer cannot, as yet, produce cotton profitably at world prices.

We can best meet these problems by the adoption of a new law which will both meet immediate needs and provide the experience from which a future long-range solution can be developed. Such a measure should meet four tests to the maximum extent possible: first, eliminate the disadvantage which the present two-price system for cotton imposes on the United States textile industry; second, strengthen the income of individual cotton farmers by enabling them to sell additional output at the world price in a combination best suited to their individual situations; third, promote sustained and expanding markets for United States cotton; and fourth, accomplish these objectives at a minimum cost to the taxpayer.

I urge that the Congress give early consideration to cotton legislation that will make this important fiber more competitive and help it recapture its markets. Ideally it should be signed into law before the end of February and made applicable to the planting of the 1963 crop. I recommend that the new law include the following:

Authorization, on a two-year trial basis, for the Secretary of Agriculture to make payments which will reduce the cost of the cotton to domestic mills by an amount sufficient to eliminate the inequity of the present two-price system, taking into account any differences in transportation costs between foreign and domestic mills and other relevant factors. This will both cure the existing inequity and help assure ample supplies of cotton textiles of good quality at fair prices to American consumers.

Within limits consistent with the need for an orderly reduction in the existing carryover, producers should be permitted to grow cotton above their basic acreage allotments for the export market at the world price. In 1963, the extra planting for export markets might be permitted up to 20 percent above the present statutory minimum allotment. Such provisions would recognize the greatly diverse conditions that prevail in different cotton producing areas, and provide fair opportunities for producers in each area. In addition, the bill could also authorize direct payments to producers, thus providing an efficient means of maintaining producer income without supporting prices at too high a level.

Research to reduce the cost of producing cotton in the United States will also strengthen the industry. For example, elimination of the boll weevil damage in the cotton crop could result in reduction in production costs of 5 cents a pound in areas of infestation. Such research will pay for itself many times over. I am therefore asking that a special effort be made to make certain that the research resources available to the Federal Government are focused on this problem. The Office of Science and Technology will review the progress and make recommendations. As actual cotton production costs fall, cotton price supports can be reduced under the stimulus of continuing research and the application of modern technology.

Dairying. The accomplishments of the American dairy industry, from processor to distributor, have been far too little recognized. Any American family can depend upon the availability of pure, nutritious milk and dairy products anywhere in the United States. This accomplishment is the product of hard work, skill and know-how and heavy capital investment.

New dairy legislation is urgently required for the benefit of both the farmer and the taxpayer. Last year I recommended to the Congress the passage of legislation to reduce the severe drain of budgetary expenditures for the dairy price support program and at the same time increase the income of dairy farmers. Failure to pass this legislation, I pointed out, would result in government costs of over $440 million a year for supporting the price of dairy products. No legislation was enacted—with the result that costs have recently been running at a rate in excess of $500 million a year, and the income of the dairy farmer has fallen by over $100 million a year. There is little prospect of any improvement in dairy farmers' income or substantial reduction in government costs unless new legislation is enacted. Under the present law surplus stocks of dairy products, especially butter, continue to pile up in government warehouses in shocking quantity. We have over 300 million pounds of butter in storage, enough to provide a year's supply of all the fats consumed by the people of Korea. Recipients of surplus foods are using twice as much butter per person as other consumers. Even with maximum use of dairy products in our food distribution programs, stocks continue to climb.

It is imperative, therefore, that the Congress apply the same successful principles of voluntary supply management to the dairy industry, and enact a program under which only producers who cooperate by reducing their marketings would receive, through market prices and payments, a return on their marketings substantially greater than the non-cooperators who choose not to join the program. Such a program would not only improve the income of cooperating farmers but also reduce government costs. . . .

Rural area development and rural electrification. The quality of housing in rural areas has not kept pace with housing in cities. A million and a half homes on farms and in our small towns are in such a dilapidated condition they endanger the health and safety of the families living in them. Another two million rural homes need major repairs. The current housing loan program of the Farmers Home Administration has made a good start toward helping rural families, who cannot otherwise obtain credit, to improve their housing. But it falls far short of what should and could be done. The need is greatest among families in the lower income levels who have neither the resources nor the credit to make any major repairs or improvements. To remedy this situation, I recommended that federally insured loans be provided for rural housing. This will broaden the opportunity of more rural families to improve their housing, and at the same time, through the substitution of private for public credit, will reduce the demands upon the federal budget.

One-third of our farm families earn only a subsistence income. Because they earn so little, they are unable to finance adequate educational and vocational training of family members, and this leads progressively to the concentration of still more poverty in rural areas. Vocational and other educational training should be made available to rural citizens who are unable to finance this training through other means. Such assistance is essential if large numbers of rural people, particularly youth and young adults, are to acquire the kinds of skills that will enable them to take advantage of new and better opportunities in an expanding economy. The alternative for many of them is a lifetime of poverty; the alternative for the whole nation is a continued waste of human resources.

Legislation is also needed to increase substantially the capacity for flood-water detention in small reservoirs in order to permit the full development, under the Watershed Protection and Flood Prevention Act, of available sites for multi-purpose use. Such action this year will supplement and strengthen the provisions of the Food and Agriculture Act of 1962 to strengthen the rural economy through more adequate development of available water and related land resources for multiple use.

It is also necessary to make provision for the lands upon which conservation reserve contracts will expire in the next few years. Some of these lands would revert to crop production; this must not happen if we are to prevent our various crop programs from being undermined. The existing $10 million limitations on authorized appropriations for land-use adjustment under Section 101 of the Food and Agriculture Act of 1962 should be raised to permit such conservation reserve lands to be treated, where appropriate, as part of an expanded land-use adjustment program. The cost will be substantially lower than it is under existing contracts.

Rural electrification and rural telephone loans have made enormous contributions to the well-being and economic development of rural America. Over five million rural customers—approximately twenty million men, women and children—receive central station electric service through over one thousand local organizations financed by the Rural Electrification Administration. Under the rural telephone loan program, local telephone companies and cooperatives have borrowed funds to finance modern dial telephone service for approximately two million rural subscribers. The credit record of REA borrowers is excellent; foreclosures have amounted to less than one one-thousandth of one percent; delinquencies on repayment schedules are equally small. . . .

To correctly reflect loan repayments in future appropriation and budget documents, I recommend that legislation be enacted to establish a Rural Electrification Administration Loan Account which will reflect the true net cost of the loan programs, showing the excess of the aggregate of the loans made over the current receipts from repayments on loans previously made. This will permit the account to be budgeted on a net expenditure basis. Funds in the loan account would not be available to the Secretary of Agriculture for loans without current prior authorization of the Congress in appropriation acts. Loan funds already authorized would remain available until expended as in existing law.

These recommendations will, I believe, accelerate progress toward our goals in agriculture while assisting in our efforts to hold down budget expenditures. With the benefit of new action in these areas, we can continue to narrow the gap between farm income and incomes in other segments of our economy, until the day is reached when efficient farm operators may be more certain of the opportunity to earn incomes equivalent to those in comparable non-farm occupations. We will also continue to reduce the excess stocks of farm commodities and to lighten the burden they impose upon the taxpayer. We will develop further our programs to conserve our resources of land and water and to redirect their use in order to supply our most essential needs—whether these be for food, timber or recreation.

We will intensify our campaign against rural poverty and our drive to build a thriving diversified rural economy. We will continue to encourage the advance of efficiency in agriculture, insuring the continued production of food and fiber at reasonable prices and in sufficient quantities to meet the needs of all Americans, and advancing the cause of economic development and security throughout the free world. A balanced and stable farm economy is essential if we are to meet both domestic and world challenges in the coming years—this program is designed to achieve that kind of farm economy.

43 : How Shall We Keep Our Manpower Employed?

CIVIC LUNCHEON
CHICAGO, ILLINOIS
MARCH 23, 1963*

I am glad to be in Chicago because I am struck every time I come by the strong public spirit which runs through this city in the determination to make Chicago second to none . . . and also by the happy spirit of community effort which joins business, labor, the civic groups

---

* This speech was part of President Kennedy's untiring campaign for the passage of his tax reduction bill. He pointed out that unemployment figures grew worse after each recession, and would be bound

and all the rest, in selling Chicago to the people of Chicago, to the country and the world. .... I don't think that there is any doubt that if this country continues to grow, if we can maintain a rate of economic vitality and prosperity, Chicago will be among the leaders.

There is, I think, the central thesis, however, that we face serious problems in this country in the decade ahead if we are going to maintain that growth, and I want to mention one of those problems because I think it concerns us all, in government, in the city, the national government, the state, labor, management, all of us as citizens. I think the number-one domestic concern of the United States is going to be in the 1960's the question of jobs—jobs for a tidal wave of men and women who are going to be hitting our labor market in the next five years. It is a concern which requires the united effort of all of us. Some people may think it strange that jobs, which were the great issue of the thirties, when we were in a depression, should also be the great concern of the sixties, when we enjoy a relative period of economic prosperity. The difficulty in the thirties was that there was an inordinately low supply of jobs for the men and women who wished to find work.

The difficulty now is the tremendously high demand for work, which exceeds the supply of jobs. But now, as then, every effort must be made by all of us to strengthen the economy so that we can find work for the people who want it. This involves not only Chicago in this country, but it involves our position of leadership in the world. Mr. Khrushchev has said that the hinge of history would move when he was able to demonstrate that his system could outproduce ours. The hinge of history will move if we are not able to find jobs for our people, not only during recessions but also during periods of prosperity. I regard this as the number-one problem we are going to face in this country in the coming years. It is serious enough to warrant a careful examination by all of us to realize that it cannot be

---

to worsen in the 1960's as the labor force increased, unless steps were taken to reverse the trend. The totals might climb to 7 percent of the nation's manpower even without a recession if the purchasing capacity was not increased.—A. N.

reduced by platitudes and hopes, and the effect of this problem is being felt and will be felt here in Chicago, Illinois, and across the country. There are three reasons for it: First is the labor released by the revolution in farm technology. Agriculture has been this nation's largest employer, engaging more people than steel, automobiles and public utilities, and the transportation industries combined.

But now one farmer can produce the food and fiber needed for twenty-five Americans, compared to only seven at the turn of the century. New fertilizers, insecticides, research and all the rest have made this one of the great productive miracles of all time—one of the great stories for the United States around the world in contrast to the failure of our adversaries—but it is a fact that since 1947 our farms have increased their output 30 percent at the very time that the man-hours worked on those farms were cut in half. Farm employment during that period declined by three million, an average of 200,000 a year; comparable to the population of the city of Akron, Ohio, being thrown out of work every twelve months. In the last two years alone, farm employment dropped by a half million, while farm production and farm income were both rising. It is estimated that, disturbing as it may sound, only one out of every ten boys growing up on the farms of the United States will find a living in agriculture.

This leads us to the second growing tide of manpower: our nation's youth.

The crest of the postwar baby flood has swept through our elementary and secondary schools and is now about to engulf the labor force. Last year, for example, 2.8 million young Americans reached the age of 16. This year, 3.8 million will be coming into the labor market at that age. Altogether, in the 1960's, 26 million new young workers will enter the labor market, an increase of 40 percent over the 1950's and a far greater number than this country has ever had to absorb and train in our history.

Already workers under the age of 25, although they comprise less than one-fifth of our labor force, constitute more than one-third of our unemployed. Last year, the unemployment rate for men age 25 and over was 4.4 percent. But for those age 20 to 24 it was 9 percent, and for those 14 to 19 it was a shocking 13 percent. Although young people are staying in school longer than their fathers, the rate of school drop-outs—four out of every ten—is too high, for job openings for the untrained are declining, in factories, mines, farms and railroads, in the construction and service industries.

Moreover, the jobless rate is always highest among the unskilled. In our modern society, even high school graduates find that their skills are inadequate. But Labor Department surveys show that their rate of unemployment is at least far below that of school drop-outs, not only in the year of leaving school but in the later years.

The latest surveys also show that unemployment rates among college graduates are much lower than among those graduated from high school. But unfortunately, only one out of every ten finish college. In short, as challenging as it will be to provide, first, jobs for the 26 million new young workers entering the labor market in the 1960's, far more difficult will be the problem of absorbing the 7.5 million who will not finish high school, including nearly 2.5 million who will not even finish the eighth grade.

I ask you to mark these figures well, for youth unemployment poses one of the most expensive and explosive social and economic problems now facing this country and this city. In the last decade, for example, arrests of youths increased 86 percent. What will the figure be for the next decade, when the net increase of potential young workers in the labor force rises fifteen times as fast as it did in the 1950's?

Finally, underlying all of these trends is the third phenomenon, both cursed and praised, and that is technological advance, known loosely by the name of automation. During the last six years, the nation increased its manufacturing output by nearly 20 percent, but it did so with 800,000 fewer production workers, and the gain in white-collar jobs did not offset this loss. Since the Second World War, the real output of the private economy has risen 67 percent, with only a 3 percent rise in man-hours.

I do not wish to be misunderstood. Increasing productivity and advancing technological skills are essential to our ability to compete and to progress. But we also have an obligation to find the nearly two million jobs which are displaced by these advances.

This city is no stranger to any of these problems. You have seen your railroads laying off machinists and boilermakers, as the proportion of diesel locomotives rose from less than 15 percent of all locomotives in 1947 to 97 percent today. You have seen your downstate coal mines laying off workers as new machinery makes it possible for forty-six men to dig the coal that one hundred men dug in 1947. And you have seen your steel mills employ seventy-nine men to produce the steel products which required a hundred men only ten years ago. Chicago, I might add parenthetically, also proves the exception to this pattern, since it now takes ten men to manage the Cubs instead of one.

This is not a blue-collar problem alone. Office and clerical workers are increasingly being displaced by automatic computers and processes. The Farmers Home Administration of the United States Government processes 35 percent more loans per employee than it did only two years ago.

This administration intends to press ahead with government economy, but we also have to find in the private economy jobs for those people who are willing.

All these trends you have seen in this city and state—workers displaced by automation, school drop-outs roaming the streets, men looking for work who have left the farm, the mine, the factory, the railroad or the distressed area. You have your share of jobless Negroes and women and older workers and all the rest, even though under Mayor Daley's hard-driving leadership this city is creating new jobs faster than almost any city in the country. The same is true on a larger scale of the nation as a whole. Our civilian labor force grew by nearly 12 million during the last fifteen years, but the number of jobs grew by only 10 million. In the last five years we saw an annual increase of only 175,000 private jobs, outside of agriculture, compared to 700,000 in each of the previous ten years. Our total Gross National Product output grew at a rate of only 3 percent, while unemployment remained continuously above 5 percent. And last year's loss of manhours, in terms of those willing but unable to find full-time work, was a staggering one billion work days, equivalent to shutting down the entire country with no production, no services, and no pay for over three weeks.

Some fourteen million Americans had some unemployment in

1962, and 28 percent of last year's unemployed were out of work fifteen weeks or longer. Fifteen percent were out of work a full six months or longer.

This nation must do better than that. . . .

Tax reduction alone will not employ the unskilled or bring business to a distressed area, and tax reduction alone is not, therefore, the only program we must put forward. To mention but a few, we urgently need to improve our schools and colleges, to reduce the number of drop-outs, to reduce the number of unskilled workers, to keep young people out of the labor market until they are ready for the jobs which automation creates, instead of those it is sure to replace.

We urgently need a youth-employment-opportunities program to give young people training and job experience instead of hanging around the streets, out of work and out of hope. We need to step up our efforts for aid to distressed areas, for the retraining of the unemployed, particularly in those areas where it has been chronic, for more security for our aged, for improving our housing and our transportation industries, and for ending race discrimination in education and employment, which helps increase, of course, the chronic unemployment of minority groups. . . .

Twenty-five hundred years ago the Greek poet Alcaeus laid down the principle which best sums up the greatness of Chicago: "Not houses firmly roofed," he wrote, "or the stones of walls well builded, nay, nor canals and dockyards make the City—but men able to use their opportunities."

Chicago is blessed to have such men at their head, and my fervent hope is that the United States of America in meeting the needs of this decade will also be peopled by "men able to use their opportunities."

44 : The Urgency of Tax Reduction

TELEVISION ADDRESS TO THE PEOPLE
THE WHITE HOUSE
WASHINGTON, D.C.
SEPTEMBER 18, 1963

Peace around the world and prosperity here at home represent the hopes of all Americans. In the next seven days, the Congress will make crucial decisions in both areas. The United States Senate will vote on the treaty outlawing nuclear tests in the atmosphere. It is the first concrete limitation on the nuclear arms race since the bomb was invented. It enables all men and women, East and West, free and slave, now and in the future, to be free from radioactive fallout. It affords us all a small sign of hope that war can be averted; that the terrible destructive power of nuclear weapons can be abolished before they abolish us; that our children can inhabit a world in which freedom is secure and the air is pure. . . .

The other crucial vote, which is in the House of Representatives, affects every individual and every business in the United States, and the taxes we pay to the federal government. No more important legislation will come before the Congress this year than the bill before the House next week to reduce federal taxes. In fact, no more important domestic economic legislation has come before the Congress in some fifteen years. It is urgently needed, and I hope you will support it in the national interest.

The federal income tax is one of those subjects about which we talk, about which we complain, but about which not very much is done. Perhaps we have heard too long about the certainty of death and taxes. Perhaps other national and international issues now seem more pressing. Yet the fact is that the high wartime and postwar tax rates we are now paying are no longer necessary. They are, in fact, harmful. These high rates do not leave enough money in private hands to keep this country's economy growing and healthy. They have helped to cause recessions in previous years, including 1958 and 1960, and unless they are reduced, they can cause recessions again.

The bill on which the House will vote next week is a sound bill and we need it for many reasons. First, a tax cut means more jobs for American workers; more after-tax money means more buying power for consumers and investors; and this means more production and the jobs our nation needs. Merely to reduce unemployment to a more acceptable level in the next two and a half years, we must create more than ten thousand new jobs every day. We cannot effectively attack the problem of teen-age crime and delinquency as long as so many of our young people are out of work. We cannot effectively solve the problem of racial injustice as long as unemployment is high. We cannot tackle the problem of automation when we are losing one million jobs every year to machines.

Second, a tax cut means new protection against another tragic recession. I do not say that a recession is inevitable without a tax cut, or impossible with one, but, excluding war years, we have had a recession on the average every forty-two months since World War II, or every forty-four months since World War I, and by next January it will be forty-four months since the last recession began. Recessions mean high unemployment and high budget deficits. Of all kinds of waste, they are the worst. We need a tax cut to keep this present drive from running out of gas.

Third, a tax cut means new markets for American business. American citizens will spend, as history shows us, an overwhelming percentage of the extra, after-tax dollars left in their pockets, and this spending will broaden markets for businessmen, put idle machines to work and require new machines and new factories to be built. The multiplied effect of these new private consumption and investment expenditures released by the tax cut will create a new market right here at home nearly equal to the gross national product of Canada and Australia combined.

Fourth, a tax cut means higher family income and higher business profits and a balanced federal budget. Every taxpayer and his family will have more money left over after taxes for a new car, a new home, new conveniences, education and investment. Every businessman can keep a higher percentage of his profits in his cash register or put it to work expanding or improving his business, and as the national income grows, the federal government will ultimately end up with more revenues.

Prosperity is the real way to balance our budget. Our tax rates are so high today that the growth of profits and pay checks in this country has been stunted. Our tax revenues have been depressed and our books for seven out of the last ten years have been in the red. By lowering tax rates, by increasing jobs and income, we can expand tax revenues and finally bring our budget into balance, and to assist further in this effort we have pledged an even tighter reign on federal expenditures, limiting our outlays to those activities which are fully essential to the nation. Spending will be controlled and our deficit will be reduced.

Fifth and finally, a tax cut means new strength around the world for the American dollar and for freedom. A tax cut can help us balance our international accounts and end the outflow of gold by helping make the American economy more efficient and more productive and more competitive, by enabling our goods to compete with those who are developing foreign factories and by making investment in America more attractive than investment abroad, and a tax cut will help us convince other countries of the advantages of freedom by helping to end the long-term poverty and chronic unemployment in depressed areas which mark our country. . . .

Recessions are not inevitable. They have not occurred in Europe for ten years, and I believe that someday in this country we can wipe them out. We already have the ability to reduce their frequency, their importance and their duration, and this tax cut is the single most important weapon that we can now add.

The support in this country for a tax cut crosses political lines. It includes small businessmen, workers and farmers, economists and educators. Very few are openly opposed, of course, to cutting taxes, but there are those who for one reason or another hope to delay this bill or attach ruinous amendments or to water down its effects. They want to deny our country the full benefits of tax reduction because they say there is waste in government. There may be, and we are working to get rid of it, but let us not forget the waste in four million unemployed men and women, with a prospect of still more unemployment if this bill does not pass.

There are those who talk about inflation when, in fact, prices have been steady; wholesale prices have been wholly steady for the last five years—a record unmatched in our history and unmatched in any other country—and when persistent slack in our economy threatens us far more with recession than inflation. Those who are opposed talk about the federal debt, when the actual burden of that debt on our economy is being steadily reduced. Since World War II, the national debt has gone up 11 percent, while our national output has gone up nearly 300 percent, in contrast to state and local governments, whose debt has risen nearly 400 percent in the same period.

Those who are opposed to this bill talk about skyrocketing federal employment, when, in fact, we have steadily reduced the number of federal employees serving every thousand people in this country. In fact, there are fewer federal civilian employees today than there were ten years ago. We have reduced waste and improved efficiency at the Pentagon and the Post Office, in the farm programs and in other agencies throughout the government.

Section 1 of this bill, as Chairman Mills of the House Ways and Means Committee pointed out, makes clear that voting for this bill is a choice of tax reduction instead of deliberate deficits as the principal means of boosting the economy and finding jobs for our people. No wasteful, inefficient or unnecessary government activity will be tolerated. We are pledged to a course of true fiscal responsibility, leading to a balanced budget in a balanced, full-employment economy.

My fellow citizens, this is a matter which affects our country and its future. We are talking about more jobs. We are talking about the future of our country, about its strength and growth and stability as the leader of the free world. We are talking about helping people, people who have been looking for work for a long time in eastern Kentucky, in West Virginia and Pennsylvania, the steel towns of Ohio, Gary, Indiana, southern Illinois, other parts of our country, some of our mill towns. We are talking about a tax cut in the pockets of our people that will help create jobs and income for everyone.

We are talking, as I said at the start, about one of the most important pieces of legislation to come before the Congress this year—the most important domestic economic measure to come before the Congress in fifteen years. It could be put off for another year. It could be cut down. It needs your support. This is not a question of party. It is a question of the growth of our country, of the jobs and security of our people. It is a question of whether our taxpayers and businessmen and workers will get the help they deserve. . . .

45 : "We Have Helped Capital, Not Soaked It"

FLORIDA CHAMBER OF COMMERCE
TAMPA, FLORIDA
NOVEMBER 18, 1963*

A little more than one year ago, when our bill to grant a tax credit for business investment was before the Congress, Secretary of the Treasury Dillon was on a plane to this state, and he found himself talking to one of the leading Florida businessmen about the investment tax credit. He spent some time, he later told me, explaining how the bill would help this man's corporate outlook and income and the businessman was most impressed. Finally, as the plane landed at Miami, he turned to Secretary Dillon and said, "I am very grateful to you for explaining the bill. Now tell me just once more why is it I am against it?"

That story is unfortunately not an exaggeration. Many businessmen who are prospering as never before during this administration are convinced, nevertheless, that we must be antibusiness. With the new figures on corporate profits after taxes having reached an all-time high, running some 43 percent higher than they were just three years ago, they still suspect us of being opposed to private profit.

---

* In this speech, one of several in a busy speaking day, the President reminded the Chamber that corporate profits were at "an all-time high." He also urged application of the Golden Rule for Negroes, and declared that domestic tranquillity was impossible unless they were given full justice.—A. N.

With the most stable price level of any comparable economic recovery in our history, they still fear that we are promoting inflation. We have liberalized depreciation guidelines to grant more individual flexibility, reduced our farm surpluses, reduced transportation taxes, established a private corporation to manage our satellite communication system, increased the role of American business in the development of less developed countries, and proposed to the Congress a sharp reduction in corporate as well as personal income taxes and a major deregulation of transportation, and yet many businessmen are convinced that a Democratic administration is out to soak the rich, increase controls for the sake of controls and extend at all costs the scope of the federal bureaucracy.

The hard facts contradict these beliefs. This administration is interested in the healthy expansion of our economy. We are interested in the steady progress of our society, and it is in this kind of program, in my opinion, that American business has the largest stake. Why is it that profits are at an all-time high in the nation today? It is because the nation as a whole is prospering. It is because our Gross National Product is rising from $500 billion to $600 billion, a record rise of $100 billion in three years—thirty-six months. It is because industrial production in the last three years has increased 22 percent and personal income 15 percent. It is because, as the *Wall Street Journal* pointed out last week, the United States now leads most of Western Europe in the rate of business expansion. For the first time in many years, in the last eighteen months our growth rate exceeds that of France or Germany. It is because, as *Fortune* magazine recently pointed out, corporate profits in America are now rising much faster than corporate profits overseas. It is because these profits have not been eaten up by an inflationary spiral. And finally, it is because we have reversed the dismal trend toward even more frequent recessions, which are the greatest enemy of profits.

By next April, with the indispensable help of the pending tax cut bill, the United States will be sailing with the winds of the longest and strongest peacetime economic expansion in our nation's entire history.

I do not say that all this is due to the administration alone, but neither is it all accidental. The fiscal and monetary policies which we have followed are the key factors in whether the economy moves toward a path of expansion or restriction. In the last three years, American business and industry have directly benefited from a host of our legislative and administrative actions, which increased corporate flow, increased markets at home and abroad, increased consumer purchasing power and increased plant modernization and productivity. And still other steps have been taken to curb the wage-price spiral. In the first six months of 1963 there was less time lost in strikes than in any other period since the Second World War.

I do not say that these actions were taken for the benefit of business alone. They were taken to benefit the country. Some of them were labeled pro-business, some of them were labeled anti-business, depending upon the viewpoint of the opposing groups. But that kind of label is meaningless. This Administration is "pro" the public interest. Nor do I say that all of these policies could please all American businessmen all of the time. So long as the interests and views of businessmen frequently clash with each other, no President could possibly please them all.

Most businessmen, though perhaps not most business spokesmen, are associated with small business. They ask the government for assistance to protect them against monopoly, to assure them of reasonable credit, to enable them to participate in defense contracts. And both large and small businesses work with the various arms of the administration every day on trade, transportation, procurement, balance of payments, and international business affairs. They do not show the hostility, which is so often described, or find that our policies and personnel are so incompatible with their own.

Businessmen are welcome at the White House, and I welcome the chance to address business meetings such as this, not because I expect that it will necessarily affect the results of elections, but I do think it can affect what this country does and how it moves ahead, and whether we are going to be able to find jobs for all the people that need them, and whether we are going to build the kind of a country in which all of us can take pride and credit. And that is the kind of cooperative effort which I invite from businessmen and from other interested citizens.

If we can keep open the channels of communication, this country can make progress ahead. To further that understanding, I would like to answer four questions that I am most frequently asked by businessmen. . . .

The first and most frequently asked question is: Is the federal government growing so large that our private economy is endangered? My answer to that is no. The federal government has been growing for 175 years. Our population has grown even faster. Our territory and economy have grown and become more closely linked. The size of our business, labor, farm and other establishments and organizations has increased. Above all, our responsibilities around the world have grown and our stake in world peace has grown immeasurably. Life itself is more complex and the American people in the twentieth century have come to expect more from governmental action. But there has been no sudden spurt in the growth of government under this administration. Leaving national security outlays aside, the federal civilian expenditures today, when measured as they should be measured in a growing economy as a percentage of our national output, are no higher than they were at the end of the Second World War—a mere 5 percent of our Gross National Product is not a threat to our economy. The real growth in government has been at the state and local level. Between 1948 and 1962, while federal civilian expenditures were rising by 65 percent, state spending, on the average, across this country rose by 227 percent—from less than $10 billion in 1948 to over $30 billion in 1962. Florida's state expenditures in that same period rose by 270 percent, or more than four times as fast, percentagewise, as the federal budget; Georgia by 331 percent; Ohio by 300 percent; Kentucky by 431 percent.

The federal government has no desire to expand the size and scope of its activities merely for the sake of expansion. Many tasks would never have been taken on by the Congress had they been able to be fulfilled at the state and local level, and this administration has made efforts to transfer to private ownership many of the financial assets held by the government, to substitute private for public credit, to reduce farm surpluses, to dispose of excess commodities and to make our transportation system less restrictive. This is a far cry, I believe, from a government too big for the economy.

Secondly, I am asked: Are not continuing deficits and the mounting national debt certain to drive us into bankruptcy? And my answer to that is no. Once again we must look at these facts in perspective. From 1948 to 1962 the total federal debt increased less than 20 percent. We had the Korean War, all our obligations abroad, a tremendously growing country, tremendously growing population. The federal debt grew by less than 20 percent, while the average for all the states was 500 percent. Or, taking only the four years from 1958 to 1962, the federal debt rose only 8 percent, while state debt as a whole went up 41 percent.

Obviously, neither the states nor the nation are teetering on the edge of bankruptcy as the result of these debts. In 1945 our national debt was 120 percent of our Gross National Product. Today it is 53 percent. Next year it will be 52 percent. At a time when our debt has gone up by the percentage I described, our Gross National Product has doubled and, therefore, as this country moves to a trillion dollar economy, which we are moving toward, it is quite obvious that as long as we maintain these proportions the fiscal credit of the United States will still be secure.

While the federal net debt was growing less than 20 percent in these years, total corporate debt—not mine, your debt—was growing by nearly 200 percent and the total indebtedness of private individuals rose by 300 percent. So who is the most cautious fiscal manager, you gentlemen or us?

It is true that the pending tax cut will add to this debt by temporarily reducing federal revenues, but the purpose of the tax cut is not to produce a deficit but to boost the economy. A full employment economy is the only way to balance the budget. A recession-ridden economy, recessions occuring every twenty-four or thirty or thirty-two months, on the other hand, is a guarantee of chronic, higher deficits and continually deeper debt. We must remember that in 1958, President Eisenhower sent up a budget to the Hill which was balanced in surplus by a half-billion dollars. As a result of the recession of 1958, that budget ended up that year unbalanced by $12.5 billion. The great enemy of the balanced budget is a recession, and it is to prevent a recession and to provide for economic growth and provide for the jobs for the ten million people who are coming into the labor market in the next two and a half years that I strongly believe in the tax cut very quickly.

Third, I am asked: Why can't this administration cut federal expenditures? And my answer is that we have cut. I recommended an additional $620 million of reductions in this year's budget since first submitting it last January. Domestic civilian expenditures—excluding national defense, space and interest on the debt—domestic civilian expenditures were budgeted below the level of last year, a feat rarely accomplished in the last fifteen years. Once 16 percent larger than state and local expenditures, our federal civilian expenditures are now 43 percent smaller. What all this suggests is not that the states have been less prudent than we have been but that this country is growing and the needs are growing. You here in Florida in this Chamber know it very well or you wouldn't have supported a $75 million debt obligation on the people of Florida. You can't tell the children of this state that they can't go to college in 1970 because you didn't take the decisions in 1963, and what we are trying to do in this state is what we are trying to do across the country. What we have to do is be prudent, responsible, selective—make our judgments about what is really necessary and valuable and what can be put aside. That, it seems to me, is the essence of responsible management by the national government, by the state government, by the local community and by private business.

We have reduced the number of federal employees serving every 1,000 people in this country. There are no more people today working for the federal government than there were ten years ago. Federal employment has not increased in the last ten years. There are less people working today for the federal government than there were a year ago. But it will go up because this country grows.

The question is, in what proportion? But I can assure you that there will be fewer federal employees serving every 1,000 people next year than there were this year.

Secretary McNamara has instituted cost reductions in the Pentagon which will save a billion dollars a year, and finally save $4 billion a year. We are constantly re-examining these programs to determine what can be done. Many of those who call for larger expenditures are forgetting the growth of our population and the complexities of our problems. And economy advocates from Florida are not opposed to the Cross-Florida Barge Canal, which was so strongly supported by your governor and by me, or the space effort at Cape Canaveral, or the Tampa Air Force Fuel Annex. They talk, instead, about Midwestern feed grain programs and Far Western reclamation projects. But out west the economizers talk about the Tampa Air Force Fuel Annex. And so the argument goes on across the country.

And fourth and finally the question arises: Will the fiscal policies of the government lead to inflation? And my answer to that is no. The danger of inflation arises when the level of total and private demand presses against our productive capacity. We are far from that today. Total output in this country would have to increase by $30 billion to reduce unemployment to 4 percent. Our productive plant still, as all of you know, is well below what you could produce operating at maximum capacity. Idle men and machines allow plenty of room for decreased taxes and increased demand without the risk of inflation. The tax cut, moreover, can be expected to stimulate productivity and growth, and thus add to our productive potential, lessening the danger of inflation. It has long been believed that a budget deficit automatically means inflation. The facts indicate otherwise. The record peacetime deficit of 1959 produced no inflation then or subsequently, nor have the deficits of recent years. In fact, most of our postwar inflation occurred in the year of budget surpluses, '47, '48, '51, '56 and '57. Recent scattered price increases have caused concern and stimulated fear that expanded demand would lead to inflation. But the wholesale price index so far shows little or no reflection of these increases. Some prices have been reduced and most prices have not moved. Many of the increases have been in the price of raw materials which have declined, and inasmuch as the trend of such prices has been stable or downward for a number of years, some recovery is not unexpected.

But the abundance of the world's raw materials would indicate that even here we do not have to fear serious inflationary pressures. Moreover, the current remarkable stability of labor costs per unit of output clearly indicates that such price increases as have occurred do not reflect a general upward surge of costs. . . .

  VIII

SCIENCE

AND EDUCATION

46 : For More Exercise and Less "Spectation"

NATIONAL FOOTBALL FOUNDATION
NEW YORK, NEW YORK
DECEMBER 5, 1961*

. . . Despite our much publicized emphasis on school athletics, our own children lag behind European children in physical fitness. And astonishingly enough, when Dr. Kraus and Dr. Weber recently went back, after ten years, to Europe, they found a basic decline in the physical fitness of European children, because in the last decade mechanization had begun to get at them too.

It is no wonder that we have such a high proportion of rejections for physical reasons in our Selective Service. A short time ago General Hershey told me that since October of 1948, of some six million young men examined for military duty, more than a million were rejected as physically unfit for military service. A good many of these men would not have been rejected if they had had the opportunity, when younger, to take part in an adequate physical development program.

To get two men today, the United States Army must call seven

---

* Speaking at the annual Hall of Fame banquet of the National Football Foundation, the President urged Americans to follow the Greeks in seeking excellence in athletics as well as in letters, art and architecture. We get too much of our exercise in climbing to stadium seats or turning on television, he said; we have too much "spectation" of sports (he coined the word) and too little participation. Jefferson, he reminded the country, had said, "Not less than two hours a day should be devoted to exercise." And he also reminded it that Gibbon had found professionalism in amateur sports one of the early tokens of the decline and fall of the Roman Empire. The Dr. Hertha Kraus whom he mentioned, long a professor in Bryn Mawr, had been director of public welfare in Cologne after the First World War. Dr. Francis J. Weber, also mentioned, is an expert in public health work. Few informal utterances of the President attracted so much attention as this speech.—A. N.

men. Of the five rejected, three are turned down for physical reasons and two for mental disabilities. To get the 196 thousand additional men that we needed for Berlin, the government had to call up, therefore, 750 thousand men; and the rejection rate is increasing each year.

I find this situation disturbing. We are underexercised as a nation. We look instead of play. We ride instead of walk. Our existence deprives us of the minimum of physical activity essential for healthy living. The remedy, in my judgment, lies in one direction—that is, in developing programs for broad participation in exercise by all of our young men and women—all of our boys and girls. . . .

We have begun this year to make progress toward this goal with the new President's Council on Youth Fitness. The idea behind our youth fitness program is to give as many American boys and girls as possible a chance for healthy physical development. . . .

The results so far show the effectiveness of what can be done and the extent of the need. In Muskogee, Oklahoma, for example, a city which prides itself on athletic achievement, which has had seven All-Americans in recent years, 47 percent of the students failed the minimum physical fitness test. Only a fraction of those who qualified could pass the more comprehensive test of physical capability. Yet only six weeks of participation in a daily fifteen-minute program of vigorous exercise brought about a 24 percent improvement among those who failed the first test.

Throughout the country we have found equally discouraging examples of deficiency and equally encouraging examples of progress. I hope that every school district in this country will adopt our minimum program. I urge every parent to support the program and his own children's participation in it. I urge our colleges and universities to lay down basic standards of physical fitness. I urge the nation's community recreation centers to provide more opportunity for those who no longer attend school. And, finally, I urge organizations such as this, with all the prestige and influence which you bring to American life, to help establish more programs for participation by American boys and girls, by Americans young and old. In short, what we must do is literally change the physical habits of millions of Americans; and that is far more difficult than changing their tastes, their fashions or even their politics.

47 : Education and World Order

UNIVERSITY OF CALIFORNIA
BERKELEY, CALIFORNIA
MARCH 23, 1962

. . . I am delighted to be here on this occasion for, though it is the ninety-fourth anniversary of the charter, in a sense this is the hundredth, for this university and so many other universities across our country owe their birth to the most extraordinary piece of legislation which this country has ever adopted, and that is the Morrill Act, signed by President Abraham Lincoln in the darkest and most uncertain days of the Civil War, which set before the country the opportunity to build the great land-grant colleges, of which this is so distinguished a part. Six years later, this university obtained its charter.

In its first graduating class it included a future governor of California, a future congressman, a judge, a distinguished state assemblyman, a clergyman, a lawyer, a doctor—all in a graduating class of twelve graduates!

This college, therefore, from its earliest beginnings has recognized, and its graduates have recognized, that the purpose of education is not merely to advance the economic self-interest of its graduates. The people of California, as much if not more than the people of any other state, have supported their colleges and their universities and their schools, because they recognize how important it is to the maintenance of a free society that its citizens be well educated. . . .

I need hardly emphasize the happy pursuit of knowledge in this place. Your faculty includes more Nobel Laureates than any other faculty in the world—more in this one community than our principal adversary has received since the awards began in 1901. And we take pride in that, only from a national point of view, because it indicates, as the chancellor pointed out, the great intellectual benefits of a free society. This University of California will continue to grow as an intellectual center because your presidents and your chancellors and your professors have rigorously defended that unhampered freedom of discussion and inquiry which is the soul of the intellectual enterprise and the heart of the free university. . . .

Yet the pursuit of knowledge itself implies a world where men are free to follow out the logic of their own ideas. It implies a world where nations are free to solve their own problems and to realize their own ideals. It implies, in short, a world where collaboration emerges from the voluntary decisions of nations strong in their own independence and their own self-respect. It implies, I believe, the kind of world which is emerging before our eyes—the world produced by the revolution of national independence which is today, and has been since 1945, sweeping across the face of the world.

I sometimes think that we are too much impressed by the clamor of daily events. The newspaper headlines and the television screens give us a short view. They so flood us with the stop-press details of daily stories that we lose sight of one of the great movements of history. Yet it is the profound tendencies of history, and not the passing excitements, that will shape our future.

The short view gives us the impression as a nation of being shoved and harried, everywhere on the defensive. But this impression is surely an optical illusion. From the perspective of Moscow, the world today may seem even more troublesome, more intractable, more frustrating than it does to us. The leaders of the Communist world are confronted not only by acute internal problems in each Communist country—the failure of agriculture, the rising discontent of the youth and the intellectuals, the demands of technical and managerial groups for status and security. They are confronted in addition by profound divisions within the Communist world itself—divisions which have already shattered the image of Communism as a universal system guaranteed to abolish all social and international conflicts, the most valuable asset the Communists had for many years.

Wisdom requires the long view. And the long view shows us that the revolution of national independence is a fundamental fact of our era. This revolution will not be stopped. As new nations emerge from the oblivion of centuries, their first aspiration is to affirm their national identity. Their deepest hope is for a world where, within a framework of international cooperation, every country can solve its own problems according to its own traditions and ideals.

It is in the interests of the pursuit of knowledge, and it is in our own national interest, that this revolution of national independence succeed. For the Communists rest everything on the idea of a monolithic world—a world where all knowledge has a single pattern, all societies move toward a single model, all problems and roads have a single solution and a single destination. The pursuit of knowledge, on the other hand, rests everything on the opposite idea—on the idea of a world based on diversity, self-determination and freedom. And that is the kind of world to which we Americans, as a nation, are committed by the principles upon which the great Republic was founded.

As men conduct the pursuit of knowledge, they create a world which freely unites national diversity and international partnership. This emerging world is incompatible with the Communist world order. It will irresistibly burst the bonds of the Communist organization and the Communist ideology. And diversity and independence, far from being opposed to the American conception of world order, represent the very essence of our view of the future of the world. . . .

48 : What the Coming Army Officer Will Need

UNITED STATES MILITARY ACADEMY
WEST POINT, NEW YORK
JUNE 6, 1962*

. . . I hope that you realize—and I hope every American realizes—how much we depend upon you. Your strictly military responsibilities, therefore, will require a versatility and an adaptability never

---

* This commencement address at West Point was delivered in the presence of the Secretary of the Army, of General William Childs Westmoreland, Superintendent of the Military Academy, of General Lyman L. Lemnitzer, who early in his career had taught at West Point, and other men of eminence.

before required in either war or in peace. They may involve the command and control of modern nuclear weapons and modern delivery systems, so complex that only a few scientists can understand their operation, so devastating that their inadvertent use would be of world-wide concern, but so new that their employment and their effects have never been tested in combat conditions.

On the other hand, your responsibilities may involve the command of more traditional forces, but in less traditional roles—men risking their lives not as combatants but as instructors or advisers, or as symbols of our nation's commitments. The fact that the United States is not directly at war in these areas in no way diminishes the skill and the courage that will be required, the service to our country which is rendered or the pain of the casualties which are suffered.

To cite one final example of the range of responsibilities that will fall upon you, you may hold a position of command with our special forces, forces which are too unconventional to be called conventional, forces which are growing in number and importance and significance; for we now know that it is wholly misleading to call this "the nuclear age," or to say that our security rests only on the doctrine of massive retaliation.

Korea has not been the only battleground since the end of the Second World War. Men have fought and died in Malaya, in Greece, in the Philippines, in Algeria and Cuba and Cyprus, and almost continuously on the Indochinese Peninsula. No nuclear weapons have been fired. No massive nuclear retaliation has been considered appropriate. This is another type of war, new in its intensity, ancient in its origin—war by guerrillas, subversives, insurgents, assassins; war by ambush instead of by combat, by infiltration instead of aggression, seeking victory by eroding and exhausting the enemy instead of engaging him. It is a form of warfare uniquely adapted to what have been strangely called "wars of liberation," to undermine the efforts of new and poor countries to maintain the freedom that they have finally achieved. It preys on economic unrest and ethnic conflicts. It requires in those situations where we must counter it—and these are the kinds of challenges that will be before us in the next decade if freedom is to be saved—a wholly new kind of strategy, a wholly different kind of force, and therefore a new and wholly different kind of military training.

But I have spoken thus far only of the military challenges which your education must prepare you for. The nonmilitary problems which you will face will also be most demanding, diplomatic, political and economic. In the years ahead, some of you will serve as advisers to foreign aid missions or even to foreign governments. Some will negotiate terms of a cease-fire with broad political as well as military ramifications. Some of you will go to the far corners of the earth, and to the far reaches of space. Some of you will sit in the highest councils of the Pentagon. Others will hold delicate command posts which are international in character. Still others will advise on plans to abolish arms instead of using them to abolish others.

Whatever your position, the scope of your decisions will not be confined to the traditional tenets of military competence and training. You will need to know and understand not only the foreign policy of the United States, but the foreign policy of all countries scattered around the world who twenty years ago were the most distant names to us. You will need to give orders in different tongues and read maps by different systems. You will be involved in economic judgments which most economists would hesitate to make. At what point, for example, does military aid become burdensome to a country and endanger its freedom rather than help to secure it? To what extent can the gold and dollar cost of our overseas deployments be offset by foreign procurement? Or at what stage can a new weapons system be considered sufficiently advanced to justify large dollar appropriations? . . .

49 : Science, Space and the New Education

RICE UNIVERSITY
HOUSTON, TEXAS
SEPTEMBER 12, 1962

. . . We meet at a college noted for knowledge, in a city noted for progress, in a state noted for strength, and we stand in need of all three, for we meet in an hour of change and challenge, in a decade of hope and fear, in an age of both knowledge and ignorance. The greater our knowledge increases, the greater our ignorance unfolds.

Despite the striking fact that most of the scientists that the world has ever known are alive and working today; despite the fact that this nation's own scientific manpower is doubling every twelve years at a rate of growth more than three times that of our population as a whole; despite that, the vast stretches of the unknown and the unanswered and the unfinished still far outstrip our collective comprehension.

No man can fully grasp how far and how fast we have come, but condense, if you will, the fifty thousand years of man's recorded history in a time span of but a half century. Stated in these terms, we know very little about the first forty years, except that at the end of them advanced man had learned to use the skins of animals to cover himself. Then about ten years ago, under this standard, man emerged from his caves to construct other kinds of shelter. Only five years ago man learned to write and use a cart with wheels. Christianity began less than two years ago. The printing press came this year, and then less than two months ago, during this whole fifty-year span of human history, the steam engine provided a new source of power. . . .

Last month electric lights and telephones and automobiles and airplanes became available. Only last week did we develop penicillin and television and nuclear power, and now if America's new spacecraft succeeds in reaching Venus, we will have literally reached the stars before midnight tonight.

This is a breath-taking pace, and such a pace cannot help but create new ills as it dispels old—new ignorance, new problems, new dangers. Surely the opening vistas of space promise high costs and hardships, as well as high reward.

So it is not surprising that some would have us stay where we are a little longer, to rest, to wait. But this city of Houston, this State of Texas, this country of the United States was not built by those who waited and rested and wished to look behind them. This country was conquered by those who moved forward, and so will space.

William Bradford, speaking in 1630 of the founding of the

Plymouth Bay Colony, said that all great and laudable actions are accompanied with great difficulties, and must be both enterprised and overcome with courage.

If this capsule history of our progress teaches us anything, it is that man, in his quest for knowledge and progress, is determined and cannot be deterred. The exploration of space will go ahead, whether we join in it or not. And it is one of the great adventures of all time, and no nation which expects to be the leader of other nations can expect to stay behind in this race for space.

Those who came before us made certain that this country rode the first waves of the industrial revolution, the first waves of modern invention and the first wave of nuclear power, and this generation does not intend to founder in the backwash of the coming age of space. We mean to be a part of it. We mean to lead it, for the eyes of the world now look into space, to the moon and to the planets beyond; and we have vowed that we shall not see it governed by a hostile flag of conquest, but by a banner of freedom and peace. We have vowed that we shall not see space filled with weapons of mass destruction, but with instruments of knowledge and understanding.

Yet the vows of this nation can only be fulfilled if we in this nation are first, and therefore we intend to be first. In short, our leadership in science and in industry, our hopes for peace and security, our obligations to ourselves as well as others, all require us to make this effort, to solve these mysteries, to solve them for the good of all men, and to become the world's leading space-faring nation.

We set sail on this new sea because there is new knowledge to be gained, and new rights to be won, and they must be won and used for the progress of all people. For space science, like nuclear science and all technology, has no conscience of its own. Whether it will become a force for good or ill depends on man, and only if the United States occupies a position of pre-eminence can we help decide whether this new ocean will be a sea of peace or a new, terrifying theater of war. I do not say that we should or will go unprotected against the hostile misuse of space any more than we go unprotected against the hostile use of land or sea, but I do say that space can be explored and mastered without feeding the fires of war, without repeating the mistakes that man has made in extending his writ around this globe of ours.

There is no strife, no prejudice, no national conflict in outer space as yet. Its hazards are hostile to us all. Its conquest deserves the best of all mankind, and its opportunity for peaceful cooperation may never come again. But why, some say, the moon? Why choose this as our goal? And they may well ask, why climb the highest mountain? Why, thirty-five years ago, fly the Atlantic? Why does Rice play Texas?

We choose to go to the moon. We choose to go to the moon in this decade, and do the other things, not because they are easy but because they are hard; because that goal will serve to organize and measure the best of our energies and skills; because that challenge is one that we are willing to accept, one we are unwilling to postpone, and one which we intend to win—and the others, too.

It is for these reasons that I regard the decision last year to shift our efforts in space from low to high gear as among the most important decisions that will be made during my incumbency in the office of the Presidency.

In the last twenty-four hours we have seen facilities now being created for the greatest and most complex exploration in man's history. We have felt the ground shake and the air shattered by the testing of a Saturn C-1 booster rocket, many times as powerful as the Atlas which launched John Glenn, generating power equivalent to ten thousand automobiles with their accelerators on the floor. We have seen the site where five F-1 rocket engines, each one as powerful as all eight engines of the Saturn combined, will be clustered together to make the advanced Saturn missile, assembled in a new building to be built at Cape Canaveral as tall as a forty-eight-story structure, as wide as a city block and as long as two lengths of this field.

Within these last nineteen months at least forty-five satellites have circled the earth. Some forty of them were "made in the United States of America," and they were far more sophisticated and supplied far more knowledge to the people of the world than those of the Soviet Union.

The Mariner spacecraft now on its way to Venus is the most

intricate instrument in the history of space science. The accuracy of that shot is comparable to firing a missile from Cape Canaveral and dropping it in this stadium between the forty-yard lines.

Transit satellites are helping our ships at sea to steer a safer course. Tiros satellites have given us unprecedented warnings of hurricanes and storms, and will do the same for forest fires and icebergs.

We have had our failures, but so have others, even if they do not admit them. And they may be less public.

To be sure, we are behind, and will be behind for some time in manned flight. But we do not intend to stay behind, and in this decade we shall make up and move ahead.

The growth of our science and education will be enriched by new knowledge of our universe and environment, by new techniques of learning and mapping and observation, by new tools and computers for industry, medicine, the home as well as the school. Technical institutions, such as Rice, will reap the harvest of these gains.

And finally, the space effort itself, while still in its infancy, has already created a great number of new companies and tens of thousands of new jobs. Space and related industries are generating new demands in investment and skilled personnel, and this city and this state and this region will share greatly in this growth. What was once the farthest outpost on the old frontier of the West will be the farthest outpost on the new frontier of science and space. Houston, your city of Houston, with its Manned Spacecraft Center, will become the heart of a large scientific and engineering community. During the next five years the National Aeronautics and Space Administration expects to double the number of scientists and engineers in this area, to increase its outlays for salaries and expenses to $60 million a year, to invest some $200 million in plant and laboratory facilities, and to direct or contract for new space efforts over $1 billion from this center in this city.

To be sure, all this costs us all a good deal of money. This year's space budget is three times what it was in January, 1961, and it is greater than the space budget of the previous eight years combined. That budget now stands at $5.4 billion a year—a staggering sum, though somewhat less than we pay for cigarettes and cigars every year. Space expenditures will soon rise some more, from forty cents per person per week to more than fifty cents a week for every man, woman and child in the United States, for we have given this program a high national priority—even though I realize that this is in some measure an act of faith and vision, for we do not now know what benefits await us.

But if I were to say, my fellow citizens, that we shall send to the moon, 240,000 miles away from the control station in Houston, a giant rocket more than three hundred feet tall, the length of this football field, made of new metal alloys, some of which have not yet been invented, capable of standing heat and stresses several times more than have ever been experienced, fitted together with a precision better than the finest watch, carrying all the equipment needed for propulsion, guidance, control, communications, food and survival, on an untried mission, to an unknown celestial body, and then return it safely to earth, re-entering the atmosphere at speeds of over 25,000 miles per hour, causing heat about half that of the temperature of the sun, almost as hot as it is here today, and do all this, and do it right, and do it first before this decade is out, then we must be bold. . . .

50 : The Urgency of Better Education

SPECIAL MESSAGE TO CONGRESS
WASHINGTON, D.C.
JANUARY 29, 1963*

For the nation, increasing the quality and availability of education is vital to both our national security and our domestic well-being. A free nation can rise no higher than the standard of excellence set in

---

* Undiscouraged by the failure of his proposed legislation for strengthening the educational system in the Eighty-seventh Congress, President Kennedy took early action to lay a new and even bolder program before the Eighty-eighth Congress. "It requires skilled manpower and

its schools and colleges. Ignorance and illiteracy, unskilled workers and school drop-outs—these and other failures of our educational system breed failures in our social and economic system: delinquency, unemployment, chronic dependence, a waste of human resources, a loss of productive power and purchasing power and an increase in tax-supported benefits. The loss of only one year's income due to unemployment is more than the total cost of twelve years of education through high school. Failure to improve educational performance is thus not only poor social policy, it is poor economics.

At the turn of the century, only 10 percent of our adults had a high school or college education. Today such an education has become a requirement for an increasing number of jobs. Yet nearly 40 percent of our youths are dropping out before graduating from high school; only 43 percent of our adults have completed high school; only 8 percent of our adults have completed college; and only 16 percent of our young people are presently completing college. As my Science Advisory Committee has reported, one of our most serious manpower shortages is the lack of Ph.D.'s in engineering, science and mathematics; only about one-half of 1 percent of our school-age generation is achieving Ph.D. degrees in all fields.

I do not say that the federal government should take over responsibility for education. That is neither desirable nor feasible. Instead, its participation should be selective, stimulative and, where possible, transitional.

---

brainpower to match the power of totalitarian discipline," he declared. Quite apart from this, no investment would yield higher returns in new products, better techniques and improved wages and purchasing power than an investment in education. He recommended a four-year effort to provide $1.5 billion to assist the states in raising teacher salaries, in constructing classrooms, and in developing special projects to solve educational problems in slum areas and depressed rural regions. This part of his program was defeated. In dealing with higher education, however, he succeeded in achieving more than any President in a hundred years, or since Lincoln signed the epochal Morrill Land Grant Act. The ideas he expounded in this field, therefore, have a special interest, and will long be regarded by educators as rearing a new landmark.—A. N.

A century of experience with land-grant colleges has demonstrated that federal financial participation can assist educational progress and growth without federal control. In the last decade, experience with the National Science Foundation, with the National Defense Education Act, and with programs for assisting federally affected school districts has demonstrated that federal support can benefit education without leading to federal control. The proper federal role is to identify national education goals and to help local, state and private authorities build the necessary roads to reach those goals. Federal aid will enable our schools, colleges and universities to be more stable financially and therefore more independent.

These goals include the following:

First, we must improve the quality of instruction provided in all of our schools and colleges. We must stimulate interest in learning in order to reduce the alarming number of students who now drop out of school or who do not continue into higher levels of education. This requires more and better teachers—teachers who can be attracted to and retained in schools and colleges only if pay levels reflect more adequately the value of the services they render. It also requires that our teachers and instructors be equipped with the best possible teaching materials and curricula. They must have at their command methods of instruction proven by thorough scientific research into the learning process and by careful experimentation.

Second, our educational system faces a major problem of quantity —of coping with the needs of our expanding population and of the rising educational expectations for our children which all of us share as parents. Nearly 50 million people were enrolled in our schools and colleges in 1962—an increase of more than 50 percent since 1950. By 1970, college enrollment will nearly double, and secondary schools will increase enrollment by 50 percent—categories in which the cost of education, including facilities, is several times higher than in elementary schools.

Third, we must give special attention to increasing the opportunities and incentives for all Americans to develop their talents to the utmost—to complete their education and to continue their self-development throughout life. This means preventing school drop-outs, improving and expanding special educational services, and providing better education in slum, distressed and rural areas where the educational attainment of students is far below par. It means increased opportunities for those students both willing and intellectually able to advance their education at the college and graduate levels. It means increased attention to vocational and technical education, which have long been underdeveloped in both effectiveness and scope, to the detriment of our workers and our technological progress.

In support of these three basic goals, I am proposing today a comprehensive, balanced program to enlarge the federal government's investment in the education of its citizens—a program aimed at increasing the educational opportunities of potentially every American citizen, regardless of age, race, religion, income and educational achievement.

This program has been shaped to meet our goals on the basis of three fundamental guidelines:

An appraisal of the entire range of educational problems, viewing educational opportunity as a continuous lifelong process, starting with preschool training and extending through elementary and secondary schools, college, graduate education, vocational education, job training and retraining, adult education, and such general community educational resources as the public library;

A selective application of federal aid—aimed at strengthening, not weakening, the independence of existing school systems and aimed at meeting our most urgent education problems and objectives, including quality improvement; teacher training; special problems of slum, depressed and rural areas; needy students; manpower shortage areas such as science and engineering; and shortages of educational facilities; and

More effective implementation of existing laws, as reflected in my recent budget recommendations.

To enable the full range of educational needs to be considered as a whole, I am transmitting to the Congress with this message a single, comprehensive education bill—the National Education Improvement Act of 1963. For education cannot easily or wisely be divided into separate parts. Each part is linked to the other. The colleges depend on the work of the schools; the schools depend on the colleges for teachers; vocational and technical education is not separate from general education. This bill recalls the posture of Jefferson: "Nobody can doubt my zeal for the general instruction of the people. I never have proposed a sacrifice of the primary to the ultimate grade of instruction. Let us keep our eye steadily on the whole system."

In order that its full relation to economic growth, to the new age of science, to the national security and to human and institutional freedom may be analyzed in proper perspective, this bill should be considered as a whole, as a combination of elements designed to solve problems that have no single solution.

This is not a partisan measure—and it neither includes nor rejects all of the features which have long been sought by the various educational groups and organizations. It is instead an attempt to launch a prudent and balanced program drawing upon the efforts of many past Congresses and the proposals of many members of both houses and both political parties. It is solely an educational program, without trying to solve all other difficult domestic problems. It is clearly realistic in terms of its cost—and it is clearly essential to the growth and security of this country.

Our present American educational system was founded on the principle that opportunity for education in this country should be available to all—not merely to those who have the ability to pay. In the past, this has meant free public elementary and secondary schools in every community, thereafter, land-grant, state and municipal colleges, and vocational education, and more recently, job retraining and specialized teachers for students with special educational problems.

Now a veritable tidal wave of students is advancing inexorably on our institutions of higher education, where the annual costs per student are several times as high as the cost of a high school education, and where these costs must be borne in large part by the student or his parents. Five years ago the graduating class of the secondary schools was 1.5 million; five years from now it will be 2.5 million. The future of these young people and the nation rests in large part on their access to college and graduate education. For this country reserves its highest honors for only one kind of aristocracy—that which the Founding Fathers called "an aristocracy of achievement arising out of a democracy of opportunity."

Well over half of all parents with school-age children expect them to attend college. But only one-third do so. Some 40 percent of those who enter college do not graduate, and only a small number continue into graduate and professional study. The lack of adequate aid to students plays a large part in this disturbing record.

Federal aid to college students is not new. More than 3 million World War II and Korean conflict veterans have received $6 billion in federal funds since 1944 to assist them to attend college. Additionally, the National Defense Education Act college student loan program has aided more than 300,000 students in more than 1,500 institutions who have borrowed nearly $220 million. In four years of operations, defaults have totaled only $700 while repayment rates are more than twice that required by law.

But as effective as this program has been, it has not fulfilled its original objective of assuring that "no student of ability will be denied an opportunity for higher education because of financial need." The institutional ceiling of $250,000 per year on the federal contribution limits loan funds in at least ninety-eight of the presently participating institutions. The annual statutory ceiling of $90 million on federal appropriations restricts the size of the program. As a result, only about 5 percent of the students enrolled in participating colleges are assisted. Additionally, the forgiveness feature for teachers is rendered less attractive as well as less meaningful by excluding those who go on to teach in colleges, in private schools or on overseas military posts. This proven program must be enlarged and strengthened.

Other types of assistance are needed. For students who cannot meet the financial criteria under the NDEA loan program, a loan insurance program—drawing on techniques well established by the FHA and other federal programs—would encourage banks and other institutions to loan more money for educational purposes.

Moreover, many students from families with limited incomes cannot and should not carry a heavy burden of debt. They must rely largely on income from employment while in college. For these students, the federal government should—as it did in the days of the National Youth Administration—help colleges provide additional student work opportunities of an educational character.

A serious barrier to increased graduate study is the lack of adequate financial aid for graduate students. Only 1,500 fellowships are permitted annually under the National Defense Education Act program, upon which we are dependent for urgently needed increases in the number of college teachers and the number of graduate students pursuing other courses essential to the nation's advancement and security. The National Science Foundation has broad authority for fellowships and training grants, but its program, too, has been restricted by limited appropriations. The President's Science Advisory Committee has predicted that the dramatically increasing demand for engineers, mathematicians and physical scientists will require that the output of Ph.D.'s in these fields alone be increased two and one-half times, to a total of 7,500 annually by 1970, and that the number of master's degrees awarded annually be substantially increased. In all fields the need exceeds the supply of doctoral recipients. The shortage is particularly acute in college teaching, where at present rates the nation will lack 90,000 doctoral degree holders by 1970. It is clearly contrary to the national interest to have the number of graduate students limited by the financial ability of those able and interested in pursuing advanced degrees. Fellowship programs can ease much of the financial burden and, most importantly, encourage and stimulate a fuller realization and utilization of our human resources.

The welfare and security of the nation require that we increase our investment in financial assistance for college students both at undergraduate and graduate levels. In keeping with present needs and our traditions of maximum self-help, I recommend that the Congress enact legislation to:

1. Extend the National Defense Education Act student loan program, liberalize the repayment forgiveness for teachers, raise the ceiling on total appropriations and eliminate the limitation on amounts available to individual institutions.

2. Authorize a supplementary new program of federal insurance for commercial loans made by banks and other institutions to college students for educational purposes.

3. Establish a new work-study program for needy college students unable to carry too heavy a loan burden, providing up to half the pay for students employed by the colleges in work of an educational character—as, for example, laboratory, library or research assistants.

4. Increase the number of National Defense Education Act fellow-

ships to be awarded by the Office of Education from 1,500 to 12,000, including summer session awards.

5. Authorize a thorough survey and evaluation of the need for scholarships or additional financial assistance to undergraduate students so that any further action needed in this area can be considered by the next Congress.

In addition, as part of this program to increase financial assistance to students, the 1964 budget recommendations for the National Science Foundation, which are already before the Congress, include a proposed increase of $35 million to expand the number of fellowships and new teaching grants for graduate study from 2,800 in 1963 to 8,700 in fiscal 1964.

Aid to college students will be to no avail if there are insufficient college classrooms. The long-predicted crisis in higher education facilities is now at hand. For the next fifteen years, even without additional student aid, enrollment increases in colleges will average 340,000 each year. If we are to accommodate the projected enrollment of more than 7 million college students by 1970—a doubling during the decade—$23 billion of new facilities will be needed, more than three times the quantity built during the preceding decade. This means that, unless we are to deny higher education opportunities to our youth, American colleges and universities must expand their academic facilities at a rate much faster than their present resources will permit.

In many colleges, students with adequate modern dormitories and living quarters—thanks to the College Housing Act—are crammed in outmoded, overcrowded classrooms, laboratories and libraries. Even now it is too late to provide these facilities to meet the sharp increases in college enrollment expected during the next two years. Further delay will aggravate an already critical situation. I recommend, therefore, the prompt enactment of a program to provide loans to public and nonprofit private institutions of higher education for construction of urgently needed academic facilities.

The opportunity for a college education is severely limited for hundreds of thousands of young people because there is no college in their own community. Studies indicate that the likelihood of going to college on the part of a high school graduate who lives within twenty to twenty-five miles of a college is 50 percent greater than it is for the student who lives beyond commuting distance. This absence of college facilities in many communities causes an unfortunate waste of some of our most promising youthful talent. A demonstrated method of meeting this particular problem effectively is the creation of two-year community colleges—a program that should be undertaken without delay and which will require federal assistance for the construction of adequate facilities. I recommend, therefore, a program of grants to states for construction of public community junior colleges.

There is an especially urgent need for college level training of technicians to assist scientists, engineers and doctors. Although ideally one scientist or engineer should have the backing of two or three technicians, our institutions today are not producing even one technician for each three science and engineering graduates. This shortage results in an inefficient use of professional manpower—the occupation of critically needed time and talent to perform tasks which could be performed by others—an extravagance which cannot be tolerated when the nation's demand for scientists, engineers and doctors continues to grow. Failure to give attention to this matter will impede the objectives of the graduate and postgraduate training programs mentioned below. I recommend, therefore, a program of grants to aid public and private nonprofit institutions in the training of scientific, engineering and medical technicians in two-year college-level programs, covering up to 50 percent of the cost of constructing and equipping as well as operating the necessary academic facilities.

Special urgency exists for expanding the capacity for the graduate training of engineers, scientists and mathematicians. The President's Science Advisory Committee has recently reported that an unprecedented acceleration in the production of advanced degrees is immediately necessary to increase our national capability in these fields. Added facilities, larger faculties and new institutions are needed. I have recommended, therefore, in the proposed 1964 budget already before the Congress, a strengthening of the National Science Foundation matching grant program for institutions of higher education to expand and improve graduate and undergraduate science facilities.

Because today's trend in colleges and universities is toward less lecturing and more independent study, the college and university library becomes even more essential in the life of our students. Today, as reported by the American Library Association, nearly all college libraries are urgently in need of additional books, periodicals, scientific reports and similar materials to accommodate the growing number of students and faculty. Additionally, they need buildings, equipment and publications to serve their academic communities, whether public or private. I recommend the authorization of federal grants to institutions of higher education for library materials and construction, on a broad geographic basis, with priority to those most urgently requiring expansion and improvement.

Expansion of high-quality graduate education and research in all fields is essential to national security and economic growth. Means of increasing our supply of highly trained professional personnel to match the rapidly growing demands of teaching, industry, government and research warrants our interest and support.

We need many more graduate centers, and they should be better distributed geographically. Three-quarters of all doctoral degrees are granted by a handful of universities located in twelve states. The remaining states with half our population produce only one-fourth of the Ph.D.'s.

New industries increasingly gravitate to or are innovated by strong centers of learning and research. The distressed area of the future may well be one which lacks centers of graduate education and research. It is in the national interest to encourage establishment of these critically needed centers of advanced learning, especially in parts of the nation now lacking them.

I recommend enactment of a federal grant program administered by the Department of Health, Education and Welfare for the development and expansion of new graduate centers. I also urge appropriation of the increased funds requested in my 1964 budget for expansion of the National Science Foundation program of science development grants, which will also contribute to strengthening of graduate education.

Our experience under the National Defense Education Act with respect to modern language and area centers has demonstrated that federal aid can spur development of intellectual talent. They deserve our continuing support, with assurance that resources will be available for orderly expansion in keeping with availability of teaching talent. I recommend that the current Modern Foreign Language program aiding public and private institutions of higher learning be extended and expanded.

A basic source of knowledge is research. Industry has long realized this truth. Health and agriculture have established the worth of systematic research and development. But research in education has been astonishingly meager and frequently ignored. A fraction of 1 percent of this nation's total expenditures for education is now devoted to such research. It is appalling that so little is known about the level of performance, comparative value of alternative investments and specialized problems of our educational system—and that it lags behind, sometimes by as much as twenty or even fifty years, in utilizing the results of research and keeping abreast of man's knowledge in all fields, including education itself.

Highest priority must be given to strengthening our educational research efforts, including a substantial expansion of the course content improvement programs which the government has supported, particularly through the National Science Foundation. Two interrelated actions are necessary:

I have recommended appropriations in the 1964 budget for substantially expanding the National Science Foundation science and mathematics course materials program and the Office of Education educational research program.

I recommend legislation to broaden the Cooperative Research Act to authorize support of centers for multipurpose educational research and for development and demonstration programs; and to broaden the types of educational agencies eligible to conduct research.

The second step to improvement of educational quality is teacher training. The quality of education is determined primarily by the quality of the teacher. Yet one out of every five teachers in the United States has either not been certified by his state as qualified to teach or failed to complete four years of college study. In the field of English, between 40 and 60 percent of the secondary school teachers lack even the minimum requirement of a college major in that subject. Thus it is not surprising that, largely because of unsatisfactory elementary and secondary school instruction, our colleges and universities are now required to spend over $10 million annually on remedial English courses.

The lack of teacher quality and preparation in other fields is equally disturbing. More than two-thirds of our 1.6 million teachers completed their degree work more than five years ago. Yet within the past five years major advances have been made—not only in the physical, biological, engineering and mathematical sciences, but also in specialized branches of the social sciences, the arts and humanities, and in the art of teaching itself.

In addition, we lack sufficient trained teachers for 6 million handicapped children and youth, including 1.5 million mentally retarded and another 1.5 million with very serious social and emotional problems. Only through special classes, taught by specially trained teachers, can these children prepare for rehabilitation, employment and community participation. Yet less than one-fourth of these children now have access to the special education they require, primarily because of the lack of qualified special teachers, college instructors, research personnel and supervisors. It is estimated that 75,000 special teachers —55,000 more than presently available—are needed for the mentally retarded alone.

The teacher training support programs of the National Science Foundation and the Office of Education have demonstrated their value. I recommend, therefore; that the National Science Foundation program for training institutes for teachers in the natural sciences, mathematics, engineering and social sciences be expanded to provide for upgrading the knowledge and skills of 46,000 teachers, as provided in my 1964 budget recommendations. . . .

51 : Our Educational Deficiencies and the Remedy

SAN DIEGO STATE COLLEGE
SAN DIEGO, CALIFORNIA
JUNE 6, 1963*

One of the most impressive, if not the most impressive accomplishment of this great Golden State has been the recognition by the citizens of this state of the importance of education as the basis for the maintenance of an effective, free society. This fact was recognized in our earliest beginnings at the Massachusetts Bay Colony, but I do not believe that any state in the Union has given more attention in recent years to educating its citizens to the highest level in the state colleges, the junior colleges, the high schools, the grade schools. You recognize that a free society places burdens upon its citizens. To govern is to choose and the ability to make those choices wisely and responsibly and prudently implies the best of all of us.

No country can possibly move ahead, no free society can possibly be sustained, unless it has an educated citizenry whose quality of mind and heart permit it to take part in the complicated and sophisticated decisions that are demanded not only of the President and the Congress, but of all the citizens who service the ultimate power.

---

* Few states, if any, had shown as much energy and foresight in meeting the tasks of public education as California. Its state-wide University of California, with eight campuses, was the most impressive structure of the kind in the nation; the Berkeley branch was among the first two or three universities in the land, and UCLA was close behind it; sixteen state colleges (soon to be eighteen) helped give every ambitious youth a chance, and more than three-score junior colleges were scattered throughout the state. The standards of the public school system on both the primary and secondary level were high. President Kennedy therefore found a receptive audience when he spoke in San Diego, and could well exhort other states to follow the California example.—A. N.

I am sure that the graduates of this college recognize that the effort of the people of California who govern the legislature, the local communities, the faculty—that this concentrated effort of mind and scholarship to educate the young citizens of this state has not been made merely to give this school's graduates an economic advantage in the life struggle. Quite obviously, there is a higher purpose, and that is the hope that you will turn to the service of the state the scholarship, the education, the qualities which society has helped develop in you; that you will render on the community level or on the state level or on the national level or the international level a contribution to the maintenance of freedom and peace and the security of our country and those associated with it in a most critical time.

In so doing, you will follow a great and laudable tradition which combined American scholarship and American leadership in political affairs. It is an extraordinary fact of history, I think, unmatched since the days of early Greece, that this country should have produced during its founding days, in a population of a handful of men, such an extraordinary range of scholars and creative thinkers—Jefferson, Franklin, Morris, Wilson and all the rest. This is a great tradition which we must maintain with increasing strength and increasing vigor.

Those of you who are educated, those of us who recognize the responsibilities of an educated citizen, should now concern ourselves with whether we are providing an adequate education for all Americans, whether all Americans will have an equal chance to develop their intellectual qualities, and whether we are preparing ourselves today for the educational challenges which are going to come before this decade is out.

The first question, and the most important is: does every American boy and girl have an opportunity to develop whatever talents he or she has? All of us do not have equal talent, but all of us should have an equal opportunity to develop our talents. Let me cite a few facts to show that we do not.

In this fortunate state of California, the average current expenditure for a boy and girl in the public schools is $515, but in the state of Mississippi it is $230. The average salary for classroom teachers in California is $7,000, while in Mississippi it is $3,600.

Nearly three-quarters of the young, white population of the United States has graduated from high school, but only about two-fifths of our non-white population has done the same. In some states, almost 40 percent of the non-white population has completed less than five years of school. Contrast it with 7 percent of the white population. In one American state over 36 percent of the public school buildings are over forty years of age. In another, only 4 percent are that old.

Such facts, and one could prolong the recital indefinitely, make it clear that American children today do not yet enjoy equal educational opportunities for two primary reasons: One is economic and the other is racial. If our nation is to meet the goal of giving every American child a fair chance—because an uneducated child makes an uneducated parent, who in another day produces another uneducated child—we must move ahead swiftly in both areas, and we must recognize that segregation and education, and I mean de facto segregation in the North as well as the proclaimed segregation in the South, brings with it serious handicaps to a large proportion of the population. It does no good, as you in California know better than any, to say that that is the business of another state. It is the business of our country. These young, uneducated boys and girls know no state boundaries and they come West as well as North and East. They are your citizens as well as citizens of this country.

The second question relates to the quality of our education. Today one out of every three students in the fifth grade will drop out of high school and only two out of ten will graduate from college. In the meantime, we need more educated men and women and we need less and less unskilled labor. There are millions of jobs that will be available in the next seven years for educated young men and women. The demand will be overwhelming and there will be millions of people out of work who are unskilled because with new machines and technology there is less need for them. This combination of a tremendously increasing population among our young people, of less need for unskilled labor, of increasingly unskilled labor available, combines to form one of the most serious domestic problems that this country will face in the next ten years. Of Americans eighteen years of age or older, more than 23 million have less than eight years of schooling, and over 8 million have less than five years. What kind of judgment, what kind of response can we expect of a citizen who has been to school less than five years—and we have in this country 8 million who have been to school less than five years? As a result, they can't read or write or do simple arithmetic. They are illiterate in this rich country of ours and they constitute the hard core of our unemployed. They can't write a letter to get a job and they can't read, in many cases, a help-wanted sign. One out of every ten workers who failed to finish elementary school are unemployed, as compared to one out of fifty college graduates. . . .

What are we going to do by the end of this decade? There are four million boys and girls born each year in the United States. Our population is growing each decade by a figure equal to the total population of this country at the time of Abraham Lincoln, just one hundred years ago. Our educational system is not expanding fast enough. By 1970 the number of students in our public, elementary and secondary schools will have increased 25 percent over 1960. Nearly three-quarters of a million new classrooms will be needed, and we are not building them at that rate. By 1970 we will have seven million students in our colleges and universities, three million more than we do today. We are going to double the population of our colleges and universities in ten years. We are going to have to build as many school and college classrooms and buildings in ten years as we did in one hundred fifty years.

By 1970 we will need 7,500 Ph.D.'s each year in the physical sciences, mathematics and engineering. In 1960 we graduated 3,000. Such facts make it clear that we have a major responsibility and a major opportunity, one that we should welcome, because there is no greater asset in this country than an educated man or woman. Education, quite rightly, is the responsibility of the state and the local community, but from the beginning of our country's history, from the time of the Northwest Ordinance, as John Adams and Thomas Jefferson recognized, from the time of the Morrill Act at the height of the Civil War, when the Land Grant College system was set up under the administration of President Lincoln, from the beginning it has been recognized that there must be a national commitment and that the national government must play its role in stimulating a system of excellence which can serve the great national purpose of a free society, and it is for that reason that we have sent to the Congress of the United States legislation to help meet the needs of higher education, by assisting in the construction of college academic facilities, and junior colleges and graduate centers, and technical institutes, and by stepping up existing programs for student loans and graduate fellowships and other student assistance programs. . . .

And finally, we must make a massive attack upon illiteracy in the year 1963 in the United States by an expansion of university extension courses and by a major effort to improve our libraries in every community of our country.

52 : The Lives of One Million Young Americans

NEWS CONFERENCE
AUGUST 1, 1963

The end of this summer of 1963 will be an especially critical time for 400,000 young Americans who, according to the experience of earlier years, will not return to school when the summer is ended. Moreover, without a special effort to reverse this trend, another 700,000 students will return to school in September, but will fail to complete the school year.

The greatest growth in labor demand today is for highly trained professional workers with sixteen or more years of education. The second fastest-growing demand is for technical and semiprofessional workers with one to three years of post–high school education. Jobs filled by high school graduates rose 30 percent, while jobs for those with no secondary education decreased 25 percent in the last decade.

We must therefore combat and intensify our efforts to meet this problem. We are now talking about the lives of one million young American boys and girls who will fail to meet their educational requirements in the next few months unless we do something about it.

This is a serious national problem. A boy or girl has only a limited time in life in which to get an education, and yet it will shape their whole lives and the lives of their children. So I am asking all American parents to urge their children to go back to school in September, to assist them in every way to stay in school. I am asking school principals, clergymen, trade union leaders, business leaders, everyone in the country, to concern themselves. Here is something that all of us can do in a practical way in the month of August and in the months to come.

One of the things which we are going to do here is to provide out of the Presidential Emergency Fund $250,000 on an emergency basis for guidance counselors in the month of August to see if we can get some of these boys and girls back to school. They will appreciate any effort we make for the rest of their lives.

53 : Science as a Guide of Public Policy

NATIONAL ACADEMY OF SCIENCES
WASHINGTON, D.C.
OCTOBER 22, 1963*

. . . It is impressive to reflect that one hundred years ago, in the midst of a savage fraternal war, the United States Congress established a body devoted to the advancement of scientific research. The recognition then of the value of abstract science ran against the

---

* The National Academy of Sciences, founded by an Act which Lincoln signed in the midst of the Civil War, was celebrating its centenary. It had been established with the stipulation that whenever any department of government called upon it, it should "investigate, experiment, and report upon any subject of science or of art." Its distinguished membership, which by this time stood at five hundred, with fifty foreign associates, had performed invaluable service during the century. During the First World War it had established the National Research Council to coordinate the research activities of the nation.—A.N.

grain of our traditional preoccupation with technology and engineering.

You will remember de Tocqueville's famous chapter on why the Americans are more addicted to practical than to theoretical science. De Tocqueville concluded that the more democratic a society, "the more will discoveries immediately applicable to productive industry confer gain, fame, and even power on their authors."

But if I were to name a single thing which points up the difference this century has made in the American attitude toward science, it would certainly be the wholehearted understanding today of the importance of pure science. We realize now that progress in technology depends on progress in theory; that the most abstract investigations can lead to the most concrete results; and that the vitality of a scientific community springs from its passion to answer science's most fundamental questions. I therefore greet this body with particular pleasure, for the range and depth of scientific achievement represented in this room constitute the seedbed of our nation's future.

The last hundred years have seen a second great change—the change in the relationship between science and public policy. To this new relationship, your own academy has made a decisive contribution. For a century, the National Academy of Sciences has exemplified the partnership between scientists who accept the responsibilities that accompany freedom and a government which encourages the increase of knowledge for the welfare of mankind. As a result in large part of the recommendations of this academy, the federal government enlarged its scientific activities through such agencies as the Geological Survey, the Weather Bureau, the Bureau of Standards, the Forest Service and many others; but it took the First World War to bring science into central contact with governmental policy, and it took the Second World War to make scientific counsel an indispensable function of government. The relationship between science and public policy is bound to be complex. . . .

In the last hundred years, science has thus emerged from a peripheral concern of government to an active partner. The instrumentalities devised in recent times have given this partnership continuity and force. The question in all our minds today is how science can best continue its service to the nation, to the people, to the world, in the years to come.

I would suggest that science is already moving to enlarge its influence in three general ways: in the interdisciplinary area, in the international area and in the intercultural area. For science is the most powerful means we have for the unification of knowledge, and a main obligation of its future must be to deal with problems which cut across boundaries, whether boundaries between the sciences, boundaries between nations or boundaries between man's scientific and his humane concerns. . . .

IX

POSTSCRIPT

Nothing was further from the mind of the American people on the morning of November 22, 1963, than the possibility that to the three Presidential assassinations in our history might be added a fourth. No President was more universally esteemed and beloved during his first years in office than John F. Kennedy had been. No occupants of the White House had ever seemed more attractive, or had won more popular affection, than Mr. Kennedy and his wife. The nation might well feel that its love raised a protective wall about him which no rational being could think of breaching; it did not realize until too late that any great society has utterly irrational members against whom it is helpless.

President Kennedy had closed October with some happy remarks at the ground-breaking for the Robert Frost Library at Amherst College. "Libraries are memories," he said, "and in this library you will have the memory of an extraordinary American." On November 21 he spoke at the dedication of the Aero-Space Medical Health Center at Brooks Air Force Base in Texas. He recalled there Frank O'Connor's statement that in boyhood he and his schoolmates would tramp across country until they came to a seemingly impassable wall, when they would toss their hats over it so that they had to follow. "This nation has tossed its cap across the wall of space," the President said, "and we have no choice but to follow it." That evening he spoke in Houston at a testimonial dinner for Congressman Albert Thomas, and then flew to Fort Worth with Mrs. Kennedy to spend the night.

Next morning he briefly addressed the Fort Worth Chamber of Commerce in a breakfast appearance—the last speech he ever delivered. He recalled that Fort Worth had once been an outpost against the Indians; that in the First World War pilots of the Royal Canadian Air Force had trained there; and that in the Second World War the Liberator bombers, one of which his brother helped fly from the city, had been a Fort Worth product. He spoke appreciatively of the newest weapon made in the city, the TFX or Tactical Fighter Experimental

*plane. At about half-past ten he and Mrs. Kennedy left their hotel
for the short flight to Dallas, reaching Love Field at 11:37 so that he
might speak to a luncheon meeting in the Dallas Trade Mart. Then
came the events that made one tragic hour indelible in the minds of
all Americans: the ride through cheering crowds, with the Governor
of Texas beside him, the shots from an upper window, the race to the
hospital, the tense minutes of waiting, and all too soon news that the
brilliant career had ended.*

A.N.

54 : Undelivered Speech for the Dallas Citizens Council, the Dallas Assembly and the Graduate Research Center of the Southwest in Dallas*

I am honored to have this invitation to address the annual meeting of the Dallas Citizens Council, joined by the members of the Dallas Assembly, and pleased to have this opportunity to salute the Graduate Research Center of the Southwest.

It is fitting that these two symbols of Dallas progress are united in the sponsorship of this meeting. For they represent the best qualities, I am told, of leadership and learning in this city—and leadership and learning are indispensable to each other. The advancement of learning depends on community leadership for financial and political support, and the products of that learning, in turn, are essential to the leadership's hopes for continued progress and prosperity. It is not a coincidence that those communities possessing the best in research and graduate facilities, from MIT to Cal Tech, tend to attract the new and growing industries. I congratulate those of you here in Dallas who have recognized these basic facts through the creation of the unique and forward-looking Graduate Research Center.

This link between leadership and learning is not only essential at the community level. It is even more indispensable in world affairs. Ignorance and misinformation can handicap the progress of a city or a company—but they can, if allowed to prevail in foreign policy, handicap this country's security. In a world of complex and continuing problems, in a world full of frustrations and irritations, America's leadership must be guided by the lights of learning and reason, or else those who confuse rhetoric with reality and the plausible with

---

* This speech, never delivered, was released to the press at noon, Central Standard Time, on November 22, 1963.—A. N.

the possible will gain the popular ascendancy with their seemingly swift and simple solutions to every world problem.

There will always be dissident voices heard in the land, expressing opposition without alternatives, finding fault but never favor, perceiving gloom on every side and seeking influence without responsibility. Those voices are inevitable.

But today other voices are heard in the land—voices preaching doctrines wholly unrelated to reality, wholly unsuited to the sixties, doctrines which apparently assume that words will suffice without weapons, that vituperation is as good as victory and that peace is a sign of weakness. At a time when the national debt is steadily being reduced in terms of its burden on our economy, they see that debt as the greatest single threat to our security. At a time when we are steadily reducing the number of federal employees serving every thousand citizens, they fear those supposed hordes of civil servants far more than the actual hordes of opposing armies.

We cannot expect that everyone, to use the phrase of a decade ago, will "talk sense to the American people." But we can hope that fewer people will listen to nonsense. And the notion that this nation is headed for defeat through deficit, or that strength is but a matter of slogans, is nothing but just plain nonsense.

I want to discuss with you today the status of our strength and our security because this question clearly calls for the most responsible qualities of leadership and the most enlightened products of scholarship. For this nation's strength and security are not easily or cheaply obtained—nor are they quickly and simply explained. There are many kinds of strength, and no one kind will suffice. Overwhelming nuclear strength cannot stop a guerrilla war. Formal pacts of alliance cannot stop internal subversion. Displays of material wealth cannot stop the disillusionment of diplomats subjected to discrimination.

Above all, words alone are not enough. The United States is a peaceful nation. And where our strength and determination are clear, our words need merely to convey conviction, not belligerence. If we are strong, our strength will speak for itself. If we are weak, words will be of no help.

I realize that this nation often tends to identify turning points in world affairs with the major addresses which preceded them. But it was not the Monroe Doctrine that kept all Europe away from this hemisphere; it was the strength of the British fleet and the width of the Atlantic Ocean. It was not General Marshall's speech at Harvard which kept Communism out of Western Europe; it was the strength and stability made possible by our military and economic assistance.

In this administration also it has been necessary at times to issue specific warnings—warnings that we could not stand by and watch the Communists conquer Laos by force, or intervene in the Congo, or swallow West Berlin or maintain offensive missiles on Cuba. But while our goals were at least temporarily obtained in these and other instances, our successful defense of freedom was due not to the words we used but to the strength we stood ready to use on behalf of the principles we stand ready to defend.

This strength is composed of many different elements, ranging from the most massive deterrents to the most subtle influences. And all types of strength are needed; no one kind could do the job alone. Let us take a moment, therefore, to review this nation's progress in each major area of strength.

First, as Secretary McNamara made clear in his address last Monday, the strategic nuclear power of the United States has been so greatly modernized and expanded in the last thousand days, by the rapid production and deployment of the most modern missile systems, that any and all potential aggressors are clearly confronted now with the impossibility of strategic victory—and the certainty of total destruction—if by reckless attack they should ever force upon us the necessity of a strategic reply.

In less than three years, we have increased by 50 percent the number of Polaris submarines scheduled to be in force by the next fiscal year, increased by more than 70 percent our total Polaris purchase program, increased by more than 75 percent our Minuteman purchase program, increased by 50 percent the portion of our strategic bombers on 15-minute alert, and increased by 100 percent the total number of nuclear weapons available in our strategic alert forces. Our security is further enhanced by the steps we have taken regarding these weapons to improve the speed and certainty of their response, their readiness at all times to respond, their ability to survive an attack and their ability to be carefully controlled and directed through secure command operations.

But the lessons of the last decade have taught us that freedom cannot be defended by strategic nuclear power alone. We have, therefore, in the last three years accelerated the development and deployment of tactical nuclear weapons—and increased by 60 percent the tactical nuclear forces deployed in Western Europe.

Nor can Europe or any other continent rely on nuclear forces alone, whether they are strategic or tactical. We have radically improved the readiness of our conventional forces, increased by 45 percent the number of combat ready Army divisions, increased by 100 percent the procurement of modern Army weapons and equipment, increased by 100 percent our ship construction, conversion and modernization program, increased by 100 percent our procurement of tactical aircraft, increased by 30 percent the number of tactical air squadrons, and increased the strength of the Marines. As last month's "Operation Big Lift"—which originated here in Texas—showed so clearly, this nation is prepared as never before to move substantial numbers of men in surprisingly little time to advanced positions anywhere in the world. We have increased by 175 percent the procurement of airlift aircraft, and we have already achieved a 75 percent increase in our existing strategic airlift capability. Finally, moving beyond the traditional roles of our military forces, we have achieved an increase of nearly 600 percent in our special forces—those forces that are prepared to work with our allies and friends against the guerrillas, saboteurs, insurgents and assassins who threaten freedom in a less direct but equally dangerous manner.

But American military might should not and need not stand alone against the ambitions of international Communism. Our security and strength, in the last analysis, directly depend on the security and strength of others, and that is why our military and economic assistance plays such a key role in enabling those who live on the periphery of the Communist world to maintain their independence of choice. Our assistance to these nations can be painful, risky and costly, as is true in Southeast Asia today. But we dare not weary of the task. For our assistance makes possible the stationing of 3.5 million allied troops along the Communist frontier at one-tenth the cost of maintaining a comparable number of American soldiers. A successful Communist breakthrough in these areas, necessitating direct United States intervention, would cost us several times as much as our entire foreign aid program—and might cost us heavily in American lives as well.

About 70 percent of our military assistance goes to nine key countries located on or near the borders of the Communist bloc—nine countries confronted directly or indirectly with the threat of Communist aggression: Vietnam, free China, Korea, India, Pakistan, Thailand, Greece, Turkey and Iran. No one of these countries possesses on its own the resources to maintain the forces which our own Chiefs of Staff think needed in the common interest. Reducing our efforts to train, equip and assist their armies can only encourage Communist penetration and require in time the increased overseas deployment of American combat forces. And reducing the economic help needed to bolster these nations that undertake to help defend freedom can have the same disastrous result. In short, the $50 billion we spend each year on our own defense could well be ineffective without the $4 billion required for military and economic assistance.

Our foreign aid program is not growing in size; it is, on the contrary, smaller now than in previous years. It has had its weaknesses, but we have undertaken to correct them—and the proper way of treating weaknesses is to replace them with strength, not to increase those weaknesses by emasculating essential programs. Dollar for dollar, in or out of government, there is no better form of investment in our national security than our much-abused foreign aid program. We cannot afford to lose it. We can afford to maintain it. We can surely afford, for example, to do as much for our nineteen needy neighbors of Latin America as the Communist bloc is doing for the island of Cuba alone.

I have spoken of strength largely in terms of the deterrence and resistance of aggression and attack. But, in today's world, freedom can be lost without a shot being fired, by ballots as well as bullets. The success of our leadership is dependent upon respect for our mission in the world as well as our missiles—on a clearer recognition of the virtues of freedom as well as the evils of tyranny.

That is why our Information Agency has doubled the shortwave broadcasting power of the Voice of America and increased the number of broadcasting hours by 30 percent, increased Spanish language broadcasting to Cuba and Latin America from one to nine hours a day, increased sevenfold to more than 3.5 million copies the number of American books being translated and published for Latin-American readers, and taken a host of other steps to carry our message of truth and freedom to all the far corners of the earth.

And that is also why we have regained the initiative in the exploration of outer space, making an annual effort greater than the combined total of all space activities undertaken during the fifties, launching more than 130 vehicles into earth orbit, putting into actual operation valuable weather and communications satellites, and making it clear to all that the United States of America has no intention of finishing second in space.

This effort is expensive, but it pays its own way, for freedom and for America. For there is no longer any fear in the free world that a Communist lead in space will become a permanent assertion of supremacy and the basis of military superiority. There is no longer any doubt about the strength and skill of American science, American industry, American education and the American free enterprise system. In short, our national space effort represents a great gain in, and a great resource of, our national strength—and both Texas and Texans are contributing greatly to this strength.

Finally, it should be clear by now that a nation can be no stronger abroad than she is at home. Only an America which practices what it preaches about equal rights and social justice will be respected by those whose choice affects our future. Only an America which has fully educated its citizens is fully capable of tackling the complex problems and perceiving the hidden dangers of the world in which we live. And only an America which is growing and prospering economically can sustain the world-wide defenses of freedom, while demonstrating to all concerned the opportunities of our system and society.

It is clear, therefore, that we are strengthening our security as well as our economy by our recent record increases in national income and output—by surging ahead of most of Western Europe in the rate of business expansion and the margin of corporate profits, by maintaining a more stable level of prices than almost any of our overseas competitors, and by cutting personal and corporate income taxes by some $11 billion, as I have proposed, to assure this nation of the longest and strongest expansion in our peacetime economic history.

This nation's total output—which three years ago was at the $500 billion mark—will soon pass $600 billion, for a record rise of over $100 billion in three years. For the first time in history we have 70 million men and women at work. For the first time in history average factory earnings have exceeded $100 a week. For the first time in history corporation profits after taxes—which have risen 43 percent in less than three years—have reached an annual level of $27.4 billion.

My friends and fellow citizens, I cite these facts and figures to make it clear that America today is stronger than ever before. Our adversaries have not abandoned their ambitions; our dangers have not diminished; our vigilance cannot be relaxed. But now we have the military, the scientific and the economic strength to do whatever must be done for the preservation and promotion of freedom.

That strength will never be used in pursuit of aggressive ambitions; it will always be used in pursuit of peace. It will never be used to promote provocations; it will always be used to promote the peaceful settlement of disputes.

We in this country, in this generation, are, by destiny rather than choice, the watchmen on the walls of world freedom. We ask, therefore, that we may be worthy of our power and responsibility, that we may exercise our strength with wisdom and restraint, and that we may achieve in our time and for all time the ancient vision of "peace on earth, good will toward men." That must always be our goal—and the righteousness of our cause must always underlie our strength. For as was written long ago: "Except the Lord keep the city, the watchman waketh but in vain."

A Chronological List of Speeches

279

JUNE 27, 1962. Matsu and Quemoy: The Basic American Position. News conference.

JULY 4, 1962. The Doctrine of National Independence. Independence Hall, Philadelphia, Pa.

SEPTEMBER 12, 1962. Science, Space and the New Education. Rice University, Houston, Texas.

SEPTEMBER 13, 1962. American Surveillance. News conference.

SEPTEMBER 30, 1962. James Meredith and the University of Mississippi. Television address to the people, the White House, Washington, D.C.

OCTOBER 22, 1962. Cuba Quarantined and Khrushchev Challenged. Television address to the people, the White House, Washington, D.C.

NOVEMBER 20, 1962. The Bombers Are Withdrawn. News conference.

NOVEMBER 20, 1962. The End of Federal Discrimination in Housing. News conference.

DECEMBER 12, 1962. How Much Real Progress in Latin America? News conference.

DECEMBER 14, 1962. Avoiding the Deficit of Stagnation. Economic Club of New York, New York, N. Y.

JANUARY 14, 1963. The Third State of the Union Message. Washington, D.C.

JANUARY 29, 1963. The Urgency of Better Education. Special Message to Congress, Washington, D.C.

JANUARY 31, 1963. Farmers and Farm Life. Special Message to Congress, Washington, D.C.

FEBRUARY 28, 1963. The Ballot, Education, Fair Employment and Other Rights. Special Message to Congress, Washington, D.C.

MARCH 21, 1963. Central America and the Development of Progressive Societies. News conference.

MARCH 23, 1963. How Shall We Keep Our Manpower Employed? Civic luncheon, Chicago, Ill.

MAY 8, 1963. The Racial Clash in Birmingham. News conference.

JUNE 6, 1963. Our Educational Deficiencies and the Remedy. San Diego State College, San Diego, Calif.

NOVEMBER 18, 1963. "We Have Helped Capital, Not Soaked It." Florida Chamber of Commerce, Tampa, Fla.

NOVEMBER 18, 1963. "Harsh Facts of Poverty and Social Injustice." Inter-American Press Association, Miami Beach, Fla.

NOVEMBER 22, 1963. Undelivered speech for the Dallas Citizens Council, the Dallas Assembly and the Graduate Research Center of the Southwest in Dallas.

INDEX

Index

285

286 : INDEX

Bolshikov, Georgi, 83n.
Bradford, William, 242-243
Brandt, Willy, 98-99n.
Brazil, 151n., 157, 159n.
Brown, Judge, 167
budget, federal, 202, 205-206, 214, 222-223, 229
Bülow, Prince, 79
business, 198-200, 227, 276

California, University of, 237, 258n.
Cambodia, 144
Castro, Fidel, 86-87, 89n.
Central America, 157-158
Chile, 151, 156, 157
China (free), 275
China (Red), 30, 59n., 85-86
Chinese Communists, 30, 59n., 85-86
Churchill, Winston, 43
civil rights, 39, 167 ff.
Civil Rights Acts, 173-174, 176-177
Civil Rights Commission, 176-177
civilian expenditures, federal, 228, 230
Clay, Lucius D., 141n.
Clay Committee, 147
Cold War, 18, 24, 27, 31, 54, 56-58, 67, 69, 71-72, 78, 89n., 119
college classrooms, 253
college enrollment, 248
College Housing Act, 253
Colombia, 146, 151, 152, 156, 157, 158
Commission on Civil Rights, 176-177
Committee on Equal Opportunity in Housing, 171

Common Market, 17-19, 29, 103n., 107, 138, 199, 208, 209
Communism, 27, 59, 86-88, 99, 158, 160, 273, 274-275
Communist bloc, 32
Communist China, 30, 59n., 85-86
Communists, 15, 30, 61-62, 66, 67n., 122n., 139, 145, 146, 147, 238-239, 274-275, 276
community colleges, 253-254
confidence, 201
Congo, 12-13, 22, 30, 33, 67, 74, 75, 135, 273
Congress of Racial Equality, 172n.
conservation, 73, 213-215
Cooperative Research Act, 256
CORE, 172n.
corn, 208-209
corporate debt, 229
corporate profits, 226
corporation taxes, 6, 277
Costa Rica, 157, 158
cotton, 209-212
Council of Europe, 134
Cromwell, Richard, 128n.
crop surpluses, see farm surpluses
Cuban crisis, xvii, 22, 30, 33, 60, 62, 66, 70, 86-88, 89 ff., 147, 158, 240, 273, 275
Cyprus, 240

dairying, 212
Daley, Richard J., 219
Dallas, 270
Dean, Arthur, 45n.
Decade of Development, 72-73, 152-153, 154-155
Declaration of Human Rights, 74
Declaration of Independence, 110
defense budget, 33
deficits, 203, 204, 222, 224, 229, 231, 272

Format by Sidney Feinberg
Set in Linotype Electra
Composed, printed and bound by The Haddon Craftsmen, Inc.
HARPER & ROW, PUBLISHERS, INCORPORATED